WOLF MAN
JOE LAFLAMME

TAMER UNTAMED

Wolf Man

Joe LaFlamme

Tamer Untamed

BY

Suzanne F. Charron

ScrivenerPress

Library and Archives Canada Cataloguing in Publication

Charron, Suzanne F., 1951-
[Joe LaFlamme. English]
    Wolf man Joe LaFlamme : tamer untamed / by Suzanne F. Charron.

Translation of: Joe LaFlamme.
Includes bibliographical references and index.
ISBN 978-1-896350-61-5 (pbk.)

    1. LaFlamme, Joe, 1889-1965. 2. Animal trainers--Ontario--Biography. 3. Animal training. I. Title. II. Title: Joe LaFlamme. English.

GV1811.L34C5313 2013   636.088'8   C2013-905317-4

French version, also by Suzanne F. Charron, is published simultaneously by Prise de parole in Sudbury, entitled *Joe LaFlamme : L'indomptable dompteur de loups*

Book design: Laurence Steven
Cover design: Chris Evans
Author photo: Rachelle Bergeron

Published by Scrivener Press
465 Loach's Road,
Sudbury, Ontario, Canada, P3E 2R2
info@yourscrivenerpress.com
www.scrivenerpress.com

We acknowledge the financial support of the Ontario Arts Council and the Canada Council for the Arts for our publishing activities.

A wolf howls and growls, somewhere on the bay, on the sea,
and then comes closer, its red eyes scrutinizing the snow
to read what is being written, to see what is being lived.

(Herménégilde Chiasson, in *Climates*)

DEDICATION

To Mélanie, Ghislain, Katrina, Jack and Avery:
May you find your passion and keep it alive!

Table of Contents

Note to the Reader, and a Request...

For ease of reading Joe LaFlamme's story, all notes on sources have been placed in a special section at the rear of the book. Notes are organized by chapter, and each note is preceded by the number of the page to which it refers, as well as by a short phrase in **bold** type drawn from the page in question.

The author does not pretend to have retrieved everything available on Wolf Man Joe LaFlamme. There are surely other documents, newspaper or magazine articles, or even other photos of Joe stored away in basements and/or attics. If the reader has any materials, anecdotal or otherwise, relating to Joe, please email a digital copy (in jpeg, with names, source, date, page, where applicable) to the author at sfcharron@gmail.com. These may be used in a future revised edition of this book, and/or sent to the Gogama Heritage Museum for display.

Acknowledgements

A book can rarely be produced by the author alone. This one is no exception. During the four years involved in researching and writing both the English and French versions of this biography, I have contacted numerous interesting people from very diverse backgrounds, and in three different countries. The gathering of the main, background, and anecdotal information on Joe LaFlamme and his era, as well as the fact-checking, would not have been humanly possible without the cooperation of all these individuals. It is with much gratitude that I take my hat off to each and every one of them.

Special thanks go to Gerry Talbot, my collaborator in research, for his unending interest, support, and patience in answering my endless questions and in researching numerous and often minute details about the history of Gogama—the village where LaFlamme lived for almost three decades. His unflagging enthusiasm and dedication to the project—from inception and continuing through writing and revision—have sustained me throughout my work. I also thank his wife Jeannine for pleasantly answering countless calls when Gerry was away from the phone. Thanks to both of you, Gerry and Jeannine!

I also acknowledge the many journalists who have written about Joe LaFlamme throughout the years, as well as the newspapers which have published the articles. Given the fact that many official documents have been lost, the reporters' often detailed accounts of LaFlamme's life and activities proved a precious source of information. Without these articles, it would have been almost impossible to construct a reasonable picture of this legendary character. Not to mention that a colourful part of Northern Ontario's history would have been lost forever. I therefore raise my hat again to all writers, past and present, who have made it not only their duty, but also their passion, to chronicle life day by day.

Finally, in listing the many people who have contributed, in one way or another, to making this book a reality, I hope I have not forgotten anyone. But if I have, rest assured it was not intentional. I also pay tribute to the people I interviewed who have since passed away: Rhéo Beauchamp, Annette Carrière, Alfred (Médé) Secord, Simone Talbot, Edelta Turgeon, Raoul Véronneau, Reina Véronneau, and Rhéal Véronneau. To the others, from the bottom of my heart, thank you:

* Charles Laflamme's family members including Gisèle and Gilbert, Guy and Diane, Huguette, Robert, Roger and Margaret, and Suzanne and Clermont; and cousin Gilles Vernier Diane, for your warm welcome and precious collaboration in my research on your great-uncle;

*Alasa Farms/Strong Family, Eunice Belisle, Wivine Bruneau, Roger (Ti-Pit) Carrière, Laurent Charbonneau, Violette Charbonneau, Gogama Chamber of Commerce, Griff Mangan, Gordon Miller, Charles Pachter, Gérald Payette, Denise Savard, Helen Schruder, Roland (Bidou) Secord, Gerry Talbot, Cécile Turcotte, Ernest (Dubby) Turcotte, Judy Turcotte, Doris Véronneau, and Marguerite Véronneau for sharing your memories of Joe LaFlamme through interviews and/or photos;

* Jean-Marie Cayen (deceased) for introducing me to the fascinating character of Joe LaFlamme several decades ago;

* Joanne Dupuis, Nicole Lalonde, Roger Lalonde, Wilfried Meyer, Gérard Violette, and Mélanie Violette for giving me valuable input during the initial revision process;

* Gaétan Gervais for your sound advice;

* L.L. Lariviere of Laurentian University for the map of Joe's territory;

* Gogama Heritage Museum for your financial contribution to the project;

* Angie O'Neil for believing in me and shoring me up with your wise words;

* my publisher Laurence Steven and editor Lisa LaFramboise for believing in my project and helping me bring it to fruition;

* Dr. Dieter K. Buse, for graciously agreeing to provide the Foreword;

* Dr. Dieter K. Buse (again) and Ruth Reid, for providing pre-publication reviews;

* my family, Gérard, Mélanie, Ghislain, Katrina, Jack, and Avery Violette, for simply being *you*!

Last but not least, I wish to thank each and every person who kindly answered my many questions when I contacted various public and private establishments during the course of this project: associations, federations and clubs of all kinds, archives, government offices at all levels, various institutions such as health and education, libraries, land registries, media, museums, genealogical and historical societies, and many more; over a hundred, actually. My dealings with these establishments may not have led to concrete information, but their service has nonetheless been truly appreciated.

Once again, a heartfelt thank you to all of you!

PHOTO CREDITS

I wish to thank all of those people and institutions who granted me permission to reproduce the photos that add so much to any biography. For all interior photos, the specific credit accompanies the photo. For the cover photos, the credits are as follows:

Front cover photo: Wolf Man Joe LaFlamme, holding one of his wolves at Alasa Farms, near Alton, New York, February 20, 1926. Photo courtesy of Alasa Farms/Strong Family.

Back cover photo: Joe LaFlamme trains his moose to climb the stairs to the balcony of his house in Gogama, circa early 1940s. Photo courtesy of Gerry Talbot.

Extensive searching has been done to determine owners of photos, and secure permission to reprint, but in some cases with no luck by the publication date. Copyright owners in this situation should contact the publisher.

Foreword

Northern Ontario has produced many engaging characters with huge personalities. Some, such as Grey Owl, the imposter who led diverse lives, and his co-ecologist wife Anahereo, have received acknowledgement in biographies and places in museums. So has the six foot nine inch Joe Muffraw, born as Montferrand, whose lumberjack and canoeing abilities have even been put to poem and song, and who is remembered with a large statue at Mattawa. Someday perhaps characters such as Mr. World, Conrad Laframboise from Espanola, or Roza Brown the fanatic royalist from Timmins, will be explored in depth.

On one of those northern personalities, we now get from Suzanne F. Charron a biography of the "Wolf Man," Joe LaFlamme of Gogama. Locals still remember him for his feats with wild animals. But, his complex life involved much more.

Charron has searched diligently and extensively. The result is a well-crafted biography. Those of us who thought we knew some of LaFlamme's exploits were surprised to learn of many more, including his brushes with the law, his abilities in defending himself, his travels and also his troubles. She has painted a full picture and provided a fascinating read.

Dr. Dieter K. Buse, Professor Emeritus of History, Laurentian University; co-author of *Come on Over: Northeastern Ontario, A to Z* (Scrivener Press).

Preface

"Wolf Man" Joe LaFlamme. The name evokes an array of feelings in those who have known him and are still alive today. Some feared the man who had no fear of man or beast. Some lauded his generosity and readiness to help a person in need. No one who knew him is indifferent to the name Joe LaFlamme. Those who have only heard about the Wolf Man are intrigued by the aura of legend surrounding him. They want to know more. I did.

Joe LaFlamme's story has been haunting me ever since I first set foot in his former house, located on Harris Street in Gogama, in Northern Ontario. On a blustery November night in 1972, a colleague, Jean-Marie Cayen (now deceased), and his wife Diane had invited my husband and me to play cards. It was raining cats and dogs and, appropriately, the wind was howling like a pack of wolves as I listened to Jean-Marie, an outstanding storyteller, relate bits and pieces of the fascinating life of LaFlamme, destined to be one of Northern Ontario's most enduring legends, alongside of but contrasting sharply with the likes of the Flying Fathers and Grey Owl. The embryonic story has been lurking in the back of my mind ever since. A few years ago, it started insisting on coming to life, on being written. Oddly, this urge made itself more pressing following my return to Ontario after having, unknowingly, lived for a few years only minutes away from Joe's final resting place in Montreal. The final nudge came at Roger and Annette Carrière's 50th wedding anniversary in Gogama, in August 2007. My husband and I were seated with our friend Gerry Talbot, and in the course of our conversation about Joe LaFlamme, Gerry and I realized that the full story had never been told. So I have seized the moment, saying to myself, "It's time!"

Here, then, is the biography of Joe LaFlamme, wolf tamer extraordinaire, who lived on this earth from 1889 to 1965. From the 1920s to the late 1940s he lived in Gogama, and his unique life there propelled him to fame on the international scene, where he became known as the Wolf Man, and later on as the Moose Man, because he understood and communicated with wild animals few of us would dare to approach. Though "tame" for him, these creatures never lost their wildness. These animals were, without doubt, more than a pastime for the tamer. They were his friends—and his vocation. To follow this unusual calling Joe often had to ignore the dictates of civilization and live his life the way he saw fit, which even meant going against the law. No social mould could contain him. Like his wild friends, he was larger-than-life.

Writing his story also came with its fair share of challenges.

As few original records have survived the passage of time, I have attempted to reconstruct the Wolf Man's character and life events based mainly on personal interviews and numerous magazine and newspaper articles, often found in the bottom of old boxes or glued in scrapbooks. Several articles were not properly identified; either the page number, the date or the name of the newspaper was missing, when it was not all three pieces of information at once! Luckily, with the help of librarians—to whom I am grateful—I have succeeded in finding most of the missing data. Nonetheless, I have spent countless hours viewing microfilm in libraries, talking with people face to face or on the phone, surfing on the web, and corresponding by email in search of as much information on Joe LaFlamme as I could lay my hands on.

I have spent hundreds of hours reading and rereading my material, trying to piece all this together—a task not always obvious given that details about earlier events were often buried in articles written years after the fact. This required constant shuffling of articles. How many times have I turned the pages of my two heavy binders of articles! In effect my search combined the work of an archeologist, patiently scouring a site in the hope of finding hidden treasures, with that of a detective, trying to piece together all the facts and clues, either written or photographed.

Needless to say I greatly appreciated, throughout my research, the generous collaboration of Gerry Talbot, a Gogama resident, who helped me regarding details of the village where Joe LaFlamme resided in Ontario. Even for the two of us it was like solving a giant puzzle. Admittedly, I haven't found all the pieces yet; certain periods of Joe's life are still a mystery. Yet, despite the holes in the chronology, I had enough material to tell the story—to bring this unforgettable but almost forgotten personality back to life.

Building the image record of this celebrity was another daunting task. Starting out with 20 or so photos, most of them unidentified, the collection now holds over 150 photos, although not all are of equal quality. Here again Gerry Talbot was a great help in collecting the photos, which then had to be identified—for source as well as content. Placing them in chronological order required numerous hours of research and study of the photos, often with the magnifying glass—but what satisfaction as I managed to lift the veil of mystery from most of the images.

In retrospect, the time was ripe for the writing of this biography. Since I started the project in 2007, several individuals I interviewed have passed away. This signals a gradual disappearance of the anecdotal information about this fabulous character. So fabulous, in fact, that some believe Joe LaFlamme was only an urban legend. Rest assured, he was not. The wolf tamer accomplished feats so out of the ordinary that he attracted considerable media coverage across North America. To date I have collected over 275 articles from Canadian and American newspapers, and from magazines such as *Life* and *Boxoffice Magazine*, not counting books and films. The bulk of the material is in English. I am sure there is still more tangible proof of the Wolf Man's existence in Canada and in the United States. (Please see my note on page eight.)

No, we are not talking of an urban legend here, but of a true legend:

through the discourse of popular culture—anecdotes or oral accounts, magazine or newspaper articles—Joe LaFlamme became, in his time, larger than life. And he deserves to continue to loom large in our heritage. Indeed, the man who was the subject of so much public attention decades ago, lived a life worthy of our examination today, if only to discover his unique approach to that life. Taming wild animals was not for the faint of heart. It required from Joe immense stamina, patience, courage, and audacious creativity. Joe's originality and free spirit can inspire us—living in an increasingly uniform society—to follow in his footsteps. For as long as he could, the Wolf Man lived his life with passion and brio. To discover and follow our own passion is therefore Joe LaFlamme's legacy to us today. I pay him homage.

Suzanne F. Charron
Greater Sudbury
May 31, 2013

1

Cracking the Whip

Joe LaFlamme once declared that, to be happy, he and his wolves needed fresh air, exercise, snow, and work. He should have added alcohol as well, at least regarding his work. Each and every one of these factors necessary for a productive woodsman's life, Joe found in abundance in Gogama, the Northern Ontario village where he lived from 1920 to 1947. And he kept a close eye on them, though one of these resources required extra vigilance. The twin boys Alfred (Médé) and Roland (Bidou) Secord, who in 1945 were only 12 years old, learned that the hard way.

Rummaging in the dark, young Alfred and Roland suddenly stumbled upon the loot. "Let's take some!" cried Alfred to his brother. In search of adventure, the twins had sneaked into the ice shed. Even without lighting, the boys could see enough to check out the sawdust piles. As refrigerators were not common back then, hotel owners kept their beer reserves cold in shacks, hiding the bottles on sawdust-covered ice until needed. That is where the boys discovered several cartons full of home-brewed beer and liquor.

They instinctively knew who owned the booty—and it was not the owner of the ice shed. Fabien Bissonnette had recently left town, leaving behind his

Poupore Street hotel and restaurant business. According to Alfred Secord, this practice was relatively common then: "People left, not even selling their homes." Abandoned buildings held irresistible appeal for the youngsters living in this village nestled in the boreal forest. Accessible only by train, plane, or boat, the village was cut off from the world, compelling its residents to rely mostly on their own resourcefulness. As for the twins, they knew how to keep busy: nothing was more fascinating than exploring all corners of their home town.

To celebrate their luck that day, Alfred and Roland decided that a little beer tasting was in order. Years later Roland recalled an after-taste of tar that made the boys spit out the brew and hurl their bottles to the other end of the shed. Then, hurriedly grabbing armfuls of liquor bottles, they scurried home like two squirrels with a newfound stash of nuts. For the boys, it was all in fun, as Alfred admitted. Nonetheless, they hoped to make a bit of spending money by selling the liquor to their older brothers. At 50 cents a bottle, this would be a lucrative deal for the two under-aged boys suddenly turned bootleggers.

But the twins were not about to stop there. A mound of bottles still lay hidden in the sawdust. So, one breezy, cloudy summer afternoon, they revisited their treasure shed. They were filling their arms with bottles when they heard a shout. Holding onto their loot, they bolted for the side door, the fear of being caught red-handed wrenching their stomachs.

Suddenly, a whip cracked within inches of their ears. The boys stopped dead in their tracks, their hearts beating like drums. Turning his head, Alfred caught a glimpse of a huge spectre in the dark corner. Towering over the twins, whip in hand, stood strapping Joe LaFlamme, the Wolf Man.

LaFlamme's glare momentarily immobilized the boys. Then, in a rush of adrenalin they darted outside and fled down the lane, praying to escape Joe's anger. Joe had no intention of harming the boys. He just wanted to scare them off and give them a lesson. And frighten them he did, which made his lodger Albert (King) Roy laugh. Alfred chuckles, "King was laughing so hard. He knew Joe would never have hit us. But we were scared. We were certain that if Joe had caught us, he would have killed us." Even though he knew they were just young lads having fun, Joe did not appreciate this intrusion into his business. He was protecting his livelihood—or at least one of his means of getting by. Most likely Gogama's most notorious bootlegger, Joe carried a large inventory of alcohol. Since his activity was illegal, he had to go to great lengths to hide his liquor from the Ontario Provincial Police (OPP), which had a detachment in remote Gogama.

Like a wolf, LaFlamme defended his territory.

2

Bootlegging at Jumping Fish

From the 1920s to the 1940s, the village was booming even though it had very few passable roads and no electricity or telephone service. The 2,000 or so residents of Jumping Fish—the meaning of the Ojibway word Gogama—lived in a world of their own, largely disconnected from major urban centres. Built on a sand esker, the village was surrounded by forests and lakes. Roughly 125 miles (200 km) south, Sudbury was the easiest centre to access because the Canadian National Railway (CNR) had a station in Capreol, just north of the city. However, Gogama boasted a Hudson's Bay Company (HBC) trading post and a branch of the *Banque d'Hochelaga* (later the *Banque canadienne nationale*).

Gogama's expansion strategically circled the train station. The transcontinental railway, the town's lifeline, wound some 220 miles (350 km) through the district from Capreol in the south to Hornepayne in the northwest. Since train engines operated on steam, a black coal chute and a huge water tank were necessary landmarks in Gogama. Timmins was not on the railway line, but became accessible with the start of the construction of the Gogama Road in 1952, which is currently known as Highway 144. Few streets existed within the town itself,

Joe LaFlamme in his mid-fifties in his sportsmen show costume and in front of his touring van, circa 1945. Photo courtesy of the Charles Laflamme family.

and motor vehicles were scarce, but at some point, Joe LaFlamme owned two. One of them was an antique car similar to one of Al Capone's vehicles: grey, very fancy, and adorned with a lot of nickel chrome on the doors and bumpers. Joe saved that one for show and used his other vehicle, a panel truck, for another business: selling and delivering slab firewood to the Gogama residents.

From left to right are: Michael J. Poupore, William H. Poupore, owner of the first sawmill in Gogama, Joe LaFlamme and possibly employees of the mill, circa 1932. Photo courtesy of Gerry Talbot.

In the LaFlamme days, the Gogama area was rated one of the best fibre-producing districts in Ontario. Lumber production constituted the town's main commercial activity. Two major sawmills, Poupore's stationary mill and the Cochrane mill, were established in the village around 1920, both on the north shore of Minisinakwa Lake. In May 1941, a major forest fire destroyed most timber limits in the area and halted the lumber industry in Gogama. Lasting for a month, it ravaged a total of 330,750 acres (133,954 ha) in 26 townships. Always looking for action, Joe helped fight this monster fire.

But Joe was neither a firefighter nor a lumberjack by trade, though he certainly had the physique for it. A handsome man in his thirties, he was well-built and had thick black hair and greenish-grey eyes. At six feet, two inches tall, he weighed a solid 225 lbs (1.9 m, 102 kg). This "bouncer" look helped him manage his bootlegging business—an enterprise meeting much demand from hard-working forestry and railway employees. Joe eased their tense, overworked muscles by offering them a good steak and a nerve-soothing potion to wash it down—for a price, of course. But Joe himself also paid the price: his bootlegging business frequently forced him to appear in court.

3

Defending His Own Cases

A quick and original thinker, Joe LaFlamme was practically self-sufficient when appearing before the judge. Lawyer Peter V. MacDonald related one case in point to the *Sudbury Star*. One day in 1937, Gogama resident Louis Labine was asked by the local police to explain the bulge in his jacket pocket. As suspected, inspection revealed a bottle of rye whisky, which then became Exhibit 1 at the trial of Joe LaFlamme, who was charged with the illegal sale of liquor. A guilty verdict could entail a sentence of three months in prison without the option of a fine. On court day, the community hall in the Catholic church L'Ange gardien was filled to capacity. People were curious to see how Joe would weasel himself out of this mess. His cunning ability to read minds and understand human nature, along with his experience as a police officer in Montreal, his deadpan humour, and his persuasiveness, made LaFlamme nothing short of a contemporary court jester.

In court, the Crown attorney had the police officer attest to his findings, about which the defense counsel Leo A. Landreville had no questions. The Crown attorney asked his next witness, Louis Labine, whether the man who sold him the whisky for $10 was Joe LaFlamme. Labine said it was. Again, there were no questions from the defense. The Crown then rested its case. At this time, defense counsel Landreville called LaFlamme to the stand, where he was sworn in. The hearing ended up being an examination led by none other than Joe himself.

Landreville: "Now, you've heard what the constable and Labine have said under oath. What is your reply?"

LaFlamme (in broken English): "When I swear to tell the troot, I tell the troot! What they said is correct, but it's only part of the story. The officer never asked me before about this and I tell him now the whole story."

LaFlamme (pointing to Labine, and surprising everyone with his tactic): "Labine, look here, if I tell a lie, stop me and say 'No!'—understand?"

Labine nods.

LaFlamme: "Your Worship, on that morning Labine come to my home. He said he has big head because of last night and he asks me if I got any liquor for sale. I tell him, NO! That's because I'm on the black list at the liquor board. Now, Labine, remember I brought you to the balcony of my home and I pointed to the alley and a pile of wood in the backyard of the house that's two doors up the alley?"

Labine nods again.

LaFlamme: "And, remember, I said, 'Go there and pull out third piece of wood from the end, on ground, then put your arm in and you'll get a bottle of whisky?'"

Labine nods a third time.

LaFlamme: "Then I said, 'Labine, for that information you pay me $10.' And you gave me $10, correct? Stand up, Labine, and tell the magistrate if that's true!"

Labine (obediently springing from his chair, shouting): "Yes, that's true!"

Landreville: "You say that's exactly what happened, Mr. LaFlamme?"

LaFlamme: "Yes, for sure."

The lawyer then argued that there was no evidence to show that the accused owned the bottle of liquor, or that he had it in his possession or on his property. In light of such a defense, the magistrate had no choice but to dismiss the case.

LaFlamme was reputed to be a lawyer's dream because he always came up with a winning defense and did most of the lawyer's work. Between 1937 and 1947, Sudbury lawyer Léo A. Landreville often defended the Gogama resident. Nothing could be easier. Joe always followed the same routine. He called the lawyer at his Sudbury office to inform him of the nature of the charge and the court date. No more, no less. When Landreville and LaFlamme met at the train station in Gogama, the lawyer quizzed him for factual details of the case. Joe was mum—always: "In court, just ask me my name and where I live and I'll tell my story." As unlikely as it may sound, Landreville related that over the ten-year period he defended Joe on average once a month and won every case—with no preparation! "Joe Laflamme would have made a tremendous lawyer, for he knew instinctively how to rustle up a reasonable doubt," Peter V. MacDonald asserted.

The 1937 case was not Joe LaFlamme's first appearance in court. His first offence dated back to March 1931, when he was owner-manager of the Moose Lodge tourist resort. He was then fined $100 for possession of liquor purchased without a permit, an offence under the Liquor Control Act.

Later that year, in June, the police were informed that Joe was trying to recover five cases of eggs and two cartons of liquor from the thief who had stolen his shipment at the train station. The investigation revealed that Joe had once again bought liquor without a permit. He appeared in court in September and defended his own case, but was unsuccessful. He was sentenced to three months in jail without the option of a fine. Magistrate Thomas Stoddart had no pity for the second time offender.

LaFlamme appealed, and this time he was represented by the King's Counsel, G.M. Miller, at a hearing held on December 19-20, 1931. Given some inconsistencies in the evidence of the Crown witnesses, Judge Edmond Proulx quashed the imprisonment charge. He amended it to a fine under section 42 of the Liquor Control Act, which allowed individuals to keep liquor in their private residence.

As a result of evidence given in court by game warden Andrew Aird, Joe lost his job as hunting and fishing guide for the Department of Game and Fisheries of Ontario. In 1930-1931, Joe had earned $108 for his services to the provincial government. How many hours of work this salary represented is not known, but the job was most likely a part-time one for the bootlegger.

Five years later, Joe was again back in court. In October 1936, he was accused of stealing an outboard motor and boat, and four drums of gasoline from Young-Shannon Mines, north of Gogama. The stolen goods were valued between $500 and $600, which made the offence serious enough for Judge Proulx to sentence Joe to 15 days in jail in addition to returning the goods to the rightful owner.

Matters did not end there. The attorney-general of Ontario appealed the conviction on the basis that the sentence was not sufficient given the nature of the offence. A week later, Judge Proulx increased the sentence to three months in jail. Since Gogama would not have a jail until 1949, jail sentences were served in Sudbury. People taken into custody were usually temporarily incarcerated in a vacant room in a local boarding house or in the basement of the house owned by Arthur L'Abbé.

According to family members, Joe was too busy to serve the three-month jail term. Instead, he coaxed his youngest brother Elzéar, also living in Gogama, to change his name to Joe and to go to jail in his place!

The two LaFlamme brothers are not the only members to have changed names in this family. Indeed, a major name change dates back to the family's establishment on Canadian soil. According to oral tradition, the family obtained the name Laflamme (with a lower case "f") from their patriarch, François Quémeneur dit Laflamme, who came from France and settled in Saint-François, on Orleans Island, in the St. Lawrence River. Close to the riverside village, there was a dangerous cliff, and to prevent ships from crashing on it, François would signal to them with huge bonfires. When the locals noticed the fires roaring, they announced to their neighbours, *"La flamme est allumée. La flamme est allumée."* (The flame is lit. The flame is lit.) Thus François acquired the name Laflamme. One has to wonder if Joe LaFlamme's name became his destiny because the man liked to play with fire, as an event that occurred in 1938 testifies.

In March 1938, Mrs. Laurent Fortin, mother of three children, was accused of setting fire to her boarding house in Gogama. The highlight of the two-day trial in June was definitely LaFlamme's cross-examination. Defence counsel J.J. O'Connor questioned him on the origin of fires having occurred at various bootlegging establishments in the community: "During the last 18 years, have you been in the bootlegging business?" Joe answered, "I don't think that has anything to do with this." The lawyer insisted on a straight answer: "Have you?" Joe's reply was unexpected: "Well, you've been in my house often enough to know." Under further questioning, LaFlamme finally admitted that he "had done a little during the past few years."

Having conceded his participation in liquor trafficking, Joe was then suspected of having purposely set fire to his competitors' properties, including that of Mrs. Fortin, also a bootlegger. O'Connor found it suspicious that Joe's own establishment had always been spared. LaFlamme answered that not only bootleggers' businesses had been burned, but also other Gogama businesses. Then the bootlegger was asked where he was on the night of the fire. Joe claimed that he was buying batteries for his flashlight when he first heard the shouts of "fire." The *Sudbury Star* reported that Joe was not surprised to see the fire at Mrs. Fortin's house. As the defence counsel objected, Joe did not get the chance to explain why—an answer that might have proven interesting.

A friend of Mrs. Fortin was finally found guilty of the arson, but one has to wonder at whose request her building was burned, since the rumour mill reported that business owners had better keep on Joe's good side if they did not want to see their enterprises set aflame. Of course, LaFlamme would not do that himself. There was always someone around who was in need of a few dollars to buy food.

In 1938, Joe was 49 years old and still unable to keep out of mischief. On October 6, he appeared before the federal court in Foleyet. He had allegedly given or sold beer to a 25-year-old Native man at a drinking party on September 19. Once intoxicated, the young man attacked the Anglican missionary and broke church windows. Joe was prosecuted and charged under the Indian Act.

Incorrigible, Joe was not deterred by court charges and continued to operate his bootlegging business.

4

Running a Clandestine Business

The bootlegging side of LaFlamme's "hotel" business obviously required a constant stock of alcohol. As regular hotels closed early at 10 p.m., many customers headed out to the bootlegger's to finish quenching their thirst. LaFlamme was always well prepared. It would not be like Joe to run out of liquor!

As there was no liquor store in Gogama in the LaFlamme era, Joe stocked up in Capreol or Sudbury as did other hotel keepers. They either ordered directly from the suppliers or went to purchase their liquor and beer in person. So, occasionally, Joe went to buy his liquor himself and came back with two metal suitcases full of alcohol. He was the only man around who could lift these suitcases, both at the same time. Was it because of his strength, or the fact he did not trust anyone with his precious cargo?

When ordered, the cases of liquor and wine would arrive in Gogama by freight car. They were kept secure in the train station until they were claimed by their rightful owners—permits and cash in hand. The purpose of the permit was to limit the amount of alcohol a person could buy. As Joe despised limits, the anecdote goes that he applied for extra permits using the names of willing accomplices. Then, saying he was sent by this and that person—with signed notes to prove it—Joe picked up the supply at the station. Obviously, controls were not very tight, though it appears that the station agents were uncomfortable when the auditors came to check the records.

But this trick was not enough to fully stock Joe's "hotel." LaFlamme therefore produced his own alcohol. As this activity was illegal, he kept his stills hidden in a remote area across the lake, nicknamed "Arizona." He had men boiling moonshine for him all year round, possibly with a slow period in the spring and fall when the lake was not safe. Joe himself held two strategic summer jobs to allow him to haul his barrels of moonshine home. Is it surprising that he was the Gogama dealer for an outboard motor company, and that he transported cargo over water for the lumber and mining companies?

Legend has it that, in winter, Joe kept a team of fast wolves to outrun the law: speed was of the essence when transporting barrels of valuable moonshine to his house from Snake Island—and possibly later from Leroux Island, across Minisinakwa Lake. He also did the moonshine run for a couple of other bootleggers who had huge stills several miles in the bush.

The liquor Joe and his men produced at "Arizona" was apparently very potent. When a subsequent owner of LaFlamme's house raised it to add a cement basement, a bottle of the original whisky was found. Wanting to test the moonshine's potency, Raymond Perreault opened the bottle, took a spoonful of the liquid, and set it ablaze. The flame burned blue and clean. According to family, Joe's whisky was 90 proof (45% alcohol) and was dubbed *la baboche*, in French.

In addition to producing spirits in the woods, Joe made an awful-tasting wine commonly known as "snub," which was as thick as molasses. His home-brewed beer was not much better; it had a subtle odour of Javex. Joe kept the concoctions hidden in his inconspicuous wood-framed, dug-out cellar. A large braided rug most likely covered the trap door to his hide-out; the last thing Joe wanted to do was alert the police who often visited his home.

On one occasion though, the police did raid LaFlamme's house. They found several wooden 25 gallon (100 litre) barrels of moonshine. Wanting to secure the illegal liquor out of sight from the bootlegger, they stored the containers in the CNR freight shed—but they did not notice that someone had seen exactly where the liquor was stashed. That night, Joe and the witness sneaked under the building, brace and bit in hand, and drilled holes through the floor under each barrel. In no time, they had drained the moonshine into other containers, thereby removing both "the moonshine—and the evidence" from the freight shed.

The cellar was not Joe's only cache. As described earlier, the moonshiner hid his loot in sawdust piles, as well as hay stacks, wood piles, abandoned homes, sheds, henhouses, and pig troughs. One of Joe's most famous hiding places was underneath wooden fence posts, as young Alfred Secord witnessed one day. He saw Joe lifting a post and shaking his leg over the hole. Wondering what the man was up to, he then caught sight of the bottle of liquor falling from Joe's pant leg into the hole. LaFlamme then put the post back, confident his treasure was safe. But Secord was now aware of the bootlegger's hiding place and knew where to get himself a good bottle of Captain Morgan rum.

Joe's career as a bootlegger started even before he moved to Gogama. It is not clear in the family's memory, but in all probability Joe started bootlegging after he resigned from the police force in Montreal in late 1916. Since he probably needed money, starting a still on some property up north was quick and easy. So was selling moonshine, especially during Quebec's short-lived prohibition in 1919. Then, in January 1920, most of the United States went dry, and border smuggling became rampant. Naturally, Canadian moonshiners, including Joe LaFlamme and his brother Elzéar, capitalized on the situation. No one knows how many times and by what means they smuggled liquor into the States, but they most likely crossed the border through Vermont since it was closest, though not dry until 1927.

On one occasion, Joe and Elzéar even crossed the border with a casket full of spirits. Good actor that he was, Joe followed the casket, sobbing, "My brother is dead, my brother is dead." No document was found to prove whether or not he was caught, but the family noticed that, after this incident, Joe seemed to be hiding from the police. Trying to dodge a warrant for his arrest may be the reason he moved to Gogama in 1920. And why not? The lumber town was in full expansion and Ontario was still under prohibition law. It was not like Joe to would miss an opportunity to run from the law and make money at the same time.

5

Settling in Gogama

Older residents recall seeing Joe and Émilie, whom everybody assumed to be his wife, getting off the train with their suitcases and trunks one summer day in 1920. But why did the LaFlammes choose Gogama? Joe told a reporter some 20 years later that he did not like living in a big city and that he felt the calling of his ancestors who were *coureurs de bois*. He came to Northern Ontario to work on the construction of a lumber mill and, as the town was booming, he decided to stay and take advantage of the freedom this land offered him.

Joe LaFlamme's origin

But who was Joe LaFlamme? Where did he come from? We know young "Joe" lived on a farm in the former district of Soulanges, Quebec, at least until the end of his teens. Born on March 9, 1889, in St. Télesphore, a small farming village southwest of Montreal, he was the seventh child of Onésime Laflamme (b.1854) and Marie Théoret (b.1858) who were married in nearby St. Polycarpe on May 2, 1876. His older siblings were Joseph (who died in his first year), a second Joseph, Louise, Albertine, Elzéar (who died in his first year), and Adélard. Four more children came after Joe: George, Aldéa, Marie-Louise, and a second Elzéar.

"Joe" LaFlamme, oddly, had an older brother also named "Joseph." So why were there two Josephs in the Laflamme family—as well as the first one, who died in infancy? In fact, on the very day he was born, "Joe" was baptized at St. Télesphore church by Father J. Pépin. He was given the name Télesphore after the parish's patron saint, who was also a pope from CE 126-137. Witnessing the baptism were the boy's father, and his maternal grandparents and godparents Bernard Théoret and Marie-Louise Poudrette, farmers from St. Polycarpe.

According to the family story, during World War I Télesphore had no desire to be drafted and sent to war. He often hid from army recruiters at his brother Joseph's farm in St. Zotique, Quebec. As a farmer, Joseph was exempt from military service. Joseph was not fond of playing this game with his sibling, but Télesphore would insist: "You have to keep me. Then after this, you will lend me your name." Not only did he take on his oldest brother's name, but he even went as far as adopting—so the story goes—his brother's youngest girls, Albina (b. 1910) and Rose-Anna (b. 1911), much to the ire of their mother, Délima. This must have happened in late 1916 or early 1917, sometime after Joe quit the police force in Montreal, thereby losing his excuse for not joining the army.

Constable Télesphore Laflamme

According to the City of Montreal archives, Télesphore Laflamme was employed with the police force from July 29, 1910 (at age 21), until November 13, 1916. His constable number was 171. There are rumours that he was asked to resign from the force because he killed someone, although an extensive search through the Montreal newspapers did not produce evidence of this action.

The *Montreal Directory* lists Télesphore as a constable starting in 1912-1913, and continues to list him until the edition of 1917-1918. In his first couple of years in the force, he was not listed as a policeman in the directory, most likely because he was in training and not a full-fledged officer yet. In the directories of 1910-1911 and 1911-1912 he was listed under the Laflamme name as "J. T. MSR conductor, 2139 St James." This indicates he was driving streetcars for the Montreal Street Railway Company (MSR), probably as a means of getting by while training or waiting for a permanent position in the police force. In the directory of 1912-1913, he was listed for the first time as

"Telesphore constable 1168 St Antoine." The following year, he was listed twice: as "J conductor 1167 St Antoine," and, under the same address, as "Telesphore constable 1167 St Antoine." This last listing appeared until 1917-1918, after which there is no further mention of Laflamme in the *Montreal Directory* until 1952. We know he came to Gogama in 1920, but where he lived from the time he left the police force to the time he left his native province is not known; neither is the reason why he resigned.

The education level required to become a police officer in the 1910s is not documented at the Musée de la police in Montreal, and the school records for the Soulanges area do not go that far back in time, so we do not know how much education Télesphore received during his youth. Family members assume he must have had at least a grade four or five, given this was the norm for boys in the farming community at the time. Even if he did not have much formal education, Télesphore received comprehensive training as a police officer. Military exercises, gymnastics, revolver shooting, first-aid, and jujutsu must have turned him into a force to be reckoned with, given his huge stature. No wonder the Wolf Man could handle ferocious wolves.

Constable Télesphore Laflamme was stationed at the No. 6 Station, on Chaboillez Street in south Montreal. Reporter Izaak Hunter, who covered the police beat, often worked out at the station gym with Télesphore and some of his police friends, J.B. Scott and Léonard Dumoulin. The latter would become, in the 1920s, a famous professional American boxer, known as Jack Renault.

The friendship with Dumoulin might have prompted Télesphore to get into wrestling. Again, no records are available for that period, but Joe himself told reporters, several years later, that he once won the heavyweight wrestling championship in Quebec. We do not know if he was in the police force at the time. The Gogama Heritage Museum has a photo of Télesphore, who appears to be in his twenties, shaking hands with another wrestler by the name of E. Chamberlin, of Sudbury. Could it be that he came to Sudbury for a competition, and that was how he found out about Gogama? In any event, he was adventurous coming to this remote community after having lived in Montreal for a decade.

POSTCARD: Télesphore Laflamme (right, aka Joe LaFlamme) shakes hands with fellow wrestler E. Chamberlin, from Sudbury, Ontario, in the 1910s. Photo courtesy of Charles Laflamme family.

Joe LaFlamme in a swimsuit, probably in Gogama in the early 1920s. Photo courtesy of Judy Turcotte.

The LaFlamme house

It was not long before Joe settled in, making Gogama his new home and "creatively" earning a living. Unorganized communities were exempt from building code regulations, so building permits were not mandatory. There are thus no records of when LaFlamme built his huge two-storey house—on a four-part lot, two parts of which he did not own until much later. The 20,000-square-foot (1,891 m²) property on the corner of Harris and Arthur Streets, in Noble Township, was divided into three parcels. Joe received from the Crown the deed for the two-lot middle parcel in 1930. He bought the other two in 1946 and 1951.

Joe's first house was built on the outskirts of town at the edge of the forest, yet not too far from the railway station. The trapper's log cabin boasted antlers on the eaves of the tar-paper roof. Once he bought his double lot on Harris Street in 1930, Joe proceeded to build a square timber structure which became the central part of the house that was built up around it over the years. The house did not have a basement originally, but apparently did later because one of LaFlamme's

Joe LaFlamme's first house in Gogama in the 1920s. Photo courtesy of Doris Véronneau.

boarders built a boat in the basement, a boat so big they had to tear down a basement wall to get it out.

The construction of the LaFlamme home was not the result of much planning, it seems. The house grew as the need did since, before long, Joe and his wife Lillie had turned their home into a boarding house. With time, a red clapboard addition was built over the main structure, making this the only part of the house that was two stories high and topped with a full attic. For some unknown reason, Joe nicknamed his attic *le p'tit Canada* (little Canada).

The east wing, added later, was only one storey. The main entrance to the house faced west, onto Harris Street. The upper level had its own entrance, also on Harris, and came complete with balcony and several steps. The stairway was torn down later, when the west wing was built. Located in the original building, the back entrance faced south and opened onto a huge backyard.

For the period, the LaFlamme house boasted an impressive "architectural design" and stood like a château next to the town's small, unpainted clapboard houses. The building, once believed to have been haunted, still stands, although it has been extensively renovated and covered in white vinyl siding. Today the large backyard is deserted, never the case when the LaFlammes lived in Gogama.

6

Trapping Live Wolves

The science of trapping wolves

It was not long before the LaFlammes' backyard was fenced in; over the years, it became home to many types of animals, wild and domestic. In the early 1920s, Joe raised Alaskan huskies, but in 1923, a distemper epidemic spread across Northeastern Ontario, killing all but two of his dogs. After this loss, Joe started to experiment with wolves while learning about trapping and the fur business.

Dave Ranger, who boarded with the LaFlammes, related to a reporter how Joe and his dog team went out with local trappers and spotted wolf tracks on Beaver Lake, now Mesomikenda Lake, 12 miles (20 km) south of Gogama. The sighting prompted him to decide right then and there to learn trapping. His fellow trappers warned him that wolves could not be caught in a trap, but Joe had a mind of his own. He set a beaver trap despite their advice. Sure enough, two days later, he caught a female wolf.

Ranger recalled how, unlike most trappers, Joe did not shoot the wolf. Instead, he cut a long pole and lay it across the animal's back, jamming her into the snow. This allowed him to tie her jaws shut and release her from the trap.

The dilemma now was how to bring the wolf back to Gogama. Hooking her into his dog team seemed like the best solution. Joe untied the rear dog and sent him home, and then tied the wolf in his place.

At first, the captive and bewildered wolf let herself be dragged on the ground by the team, but eventually she decided to get up and start running with the dogs. This enticed the team to pull hard, each dog probably thinking it was being chased by the wolf. Indeed, the team ran so fast it beat the other trappers to Gogama.

This successful first experience with the wild beast gave LaFlamme the idea to start hitching wolves to a sleigh. He therefore continued to trap live wolves. During the winter Joe lured one by putting a trap inside a partly eaten deer carcass he found in the bush. But when he later checked the trap, the carcass was gone. He then followed the trail in the snow. It turned out that a female wolf had gotten caught in the trap and had dragged the carcass over half a mile (0.75 km) until the trap got tangled in the brush and pulled away from the carcass. When Joe found the wolf, he threw a harness over her and took her out of the trap. Soon she became part of his first wolf-and-dog sled team.

By the summer he had more wolves than he needed to make up a team, so in June 1923 he delivered one to the Toronto Zoo, carrying the 65 lb (30 kg) female timber wolf under his arm. Joe did not always trap his wolves. In later years, since he had increasingly less time on his hands, he obtained his wolves either from local trappers or the Natives, who sold the animals for $10 each. He also ordered some from the Hudson's Bay Company, which often got them from the western provinces. His most beautiful silver-grey wolf named Tommy came directly from British Columbia.

In 1925, Joe told a *Toronto Daily Star* reporter that, so far, he had succeeded in trapping eleven wolves, five of which he kept in captivity in Gogama and had trained to pull a sleigh. They were relatively easy to catch since the population was reaching a peak. "They are breeding rapidly, and right now the woods are full of them," he said. In fact, in the mid-1920s, the wolf population was endangering wildlife in Northern Ontario, especially the deer in Algonquin Park. At the time, Joe believed that waging war against the wild canines would help protect other wild and even domestic animals. He did not recommend using posses and rifles, as had been attempted in Sault Ste. Marie the previous December. Wolves, he argued, were too fast for the average rifleman. A marksman himself, he recalled how, a few days earlier, he had seen a pack of 13 wolves across the lake. Wanting to scare them, he raised his rifle, but before he could pull the trigger, the wolves had disappeared. "You put up your rifle and whist! Mr. Wolf is gone… Shooting is no good," he said to the reporter. "Trapping is the only way to do it, and even that must be done by experienced and crafty woodsmen."

LaFlamme had his own theory on trapping wolves humanely. When a wolf's paw got caught in a steel-jawed trap, it would fight to free itself, often considerably damaging the leg. To prevent this, Joe padded his No. 3 beaver traps with heavyweight canvas. For bait, he used meat from moose, skunk, partridge, or hare. Though this

Joe LaFlamme, all dressed up, brings a wolf to the Toronto Zoo in June 1923. Photo courtesy of *Toronto Star*/GetStock.com #2086200443

worked well in winter, he admitted getting better results in summer when he could more easily camouflage the bait under moss, grass, or leaves. In addition, he left his traps free, so that when a wolf got caught in one, it simply dragged the trap instead of struggling to shake it loose from a tree and risking damage to its leg. Joe could always follow the trail and release the wolf from the contraption to bring it home.

The science of training wolves

LaFlamme kept his first wolves in large cages. To train them to run in a team, Joe lured each animal with food to a smaller pen. He then knelt before the snarling animal and took it in a stranglehold. Next, he slipped a muzzle on its mouth. The muzzled wolf was dragged by a steel chain to the sled, where a harness was snapped on. Joe repeated this method until all wolves were harnessed to the sled. Only then did he take off the muzzles, because otherwise the animals refused to pull.

Joe's first sled was very basic. Short and low, it resembled a child's wooden flyer sled, but without the transversal bow at the front. To train his wolves to harness, Joe used his muzzle method. But when he took off the muzzles, the wolves' gut reaction was to chew the harness to regain their freedom—and chew they could. Joe later explained to another reporter how his lead wolf once chewed a three-quarter-inch (2 cm) rope in two—without straining his jaw muscles. A fully grown wolf has 42 teeth, including four canines measuring two and a half inches (6 cm) long. The wolf's muscular jaws can exert a pressure of 330 lbs (150 kg) on whatever it decides to chew. No leather, however thick, can withstand such carnivorous fangs. Joe once told reporter Maurice Desjardins that wolves eat leather as if it was candy. Young Alfred Secord found this out the hard way when he ventured into an abandoned building where Joe kept some wolves. Alfred's leather shoelaces were untied and dangling on the ground, and one of the wolves couldn't resist and jumped on the laces, devouring them: "He wouldn't let go, as if the laces were quite a snack," recalled Secord years later. Thinking like a wolf, Joe replaced the leather lines with chains and made all his harnesses out of canvas. The wolves then had no choice but to submit to their master's commands.

7

Racing Wolves for the First Time

Harnessing timber wolves obviously presented a greater challenge than doing so with huskies. Author Laurie York Erskine had actually seen Joe's first team in operation, and he painted a picture of the wolves taking to the harness somewhat reluctantly. With heads down and tails between their legs, they seemed to despise the task at hand. With time, Joe would gain enough experience in taming wolves so that they would pull without hesitation.

In the winter of 1924, the tamer decided to try racing his wolves competitively. He put together a team of nine brawny timber wolves, weighing 70-95 lbs (32-43 kg) each. Travelling to Montreal, most likely by train, Joe entered his team in the city's winter carnival derby. The organizers of the February 9 event probably did not even know about the makeup of Joe's "dog" team. In all likelihood, though, the team had at least one husky to act as lead dog, since Joe would not succeed in training a wolf to lead the team until the late 1930s.

The 30 mile (50 km) race started on Sherbrooke Street West, in front of McGill University. Curious bystanders literally crowded the participating teams, often hindering their departure. The competition involved three races on the same circuit, which followed Sherbrooke and Durocher Streets, then went from Avenue des Pins to the actual Mont-Royal, onto Ste. Catherine Street and Queen Mary Road, and then to Décarie Boulevard and Côte-Saint-Antoine, finally returning to the starting point on Sherbrooke.

LaFlamme missed the third prize of $200, coming in a mere five and a half minutes after the James Strachan Ltd. team. Completing the circuit in 3 hours and 38 minutes, he was still 24 minutes ahead of his next opponent, Madden & Son. The first prize of $500 went to the Holt-Renfrew team driven by Quebec City's Hector Chevrette, who ran the circle tour 31.5 minutes faster than LaFlamme. The C.-E. Letourneau team, from Montmagny, won the $300 second prize.

To celebrate the winners, the organizers invited participants to a banquet at the Queen's—the same Queen's Theatre visited by author Charles Dickens and his wife Catherine in 1842. In all likelihood, Émilie also attended this celebration as the social column of the Ottawa daily *Le Droit* reported that Mrs. Jos. LaFlamme participated in Montreal's winter carnival with her husband.

While Émilie probably visited her friends, Joe camped out in a tent at Dominion Square, where he could show the public his wolves and their obedience to his commands. A bushwhacker to the core, at night Joe wrapped himself in a moose hide and slept like a log.

Lillie LaFlamme in Joe LaFlamme's sleigh, either in Montreal in 1924 or in Toronto in 1925. Photo courtesy of Denise Savard.

8

Earning His Place in Toronto's Galaxy of Stars

Born with a streak of showmanship, Joe had been galvanized, in 1924, by the crowd's response in Montreal, then the largest city in Canada. He wanted more. Why not mush with his wolves in Toronto—the second largest city in the country? The 1925 winter carnival provided the perfect opportunity.

Whether Joe contacted the *Toronto Daily Star*, or the paper approached him, is not known. We do know, however, that LaFlamme, his wolf-husky team, and handlers French-Canadian Bill Fortin and Ojibway Isaac Lewis (William) were guests of the *Star* for one full week during the 1925 winter festival. Joe and his team would be involved in several activities to give as many Torontonians as possible a chance to see the northerners and their wild animals in action. This was Joe's chance to make a strong case for the North, still considered by many to be an untamed frontier.

Day one: Monday, January 26, 1925

Having travelled in an express car, the leashed dogs and wolves, along with their master and the handlers, arrived at the Union Station on the early morning train. Joe wasted no time and, to the amazement of the railway workers, har-

42

nessed his team right on the spot: ten huskies, four timber wolves, and his lead dog, a Belgian shepherd named Billy. The three men loaded their heavy gear onto the sled. Then, having a general idea of his destination, Joe emphatically commanded "Mush!" and off they went, heading north via Simcoe Street. Billy led by trotting. Wagging his tail, he maintained his position by wits more than muscles; he was no match for the howling and snarling huskies who were straining at their harnesses and the wolves who were crouching and hugging the ground as if wanting to disappear in the snow. Fortin and Lewis ran alongside the sleigh, occasionally riding in it. LaFlamme stayed at the rear, guiding the team with a rope.

Nearing Queen Street, Joe had to stop and check the street name. But how did one stop a racing dog-and-wolf outfit with no brakes? As Joe's service sleigh did not have brakes, he relied on an old musher's trick. Running alongside the sled, he swung his rope around a telephone pole and jerked the team to a halt. Noting the direction to take, Joe signaled to Lewis, who then shoved the sleigh into the turn, and off they went again. Further on, the musher shouted, "Haw!" and the team swung left onto University Avenue. On the wider street, the pace became steadier, averaging 10 miles per hour (16 kph). The musher again snubbed his rope around a pole to take his bearings. Taking Elm Street and making a right on Duke Street, they finally reached their destination, a veterinary hospital, a little over one and a half miles (two km) from Union Station.

Since the animals would lodge at the hospital's stables for the first few days, Joe took their harnesses off. Most of them were happy to be unhitched, but one of the two wolf pups thought otherwise. When Joe reached the animal to undo its hitch, it snarled and snapped at its master. Unfazed, Joe put a rope over its neck, pulled it snug, and with an experienced flip, threw the wolf on its back. Tightening the rope to prevent the wolf from biting, he picked it up and put it in a shed. Fortin unhitched another snarling wolf by grabbing the back of the harness. Swinging the wolf under his arm, he threw it into the shed.

Soon LaFlamme and his team were settled in and were preparing to spend their first night in southern Ontario, far away from the cold northern country. Little did they know that they were about to experience some of Toronto's coldest weather.

Day two: Tuesday, January 27, 1925

Toronto's temperature plunged to -11° Fahrenheit (-24° C) by early afternoon. This was unusually cold for the city. With high humidity coming from Lake Ontario, the below-freezing weather was bone-chilling, making it hard not only on humans, but also on automobiles. Even milk bottles sitting at the door were breaking by the hundreds as a result of the cold. But that did not deter the three northerners, much less their thick-haired pets.

A character study of Joe LaFlamme and his wolf Tommy done by Gilbert A. Milne, at the Milne Studios in Toronto, on January 27, 1925. Photo courtesy of *Toronto Star*/GetStock.com #2086200446

Their second day in Ontario's capital was spent playing movie stars. Impressed with the looks of Joe and his animals, professional photographer Gilbert A. Milne had phoned the *Toronto Daily Star* earlier in the morning requesting permission to do character studies of them. The *Star* sent the three northerners to Milne Studios. The musher, accompanied by his pet wolves Pete and Tommy, got into a taxi, the two animals taking over the entire back seat.

At the studio, Tommy displayed great nervousness. His master patted, caressed, and even kissed the wolf to quiet him down long enough for the photographer to take good pictures. Milne intended to exhibit the collection "as examples of northern racial expressions." Once the session was done, Joe left, carrying Tommy in his arms to the taxi.

Day three: Wednesday, January 28, 1925

LaFlamme intended to thrill Torontonians and give them a chance to experience one of the North's unique lifestyle features. So, at noon, Joe and his equipage did a run in the east end of the city, starting from the Bloor Street Viaduct—a great vantage point for curious boys. They headed east along Danforth Avenue, on to Main Street south to Gerrard west, then to Broadview south up to King, steering west toward their home base.

What a spectacle this must have been for big city dwellers! Wanting to catch a glimpse of this once-in-a-lifetime happening, Torontonians flocked to the streets on the way to their offices. Imagine a dogsled train 65 feet long (20 m), the length of a transport truck, rushing through the city, men in tow. The sheer length of the harnessed team and sled presented a communication challenge for the musher and his lead dog. Joe experimented with a telephone receiver which he hung close to the canine's neck. This allowed him to give commands to Billy through a mouthpiece. The leader apparently adapted quite well to the innovative communication tool.

Once the 9 mile (15 km) run was over, the whole northern outfit went to Queen's Park to pay a visit to George Howard Ferguson, premier of Ontario and leader of the Progressive Conservative Party. Also present was Charles McCrea, then the Sudbury MPP who served as Minister of Mines. During his meeting with the politicians, which naturally was held outdoors, Joe invited himself and his entire train into the Ontario Legislative Building. The musher, his 15 animals, and their sleigh all climbed the stone steps to enter by the front door.

For the occasion, Joe was wearing what would become his signature costume for sports shows and other public events involving wildlife. The most striking piece was a fingertip-length version of the capote, or wrap coat, made from a Hudson's Bay Company point blanket. His was pullover style, emerald green, and trimmed with fox fur at the neck, wrists, and hem. Wrapped around Joe's waist was a multicoloured Assumption sash or fur-trader's belt, better known as the French-Canadian *ceinture fléchée*. As the coat does not seem to have had pockets, he folded his woolen mitts over the belt. A cone-shaped wolf-fur hat complemented his outfit. The trapper also sported dark woolen pants and socks, the latter decorated with stripes and side tassels. He wore ankle-length leather boots. To complete his musher's attire, he hung his 40 foot (12 m) moosehide whip like a necklace around his neck.

LaFlamme's assistant Bill Fortin (left), Joe LaFlamme, Ontario Premier George H. Ferguson and an unknown dignitary with LaFlamme's sleigh, at Queen's Park, in Toronto, on January 28, 1925. Photo courtesy of Gerry Talbot.

What outdoorsman Joe LaFlamme and Premier Ferguson discussed during their meeting was not reported in the papers. In one of the photos in the Gogama Heritage Museum's collection, it looked like they were pondering Joe's mishap with the sleigh, probably when it was dragged up the stairway to the Queen's Park building. The left handlebar and a stanchion were broken and Joe seemed concerned about his predicament. Rightly so, as this was his main sled and he still had a few more runs to make in the city as well as several other activities planned for the following weekend on Grenadier Pond, a large body of water bordering the west side of High Park, southwest of downtown Toronto.

In the evening, Joe visited the winter carnival held at the Varsity rink in the stadium. Because the enclosure available at the site was not large enough to contain his whole team, he decided to hitch four animals, a mix of dogs and wolves, to one of his smaller sleds.

The January 28 edition of the *Star* carried a warning that LaFlamme's wolves and dogs were not the petting zoo variety: "Although Joe Laflamme has his wolves and dogs under good control, the general public is warned against going too near them. Please keep away yourselves, and don't let your children or dogs go near. Take this unique opportunity of seeing a northern bush outfit. It is both educational and entertaining. But don't come too near."

Day four: Thursday, January 29, 1925

Thursday's parade got off to a rocky start. Right before the animal train was set to leave for its noon run, Knabey, the six-month-old wolf pup, escaped. Darting from the stable on Duke Street, he rushed through the neighbourhood in search of a way home. News of the getaway flashed through the city and created a wave of excitement far exceeding that of the massive wolf expeditions organized in Sault Ste. Marie the previous December. Apprehension soon settled in, especially in the High Park area, where the wolf was supposedly headed. Before long, all and sundry joined in the wolf hunt, though, understandably, no guns were allowed. Nonetheless, the police had the order to shoot the animal if they saw him and could hit him without missing their target or hurting anyone else. Through the day, they received numerous reports of sightings; unfortunately most were dogs mistaken for Knabey.

The wolf pup had to be retrieved, and Bill Fortin was in charge of searching for him while Joe honoured his commitment to the *Toronto Daily Star*. Scheduled for noon sharp, the run started an hour late. The departure point was the *Star*'s office, at the corner of King and Yonge (which Joe rhymed with "lunge") Streets. The itinerary included travel on King West where the team also had to contend with streetcar tracks in the middle of the road. Large, enthusiastic crowds cheered them on. The skyscrapers on King and Yonge were empty, as was the Bay Street financial district. As the *Star* reported, Joe drew "all Toronto's Wall Street from the New York ticker and the sensational swoops and swings of $2.00 wheat."

They continued on to Bay Street. In this downtown area, the lead dog had to manoeuvre in order to guide his team between tight crowds of people lining the streets. This was not an easy task, with the sleigh piled high with the canvas tent, dunnage bags, and food. Joe and his team were moving to another location. The dog-and-wolf team could take the load, though at a slower pace than on well-beaten trails where a team of 10 dogs could easily pull 600 lbs over a distance of 100 miles (275 kg over 160 km).

After tying up traffic for blocks, the outfit continued its trip from Bay to Bloor West, then up the long hill on Bathurst, reaching Wychwood Park Avenue. There, Joe halted and gave his dogs and wolves time to recharge their batteries before undertaking the arduous climb up the hill to Wychwood Park. It was well worth the effort. With the thick white snow and the tall pines, the park area was reminiscent of a northern landscape. Here, far from the "chrome yellow lower town…a Gogama, go-get-em dog had room to breathe and stretch his legs."

Picking up speed going downhill, the team was heading straight for the railway crossing. Onlookers would swear it was going to crash the gates! Joe shouted a command in French and Billy instantly brought the team to a halt. No one could deny the musher's amazing control of his team. It was with relief that the train conductors saluted him.

The team was now headed west on St. Clair toward Keele Street, and down Keele to High Park Avenue. Pulling the heavy sled on the sanded streets was challenging. Given that the temperature had risen in the past few hours, the scant snow was melting and soaked with motor oil from the vehicles.

The downtown crowds were enthusiastic, but nothing to compare with the wild screams of school children at Bloor, Bathurst, and St. Clair. With capacity audiences at every corner, there was magic and mystery in the air, just as with the annual Santa Claus parade. The trees and snow banks were dotted with a lot of red toques worn by excited youngsters. Not only were they thrilled to have the afternoon off, but they also felt blessed that Billy acknowledged them. They greeted him by name whenever the big dog approached. When he looked at them straight in the eye, children believed that he was personally thanking them for cheering on his team. So they cheered even harder, with dozens of them running in the trail of the Gogama dog-and-wolf express.

Crowds were still strong at Keele and Dundas, and the atmosphere was carnival-like. On the last eight miles (14 km) to High Park, the team was even accompanied by a group of *coureurs de bois*, part of High Park's reception committee. Over Bloor Street, the northern train headed for the road on the east side of the park to circle the lake end, inside the railway embankment. Then it was uphill to the old Howard residence.

The downhill slope to Grenadier Pond was steep. Would the heavily loaded sleigh lag behind or slide forward among the animals? Here again, Joe demonstrated a complete understanding of the dynamics of his team and of the sleigh's brake system. With expertise, he managed to keep the line taut and the sleigh at the back. They slalomed down to the pond, and once on the snow-covered ice, galloped full speed to its new location just south of the ski-jump. The long train of dogs, wolves, and sled running on Grenadier Pond against a background of abrupt hills and rugged pines was truly a scene from the Canadian wilds.

Public curiosity about the bushwhackers and their wolves and huskies was increasing daily, more so after Knabey's dash for freedom. The lure of the North and the free-spirited lifestyle it evoked struck a chord in the city dwellers. The *Star* reported, "Not for a long time has there been such widespread interest and excitement as occasioned by the visit of Joe Laflamme and his outfit from Gogama as guest of the *Star*." Thousands of people wanted to see them, and over the weekend they would have many opportunities to do so up close. A born salesman eager to instill awe at the ruggedness of life in Northern Ontario, Joe had decided to set up a real winter bush camp on a small wooded promontory close to the base of the ski jump. On the shores of Grenadier Pond, the whole crew would camp out in the cold right through to Saturday evening, and the public was invited to come and see with their own eyes how one survived the harsh winter in the bush.

Meanwhile, Fortin continued his search and, shortly before five o'clock, finally located Knabey under the CNR freight sheds at the corner of Simcoe and Frost Streets, many kilometres away from his temporary home. Several railway and freight employees had seen the wolf abandon the tracks just east of Spadina around noon, slinking away from one freight car to another. Quite a few men chased the animal, which played hide and seek with them. Finally, he took cover under the sheds where Fortin found him. Locating the animal was a good start, but the challenge was getting him out of hiding. Fortin had no choice but to crawl under the sheds and fetch the wolf himself. Needless to say, a crowd of employees were soon hustling to grab front-row places to cheer on the courageous young French-Canadian.

Bill watched the wolf until, wanting to hide further, the animal finally cornered himself at the west end of the sheds. All Bill had to do was to grab the dragging end of the chain and pull the wolf out. It sounded easy enough, until the wolf got caught in between two beams. With the intention of freeing the wolf, quick-thinking Bill crawled further underneath into a dark eight-inch-high space (20.3 cm). When he presented his foot to Knabey, the wolf tried to snap it. Bill now grabbed the animal's chain and pulled it hard enough to get his head locked between his legs. He then muzzled Knabey with the chain and dragged him out with the head still between his legs. A couple of men then pulled Bill by the arms to get him from under the sheds. The brave lad was lucky to have gotten out scot-free, except for a gash on one finger. Undoubtedly, Joe felt relieved the ordeal was over with no harm done to his companion, his wolf, and the Toronto public. The event was surely the subject of many coffee breaks thereafter.

In the meantime, even after dusk crowds of Torontonians hung around LaFlamme's bush camp, which came complete with wolves and huskies hitched to trees. Joe and his companions roped off a 50 ft. (15 m) area to keep the curious from befriending the animals. The campsite had become "an island in a sea of wolf fans." Adding to the romantic novelty of the scene were moonlight and a log fire shedding a warm glow. At bedtime, the three men snuggled up in the unheated tent, bundling themselves in furs. The cool lake breeze soon lulled the tough bushwhackers to sleep—with some snoring probably heaving the tent walls.

Day five: Friday, January 30, 1925

Starting at eight o'clock on Friday morning, a steady stream of visitors lined up at the encampment to check if the campers had survived the night in their alfresco abode. The only one who complained was Isaac Lewis, commenting on his bedroom being too hot. He sounded more as if he had caught heatstroke than chills.

At 11:30 a.m. sharp, Joe and his Gogama dog special went out on an exhibition run. The wolves were left behind, tied with steel chains to the pine trees, with no chance of escaping this time unless they uprooted and dragged the trees with them. The 11-dog train left Grenadier Pond with Billy, who knew his path by heart, leading his team uphill around the curve. They circled Howard Park past the car barns well before noon. Joe raced his team full speed, as if he were on an urgent mission. At Dundas Street, the animals dashed down the incline of the long bridge that spanned the railway tracks, and then sped through the College and Dundas intersection, dispersing the tight crowd of children like Moses parting the Red Sea.

At Dundas and Bathurst, Joe braked the train with his foot: "Whoa!" The dogs came to a full stop, probably recognizing Émilie, who was waiting for Joe at the corner. She had taken the 7 p.m. train from Gogama the night before and arrived in Toronto that morning, accompanied by her own gentle brush wolf, named Sparky. Playful, the small female wolf was much tamer and easier to handle than Joe's wild timber wolves. When Émilie took a seat on the sled, Sparky sat obediently in front of her. Off went the "Eskimo limousine," crossing University Avenue, always greeted by the shrieks of numerous delighted children. At the signal "Haw!" Billy led the team on a left turn onto Yonge.

At the corner of Yonge and Adelaide streets, Joe spotted the cameraman who had been following them all over downtown. Both the musher and his huskies disliked the huge tripod and whirring camera. The movie man had been trying, without much luck, to get good action shots of the northern team. None too happy to meet him again, Joe purposely sabotaged the cameraman's efforts by ordering his dogs to stop on the spot, right in the middle of one of Toronto's busiest intersections.

This time, the cameraman had had enough and walked up to Joe, protesting about his lack of cooperation. Joe only smiled, smug in his knowledge that his team would not budge until he said so. He did not care if honking cars and yelling horse-sleigh drivers were forced into a wide detour to avoid him and his beasts. He didn't even care when a traffic policeman finally came and ordered him to get his team out of the way. "You move 'em," he offered the officer. After pondering the situation, the policeman declined the invitation; handling wolf-like dogs was not his cup of tea. So Joe had his team sit on their haunches until the frustrated cameraman lost his patience, packed his gear, and moved on. Only then did Joe's command to "Mush!" get the team trotting up Yonge.

At one intersection on Bloor, a traffic policeman cleared the way for Billy and allowed him the privilege of making a left turn, a move forbidden to motorists. A sensible dog, Billy showed his gratitude by circling the officer like a high-stepping harness horse and producing an impeccable turn. Joe probably grinned with pride at his dog's showmanship. Then it was homeward bound for the bushwhacker and his team, with a Royal Canadian Mounted Police officer leading the way and marathoners following in the dog-and-wolf train's wake. Children in a festive mood were again lined up along the streets as the outfit ran west on Bloor to Queen's Park, through the west side of the park to the University of Toronto gates, across the university grounds to College Street, then west on College to Landsdowne, Dundas, and back through Howard Park. There they ended their day's 11 mile (18 km) circuit with a spectacular manoeuvre. Zigzagging beautifully down the steep and slippery hill at the ski jump, they made a breathtaking landing, untangled, on the ice, literally dropping into their encampment. A ski jumper's dream!

After many hours of mushing, the team rested, but not before eating. To satiate the famished animals' hunger, Bill dragged three quarters of beef near the fire and cut them, with an axe and a knife, into five-to-nine-lb (2-4 kg) chunks. The onlookers were amazed at the speed with which the strong teeth and powerful jaws tore the flesh and crushed the bones. Who would have dared steal their meal? When they were finished, Joe gave his animals a final inspection before retiring for the night: "Now they be in first-rate shape for big day tomorrow." As for Mrs. LaFlamme, she probably checked in at a local hotel for the night—but not her Sparky.

The spine-chilling howling of wolves surely kept many a city dweller awake that night, including the *Star* reporter who described in great detail the wild medley that echoed several times in High Park. The keynote was given by Pete, a shaggy-haired, white-fanged, sure-footed, bushy-tailed, 75 lb (34 kg) wolf that had been snapping and snarling all week long. Joe usually kept him muzzled. Baying at the moon, Pete let out a long-drawn, mournful, bloodcurdling howl, breaking the silence that had settled over Grenadier Pond and the High Park neighbourhood. Soon to follow the lead was the gaunt and towering 90 lb (41 kg) Tommy with a deeper and sadder wail, all the while clanging his chains, trying to break loose. Naughty Knabey and quick Weeweep, secured in a cage, joined in the chorus with half-barks and half-howls. Sparky cried faintly in the distance.

Not wanting to be outdone, all but one of the huskies contributed to this midnight serenade to the moon: La Petite; Pete's son Maheggan; Sawn the yellow; Huskie; Fidel the faithful; Flossic; Waugouch the fox; Dick; Paddy the pup; and Mokooman the knife. As for police dog Billy, he had no time for chorus singing; he was too busy pacing back and forth in front of his master's tent, guarding the three sleeping trappers.

The ode to the moon would last a minute and a half and then abruptly stop. Silence would again reign over Camp LaFlamme, until, an hour later, Pete got up again, sat on his haunches, and restarted the chorus, inviting his brethren to join in the howling session. This went on all night, at varying intervals.

Day six: Saturday, January 31, 1925

An article in one of Toronto's morning papers cast a doubt on the makeup of LaFlamme's team, suggesting that all 15 animals were dogs. Self-assured, Joe not only took the remarks with his usual sly humour, but also challenged readers to come and check out the wolves for themselves. He even offered a prize to the successful contestant: "If anyone will come to High Park and take away one of the wolves with him, without shooting him, of course, I'll give him $100. I mean, of course, a wolf without his muzzle on. Let anyone try it today. If they are all huskies, with no wolves, it will be easy enough for the challenger to walk away with any of them. Let him try to take away one of my wolves from the pack. To make it fair, I'll let the challenger fix the wolf's chain to himself, then let him see what will happen." There were no takers!

LaFlamme's activities were the main attraction of the *Star*'s winter carnival. Record crowds of over 50,000 people (conservative estimate) gathered around Joe's bush camp at High Park—or rather exhibition park given all the events put on by the *Star* and its guests from the Northlands. Joe and his companions gave spectators plenty to see: a rustic tent; a log fire; huskies and wolves resting by the trees, tied, of course; sled and toboggan races, stunts, and jaunts up the hill and through the park. The Toronto Transportation Commission dealt with the unprecedented influx of cars in the west end by adding special street car service on the Beach (Queen) and Carlton lines in the direction of High Park. Even though LaFlamme's races were scheduled for the afternoon, early-birds arrived at Grenadier Pond hoping to get a close view of Joe and his animals in their encampment. Miss Canada, a Torontonian, also partook in the celebrations. She even dared to hold one of the wolves: the docile and cooperative Sparky. A reporter commented on the woman's expression, noting that her smile might not have been so spontaneous had she been holding one of Joe's snarling wolves.

As for the burly Gogama musher, he felt quite comfortable in dark woolen trousers, a heavy wool sweater and pompom beret, and knee-high boots. Confident in his knowledge of his animals, Joe loved being the centre of attention and went all out to impress city dwellers. They would remember the show for years to come.

By two o'clock, thousands of people flocked single file through the park down to the pond. Coming from all directions, they travelled to Camp LaFlamme on foot, on snowshoes and skis, on toboggans and bobsleds, and by motorcar, tramway, and bus. The *Star* reported that the scene "with its innumerable spots of…red, yellow, green, violet, and so forth, looked like a canvas painted by the dot and dash method." In this case, it was not the painting that was roped off from the public, but the wolf camp itself. Authorities were not taking chances: wolves' fangs could make a quick meal of little hands outstretched to pet the wild beasts. But some young boys managed to escape police surveillance and snuck under the rope to approach the animals. They were lucky the wolves were not hungry at the time, because when the wild canines open their jaws almost at a right angle, their white teeth look "like a combination of a saw mill and a surgeon's kit."

The spectators covered the hill near Grenadier Pond from top to bottom. Some were standing on tip-toe while others were digging their heels into the slippery hill to stop from sliding down. The desperate broke the ice at the pond's edge and stood in slush up to their ankles. All wanted to grab the best vantage point to see LaFlamme in action. The favourite act in the show was Joe harnessing his dogs and wolves. The crowds pressed so close, despite the rope enclosure, that it was amazing Joe and his crew of "wolf charmers" had room to manoeuvre.

For the upcoming exhibition race, two teams were harnessed. The first one was made up of four huskies eager to go to work and pull the sleigh. They did not even mind being petted by hundreds of little hands while they waited for the other team to be harnessed. The 11 other animals were a different matter, the dogs probably influenced by the untamed wolves' behaviour. Snarling and snapping at their master, the wolves resisted the harness, until Joe, unfazed, got the upper hand. Confident in his wolf-handling skills, the strong man jammed each wolf's hindquarters between his legs, and pulled the animal's chain tight enough to prevent it from moving his head. All this careful handling did not prevent Joe from getting the odd leg butt from a wrestling animal. Yet he methodically pulled the harness over the wolf's head, and coaxed the busy feet through the straps. Then he and his assistant, one pulling tightly at the wolf's head and the other holding the tail end taut, carried the trembling animal to the steel gangline attaching the wolves to the sleigh. The truly fascinating feat was repeated four times to the delight of the public.

The climax was definitely the muzzling of two of the wolves. The Wolf Man himself thrilled the crowd when he put his hand alongside the snarling wolf's mouth. The keen observer quickly learned that the secret to wolf-handling was to never give the beast slack. Joe had probably learned this the hard way. But no one among the thousands of spectators cared to test the trade secret by taking up LaFlamme's $100 offer to come and harness a wolf.

The four wolves, now harnessed to the gangline, threw themselves wildly on the ground. But when Billy got the order to "Mush!" every team player got in line and started running and pulling. Joe grabbed the handlebars, cracked his long whip, and directed the Gogama express between two solid walls of cheering humans. In fact, the police had to clear the way.

Heading northward, the musher reached the pond in no time. His team soon galloped over the frozen rush-covered marsh, with Émilie and two little boys from the crowd in the sleigh. But, on the home stretch, Joe noticed that the ice on Grenadier Pond was cracking. With 15,000 onlookers on the ice, quick thinking was in order. They were still a mile (1.5 km) from shore. At the end, Joe led his team swiftly over the hill in an attempt to lure the crowds to firmer ground. Luckily, it worked!

After the race, Joe and Camp LaFlamme remained the centre of attraction until nightfall. Meanwhile, in honour of their northern denizens, the *Star* organized a mid-afternoon "wolf hunt," complete with prizes for the successful "hunters." The unique event was a glorified paper chase, where the participants, children, and adults on snowshoes or skis hunted three members of the Toronto Ski Club. President Sam Cliff, secretary Charles Punchard Jr., and membership committee chairman Alex Duncan frantically skied on different trails, trying not to get caught.

Hundreds of people took up the challenge, but given the rough terrain and sticky snow, only about 30 people lasted until the end. Skis were offered to the three adults who caught the "wolves": Cliff Chilcott, A. Leaneater, and R.S. Godfrey. The junior winners were Lorne Mickelborough, Teddy Howard, and Harvey Jackson.

The week had been packed with crowd-pullers put on by Joe and his huskies and wolves. Not only had LaFlamme, Fortin, and Lewis given big-city dwellers a taste of Northern Ontario's vastness and wilderness, but they had also managed to draw huge crowds to a part of Toronto most never even knew existed. Joe and his animals had captured the hearts and imaginations of Torontonians. They now considered the northerners among their beloved heroes, along with cartoonist George McManus, the creator of *Jiggs and Maggie*; Tiny Tim, from Charles Dickens's *A Christmas Carol*; Canada's marbles and jacks champions; and several others. The *Star* reported, "Now Joe Laflamme and his wolves have carved a place in this galaxy of stars."

9

Meeting Mrs. LaFlamme

Joe's fame now followed him wherever he went, even as he headed out for the races in Quebec City and Lake Placid, New York. Throughout the coming months, it reached the ears of thousands of Canadians—even those of the Governor General of Canada, Sir Julian Byng, and his wife Marie Evelyn. On June 17, 1925, the couple was travelling west when the train stopped briefly in Gogama. To replenish the supply of coal and water for the steam engine usually took about 15 minutes, but the Governor General and his wife wished to extend the stopover to meet Joe LaFlamme and his wolves. Whether they actually went to Joe's house is unknown. If they did, no doubt Mrs. LaFlamme was well prepared. Her many years in Paris as a young woman had instilled in her both taste and style.

Mrs. LaFlamme's origin

Émilie Ernestine Hélène Haigneré was born on Friday, August 18, 1893, in the fishermen's village of Étaples-sur-Mer, in the department of Pas-de-Calais, in northern France. The daughter of Auguste Pierre Josse Haigneré and Augustine Dalila Gosselin was baptized on August 23, probably at Saint-

Michel, the only Catholic church in town. In all likelihood, she inherited her first and middle names from her godparents, Émilie Carlu and Ernest Altazin.

Émilie came from a long line of *Étaplois* seamen. Her parents were married on May 3, 1890. According to the 1911 census records, Émilie had an older sister named Élisa; two younger sisters, Georgette and Augustine; and a younger brother by the name of Auguste. Émilie herself was not mentioned in this census, and it is possible that she had been placed with a relative in Paris at a young age, since she claimed to have lived the greater part of her life on the banks of the Seine River.

It is difficult to imagine Émilie living a rustic life in remote Gogama, lacking basic amenities such as electricity, running water, and indoor plumbing. According to a *Toronto Daily Star* report, Émilie was 4 feet, 2 inches tall and weighed barely 100 lbs (1.3 m, 45 kg). While this record of her height seems questionable, there is general agreement among her sources that she was under 5 ft (1.5 m). The petite auburn-haired lady was known in Gogama as Lillie, but mostly as *la p'tite femme* (the little woman), a nickname Joe himself had given her. Locals remember her as being very smart and a fancy dresser, always wearing the prettiest dresses. Most of her winter coats were adorned with a fox collaret, which she complemented with a brimmed hat and stylish boots. Relatives in the Montreal area also remember her as a fashion-conscious woman who was no stranger to makeup, jewelry, and heels. When the ex-Parisian visited her husband's family during the cold season, she often sported a beautiful leopard coat and hat, and white boots, very much *à la mode de Paris*.

Yet despite the ruggedness of her life in the north, Lillie would not have traded it for all the comforts she once enjoyed in Paris. In January 1925, she told the *Toronto Daily Star*, in rather broken English, that she had come to love Canada: "You see, I hafe so many t'ings nice to own. In zee summer a jardin, ah un beautiful jardin, seex canarie, and cheeken, and peegion and skenks—t'ree of dem, just for pet." Smilingly, she reassured the reporter: "Dey are nice—no smell you know." She also had Sparky, or *Teet Loup* as she called her small wolf.

Lillie did admit that she had been lonely when she and Joe first moved to Gogama. "Ah, oui, dere were just one cabin dere when we go fife year ago, but now one hun'red and feefty famil', church, école, and two méell...Mostly all come in las' two year." Émilie's comment was a slight exaggeration of the truth as there was definitely more than one house when the LaFlammes arrived in Gogama in 1920. One of the earliest residents, Arthur L'Abbé, came to Gogama in 1917 and became postmaster and general merchant. As there were already two mills in town, he soon built a poolroom. After the 1922 arrival of Gogama's first resident priest, Monsignor Achille Cournoyer, the poolroom doubled as a church for the Catholic parish of L'Ange gardien. It is not until 1947 that an actual church was built, and then renamed Notre Dame du Rosaire. The HBC also put down roots in 1922. Gogama was definitely growing, all the more reason for a bootlegger to settle in the community.

Independent and spunky, Émilie continued, "Me, I am nefer lonely. Eef Joe away in zee winter an' I wish to go some place I just take a team an' I go out...Mais oui, I can heetch up a team of dogs—a small team, you know." Because she had a girl to help her with the boarding house, she was free to leave as she pleased, though she commented on the vast distances up north. If Joe did not agree, undaunted, *la p'tite femme* knew how to play her ace. For example, when he went to Toronto in January 1925 she wanted to come along, but Joe insisted that she was not strong enough for this kind of trip. To his remark she replied, "Eef I no go I keep Bilee home too, den who lead your team for you?" Billy was her police dog, not Joe's. She finally took the train for Toronto a few days after Joe.

Joe had good reason to worry about Lillie's strength. Canada's harsh winters and hot summers had taken their toll on her health: "Me, I was plump—nice, but I lose forty poun' in seex year." This was since she first came to Canada in 1919 at the prodding of two friends who had married Canadian soldiers. Not long after she arrived in Montreal, she met Joe: "Hee ees fonny. He love all zis life up nort'—zee dog an' hunt an' trap. He go up zere an' I go too. When one marry she go wix zee hosban' an' be happy." She claimed to have married him a year after the war, which would be the same year she arrived on Canadian soil. No record of this marriage has been found. Since Joe's first marriage was officiated in a Catholic church, he would have had to get an annulment before remarrying within the church.

Joe LaFlamme's first and only marriage

In all likelihood, Joe and Lillie just decided to live together without the Catholic rites that had been performed five years earlier at Joe's marriage to Florence May West. The marriage ceremony was held on April 28, 1914, at Florence's Saint Aloysius parish church in Montreal. The marriage banns were announced prior to the event at both her church and his, which was Ste. Elizabeth, also in Montreal. Three weeks before the wedding, Florence was baptized into the Catholic faith. The marriage was blessed by the parish priest, Father M.L. Shea. Witnessing the nuptial vows were Joseph Laflamme, the groom's oldest brother, and Joseph Roberts, a relative of the bride. Florence's parents were William-Henry West and Christie-Anne Roberts, both from the Gaspésie region of Quebec.

It appears that the couple took a belated honeymoon in March of the following year, travelling on the *Olivette* from Havana, Cuba, to Key West in Florida, where they would have boarded another boat to Montreal.

The cause and date of the relationship's rupture are not known. There are no records of Joe's and Florence's separation or divorce, as there are no records of the couple having had children. But we know that on July 19, 1914, Joe and Florence were still married because they both signed a baptism registry for Jean Télesphore Adrien Laflamme, son of constable George Laflamme, one of Joe's younger brothers.

On November 19, 1915 Joe was again godfather, this time to Jos. Télesphore Maurice Laflamme, son of Joe's older brother Adélard and Marie Anne Comtois. He shared the responsibility with his mother Marie Théoret. It was possible that Joe and Florence were separated by this time, but not necessarily. Family traditions, preferences, or circumstances could have dictated the choice of godparents other than a married couple.

Joe and Émilie

How Joe and Émilie met in 1919 is anybody's guess. Records show that Émilie Haigneré left the port of Liverpool, England, on the RMS *Melita*, to arrive in Saint John, New Brunswick, on March 6, 1919. Why did Émilie choose Liverpool as her port of departure? At the time, Liverpool was the major freight port in Europe, thus offering the cheapest fares to travellers immigrating to North America. Furthermore, because the port boasted frequent departures, this reduced costly waiting time in the city. As Émilie was a domestic leaving for Canada with a meagre sum of 130 French francs in her pocket (not much, given the weakness of the postwar franc), Liverpool was the most economical choice for her.

Though her destination was the port of Montreal, Émilie landed at Saint John because, until the 1950s, the maritime port functioned as Montreal's winter port, since both the Gulf of St. Lawrence and the St. Lawrence River were frozen. The 25-year-old French traveller most likely reached Montreal by way of the Canadian Pacific Railway (CPR) through the state of Maine, USA. Being single, the young woman gave as reason for her immigration, "to marry." Indeed, marrying a British subject in Canada would automatically make her, later on, a British subject and a Canadian citizen, thus allowing her to forego the naturalization process.

We know that the young couple did not stay in Montreal for very long since they moved to Gogama in the summer of 1920. The move to Northern Ontario completely changed the former Parisian's lifestyle. A few years later, she would admit to a *Toronto Daily Star* journalist that she did not think anybody could live the life she was living in the northern bush.

Despite her hectic routine, Émilie found time to practice her pool game and she excelled at it. Proud of his wife's skills, Joe matched her up against his male visitors, and invariably she won the game—and he probably won the bet. Joe himself was also "the very devil with a billiard cue."

As rough as her life was in the pioneer village, Émilie did not lose her taste for the niceties of life, as was reflected in the wedding gift she and Joe gave to a Gogama couple. In May 1937, Dave Ranger, who was still boarding at the LaFlammes, took the train to Sudbury with his fiancée Simone Morin to be secretly married in Sainte-Anne-des-Pins church, thus foregoing any public celebration of their wedding. The LaFlammes' gift was one of the few the couple received. The beautiful cake platter and lifter were surely chosen by Lillie.

The yellow platter was round with a thin royal blue border repeated near the white centre which, in turn, was decorated with a decal depicting an

English country scene with a young woman in a pink crinoline. The pattern was repeated on the matching lifter. The bone china cake set was made by Hollinshead & Kirkham Tunstall, a reputed company in England. It was not bought in England, however, as there is no evidence that Lillie ever returned to Europe. She once mentioned to a *Toronto Daily Star* reporter that, if and when Joe made enough money, she would like to visit Paris again, "to have [a] good time."

10

Having a Good Time in New York

Joe LaFlamme's week-long stay in Toronto in January 1925 had whetted the wolf tamer's appetite for public attention. He wanted more. The lure of the crowds and of adventure brought him to travel 700 miles (1,150 km) with a team of eight huskies, one half-breed wolf, and four full-blooded timber wolves, sleigh and gear included. How he travelled to New York is unknown, but he most likely did not mush down to the Big Apple all the way from Gogama, as one *New York Times* article suggested: "Mushes 700 Miles with Dogs to See Hockey Here Tonight."

He did get to mush down Broadway on the morning of Saturday, January 23, 1926. Imagine coming to Manhattan from the Canadian wilderness with wolves—it would be like Crocodile Dundee arriving from the Australian outback with a float of crocodiles. Joe did it, and it proved to be one of the most thrilling moments of his career—one he would undoubtedly remember all his life. How could he not when he was welcomed by thousands of people who lined the streets cheering him on?

That same evening, the Wolf Man of the North had the honour of dropping the puck at the start of the New York vs. Boston hockey game held at

Madison Square Garden. He then drove his team around the ice during the intermissions. The crowd of 10,000 spectators was both excited and amazed at seeing real timber wolves in action right on its own turf. Whether the wild beasts were true to nature in such a foreign setting seems doubtful, though, as is evident in *New York Times* journalist Harry Cross's comment, "The timber wolves and dogs from the frigid North acted as if they knew they were far from home." Not so for the Boston team, who won the game 3-2 in overtime. The Canadian musher and his wolves also attracted huge crowds at several other hockey matches.

Joe must have been thrilled to be on the ice with international sport stars, especially given that his family members were avid hockey fans. To top it all, he did so in the biggest city in North America at the time (the second largest city on the planet). In 1926, New York's population exceeded seven million people. Was Joe just experiencing a thrill, or was it the power to be able to accomplish feats never done before? At 36, Joe had boundless energy and drive, a flair for showmanship, and most of all, an untamable spirit that got him what he wanted. Afraid of nothing, or so it seemed, he knew how to play with life.

LaFlamme seemed instinctively to know how to be in the right place at the right time, and how to approach individuals. For example, on a train trip near Toronto he met Al Greene, night wire chief for United Press. Greene then brought Joe to the attention of George Lewis "Tex" Rickard who was, at the time, the number one sports promoter in the United States and the founder of the New York Rangers. Rickard held the rights to promote live events at the brand new Madison Square Garden, which had offically opened on December 15, 1925. Since Joe LaFlamme was as good a live show as he could get, Rickard sponsored him and his dog-and-wolf team for a two-week engagement at the Garden. The exhibition contract was made in connection with the Westminster Kennel Club's dog show.

Prior to the dog show, on the weekend of February 5-7, 1926, Joe headed out to fashionable Jackson Heights, on Long Island, bringing in the carnival queen, Janet Crombie, in his dog sled.

To advertise the dog show, a photo of two muzzled wolves being held by LaFlamme, his assistant Paul Giroux and Marilyn Gerndt appeared in the

New York Evening Graphic. The caption stated that the "dangerous dogs" were on display at the show. The organizers were quick to form an opinion about LaFlamme's "dangerous dogs." Despite having been set up in a corner of the Garden, Joe's wolves managed to stop the show. All eyes were on the Canadian trapper's wild canines. Only the judges paid attention to the show dogs.

Once all shows were over, the wolf tamer took advantage of his trip to the State of New York to contact an American friend. In fact, he had intended to pay Alvah Griffin Strong a visit in January but, unable to refuse Tex Rickard's fabulous offer, he had postponed his trip to Alton, some 300 miles (500 km) north of the Big Apple. On Thursday, February 18, Joe, Paul, and the 13 animals arrived at the Alasa Farms, all in great shape for the weekend races.

Joe LaFlamme at 36 years old, at Alasa Farms, in February 1926. Photo courtesy of Alasa Farms/Strong Family.

11
Making History at Alasa Farms

A **one-of-a-kind race**
Alvah Griffin Strong's 1,600 acre (648 ha) country estate offered a posh welcome to the northern bushmen and their canine wards. Strong was the grandson of Henry Alvah Strong, first president of Eastman Kodak in New York City. Alasa Farms, located high on the rolling hills of the south shore of Sodus Bay, boasted more than five miles (eight km) of shoreline, about 100 acres (41 ha) of apple trees, and plenty of open fields. The large house had been built by Shakers nearly a century before. Strong raised milking Shorthorn cattle, exhibition hackney ponies, and Alaskan huskies. His splendid kennel house was now home to LaFlamme's rugged animals.

It was because of this kennel that Strong and LaFlamme had met. The previous summer, Alvah had gone to Gogama to buy some Alaskan huskies from Joe. How did he find out that the Gogama resident had dogs to sell? Maybe Joe advertised in the newspapers or through dog breeders' associations or kennels. Among several other dogs, Alvah had bought Gogama, the mother of LaFlamme's lead dog Fidel. Unfortunately, she died a short time before Joe's visit to Alasa Farms.

True men of the woods, both in attire and demeanour, Joe LaFlamme and 26-year-old Paul Giroux—and the animals—were enjoying the vast open spaces and the fresh air, as Joe confided to a reporter: "New York is all right, but it's too crowded, too noisy. We are glad to be away. The wolves stood the 375-mile [600 km] trip from Gogama to Toronto better than the dogs, but they could not stand New York and being inside. The dogs can stand that best. It was hard on us all; we need cold air, exercise, snow and work—and we miss the trees." Exercise they would as they prepared for a historic race, the first event of its kind in the world. Approximately 300 people, driving on snow-drifted roads from as far as Rochester, were about to witness extraordinary entertainment. Each guest had received a written invitation from Alvah himself. Before the exhibition race, a course was laid out on the snow-packed hills of Alasa Farms.

Saturday, February 20, was a partially cloudy day, and, according to Joe, the weather was excellent for his dogs and wolves. The race was set for 2 p.m., and the spectators, lined up between what seem in the photos to be the house and the barn, got to see the preparations first hand. Among the group of bystanders was one tall, gangly country boy who did not feel comfortable in close proximity to wild wolves. He carried a sawed-off shot gun, and when Joe brought his wolves out of the kennel house, the boy discreetly tried to slip a

Alvah G. Strong (right), owner of Alasa Farms, with Joe LaFlamme and his wolf on February 20, 1926. Photo courtesy of Alasa Farms/Strong Family.

shell into the gun's magazine. Another youth asked the lad why he was loading his gun. Spitting tobacco juice in the snow, the country boy was unrelenting: "I ain't taking no chances when wolves is about."

The young man was probably wise not to take chances, unlike others who thought that Joe's wolves were nothing but "dangerous dogs." Joe protested adamantly: "[It] is absurd, they do not know a dog can bark, the wolf can only howl. I have dogs with me and I have wolves. If any man thinks that they are dogs, I will

Joe LaFlamme and one of his wolves at Alasa Farms near Alton, New York, on February 20, 1926. Photo courtesy of Alasa Farms/Strong Family.

give them to him—let him take them home. . . . If any man is tired of his wife, I will give him one, it will help—if he can take it home."

Wolves and dogs were indeed "about," in pre-race frenzy. The competition would be tight; Strong owned an exceptionally good team of huskies. The wolf trainer also had an excellent team, but the challenge was to put it together. To harness the free-spirited beasts required tremendous energy. Joe and Paul first worked hard to muzzle the wolves, put on their webbing harnesses and get them out of their cages. Another battle ensued to attach the wolves' short chains to the sled's long gangline. As the animals were set up in pairs, removing their muzzles required an experienced and swift hand, especially for the second wolf in the pair. But the musher and his handler were getting quite adept at avoiding vicious bites and pulling the team together.

The Canadian musher's team comprised two pairs of wolves at the rear, preceded by another half-breed wolf, then by Fidel in the lead. The American musher's team would be led by none other than Billy—the dog that had performed so well for LaFlamme in Toronto the year before. Teaming up with him were Yak, the finest husky the Canadians had seen; Husky; Nugget, an Alaskan husky exceptional in both size and beauty; and Jumbo. Both teams were now eager to run, waiting for the start signal.

"Anamoosh, maheegan!" At LaFlamme's Indian command, the excited timber wolves lunged and the gangline tightened. "Quich!" Fidel sprang forward and the wolves followed his lead. "Fidel, Gee!" beckoned the lead dog to the right. Later, a cry of "Fidel, Haw!" got the wolf team to veer to the left until

Joe LaFlamme's wolves and dogs in harness at Alasa Farms, on February 20, 1926. Photo courtesy of Alasa Farms/Strong Family.

the musher's shout to "Quich!" set the pack on a straight course once again.

The animals were surely enjoying their run in the open fields more than their cages and muzzles. Yet Fidel, who was a born leader, knew how to pace the wolf team. As for the wolves, because of their keen pack instinct, they could be trusted to follow their leader. Joe could read his animals and communicate with them, demonstrating a masterful control of his team. That was why he was called the Wolf Man, a title he relished. The title was now earned more than ever, as LaFlamme was the first man in the world to succeed in harnessing timber wolves and training them to race and do sled work.

Wolf Man Joe LaFlamme, with one of his wolves at Alasa Farms, near Alton, New York, February 20, 1926. Photo courtesy of Alasa Farms/Strong Family.

LaFlamme's working partners

Indeed, LaFlamme's wolves were not only show animals but working partners as well. In Gogama Joe supplemented his bootlegging business by delivering supplies to lumber camps and, on occasion, by bringing injured men to first-aid stations when horses were impractical in six and a half feet (2 m) of snow. Sledding dozens of miles through otherwise impassable trails in forests, and over marshes and lakes, Joe needed a dependable and strong team. Northern lakes were often slushy due to water seeping up through the ice after thick snow cover. When huskies travelled on those lakes, their paws would get wet with slush and then freeze. The rugged wolves, on the other hand, were hardly inconvenienced by the slush. Led by a good guide dog, they could hold their own in hard, physical labour like hauling the 16 tons of supplies Joe had brought to the bush camps since he first harnessed wolves in 1923. And, in the midst of all this work, LaFlamme managed to have fun too.

Since he sometimes harnessed the wolves to a long toboggan instead of a sleigh, Joe learned how to ride standing up. Once he could find his balance, he thoroughly enjoyed the ride, especially when the toboggan was pulled by a fast team on smooth terrain and frozen lakes. Joe compared it to "sailing in fair and steady winds." On the other hand, when the trail was rough, it was like "riding a camel" or "shooting the *chutes.*"

Working with sled wolves had definite advantages for LaFlamme. The only downfall was when a pile-up occurred on a downhill trek. Huskies usually stayed there, quietly waiting for the situation to straighten itself out. Wolves, who did not wear their muzzles when working, would start fighting right away, chewing each other's ears off. Now, imagine trying to untangle those mean beasts! But, once they were back on the trail, they showed great stamina. As the Wolf Man later told a reporter: "[Wolves] are stronger, can do more work and don't get sick like dogs."

If a wolf occasionally got sick Joe knew how to handle it—with some help from an assistant. He would hold the wolf gently around the neck, with one hand on the animal's upper back. The assistant would then force the wolf's jaws open with a wooden stick. Joe would then stand up and, carefully watching his fingers, shove a pill down the beast's throat. Obviously, the wolf would squirm and struggle to free itself. After having stabilized it, the trainer would pour some diluted goose-grease down its throat as a chaser, directly from the bottle. This last step would be repeated two or three times to prevent the wolf from spitting out the medication. Before long, in most cases, the animal would have regained its strength and would be ready to work again.

The LaFlamme-Strong friendship

Alvah G. Strong and his guests had the opportunity to witness the wolves' strength and endurance during an exhibition. Fastened to trace chains, the beasts not only easily pulled heavy logs, but also a Ford automobile weighing some 1,200 lbs (550 kg). Strong must have been glad he had invited his Canadian friend and his timber wolves to his estate.

As for the results of the historic race—none of the articles consulted reported a winner. Given each man's propensity for entertainment, winning the race was probably of little importance.

The two men had a lot in common besides raising and racing dogs, but it was certainly not their height, since Joe stood at least a head above Alvah. According to anecdotal information, Joe's English skills were basic and Alvah did not speak a word of French. Alcohol was therefore the translator for both fellows. A glass of liquor and an honest pat on the back were definitely universal camaraderie builders.

As all good things must come to an end, it was time for the Wolf Man and his party to leave Alasa Farms and head to Rochester, where Joe had a two-day public engagement. Probably impressed by Saturday's performance, the *Rochester Democrat and Chronicle* had invited the Canadians to race on the old Oak Hill golf course on February 24-25, courtesy of the University of Rochester and the Oak Hill Country Club.

Alvah G. Strong (left) wears Joe LaFlamme's parka and fur hat. In the middle is probably the wolf tamer's assistant Paul Giroux, sitting next to LaFlamme (right), at Alasa Farms, on February 20, 1926. Photo courtesy of Alasa Farms/Strong Family.

12

Wooing the Crowds in Rochester

In all probability, Joe LaFlamme, Paul Giroux, and the 13 animals travelled the 30 mile (60 km) westerly trip to Rochester by truck either Tuesday, February 23, 1926, or the following morning. On the day of the first race fine weather still prevailed and Joe was excited: "I have been told that the Oak Hill golf course, where I will exhibit my wolves under the auspices of the *Democrat and Chronicle*, is an excellent place for such an exhibition and I feel sure that we will be able to interest the people of Rochester." Sporting a bushy black beard and his traditional costume, Joe was ready to put on a good show; but just in case the show went wrong, Public Safety Commissioner Curtis W. Barker would be on hand to ensure that onlookers were safe.

Early Wednesday afternoon, on February 24, hundreds of people started lining the streets in downtown Rochester, waiting for the musher and his animals to appear. Meanwhile, Joe and Paul were harnessing two teams at the Webber Animal Hospital on Andrew Street. The Canadian musher would drive a team of four full-blooded wolves drawing a small sled. His assistant would pilot a team of eight huskies and a half-breed wolf hauling a long wooden sleigh and gear. At 2 p.m., all were ready and eager to start the rigorous trek through the city to the old golf course, some 13 miles (21 km) away. This exhibition run with harnessed wolves was also a first in Rochester.

Their itinerary went from Andrew Street to Church, then on Plymouth Avenue North to Main Street East. The hills of East Avenue proved challenging. Then from Alexander Street, the route led on to Mount Hope and Elmwood Avenues. The pavement on Elmwood being almost bare in some places, Joe was forced to drive his team on the snow-covered sidewalk.

Just before reaching the Lehigh Valley railroad tracks, the Wolf Man spotted a woman pushing a baby carriage on the sidewalk in front of his team. He called out to her to clear the way because his running wolf team might be difficult to stop. The woman panicked and ran onto the street, leaving baby and carriage behind. A police officer escorting the musher quickly picked up the carriage and brought it to safety. After the incident, Joe admitted that he would have been able to stop his team before reaching the woman. Was this LaFlamme's flair for showmanship at work again?

Now and then the two teams stopped in the downtown streets to rest. In all likelihood Joe seized the opportunity to talk with the onlookers about wolves and life in Northern Ontario. Then it was onward to the old golf course.

A crowd of six to seven thousand people waited at the Oak Hill, where the Canadian musher and his party were scheduled to appear at 4 p.m. Automobiles were parked everywhere, even as far north as the intersection of Brooks and Plymouth avenues. Half the crowd swarmed around the dogs and wolves as they rested briefly from their long run. Joe and Paul then unharnessed and attached the dogs to another sled before leading both teams to the top of the hill, formerly known as No. 1 Tee. For the next race, Joe's team consisted of the four wolves and the half-breed, with Fidel in the lead.

The dog-and-wolf teams raced side by side down the hill, with the two mushers calling out to their animals. "Ally-mush! Ally-mush!" Joe's command prompted the wolves to go even faster. He occasionally prodded the team along by snapping his rawhide whip over their heads. Again, the outcome of the race is not known.

In the hour following the race, the Wolf Man showed the crowd how he handled wolves when they hauled supplies to the remote bush camps.

It was clear who was master because a word from LaFlamme would get the wild canines to rise and start trotting over the hills. After the exhibition, Joe extended his showmanship by offering a ride to several school girls in the crowd.

The Thursday event was to be similar, starting at 2:45 p.m. with a march along the same streets up to Monroe Junior High School, on Alexander Street. Once there, the wolves and dogs would be taken off their sleds and trucked the remaining distance to Oak Hill. The last race and exhibition were set for 4:30 p.m., a half-hour later than the previous day to allow school children more time to get to the golf course.

On Thursday, however, the fine weather spell was over, and the events were postponed until Friday because of rain. Instead of amusing the public, the Wolf Man entertained his hosts for the night. Doctor and Mrs. Willard A. Gray, living on Shellwood Road, listened earnestly as Joe related how he trapped wolves several hundred kilometres north of his Gogama residence.

Finally, after the exhibition on Friday, February 26, Fidel returned to Alasa Farms to stay with his new owner, Alvah G. Strong. As for the rest of the Canadian party, they headed straight to Gogama, taking several days to complete the 543 mile (900 km) trip.

13
Everyday Life in Gogama

Mink farming

Satisfied—for a while at least—with his adventures, the Wolf Man now settled into a routine at home. So did his wolves, pacing the dirt floor in their large pens. Other little feet were also pacing in their cages: in 1926, Joe was listed by the Dominion Bureau of Statistics as an Ontario mink rancher. He was still in this business a few years later; Dave Ranger told a reporter that he looked after LaFlamme's fur farm from 1928 to 1930.

There were, at the time, hundreds of other fur farmers in Ontario, some of whom also operated huge traplines in the northern part of the province. One of them was R.G. (Bob) Hodgson, editor of the *Fur Trade Journal* and author of the book *Let's Go Fur Farming*. One January day he paid a visit to his friend Joe, a visit "that gave his adrenal glands a workout." As the story goes, Hodgson and Frank Johnston headed out to Gogama in January to study wolves up close. Joe had some very impressive and ferocious specimens, some of them, like Pete, weighing close to 100 lbs (45 kg).

While both men were at the LaFlamme home talking to Lillie, they heard a lot of noise outside the door. In came Joe with Pete and another huge wolf, both of them on leashes, of course, but not for long because Joe proceeded to remove their chains. The wolves then started walking around the small room. Bob and Frank immediately hid behind their chairs, while searching for a better means of protecting themselves. Hodgson commented, "I do recall that while it came to my mind then that wolves had never been known to attack humans, it was extremely difficult to convince my feet of this fact." But there was no need to worry: Joe had control over his wolves. Satisfied that his guests had had a little bit of fun, he put the chains back on the wolves and took his pets outside. As for Hodgson, he described LaFlamme, whom he had known for several years, as "a real character of the north, of which there will possibly never be another just like him and would himself be an attraction to the general public."

Joe's generosity

Like his sense of humour, LaFlamme's everyday speech was sometimes hard to decipher. Being moderate in delivery, it was often sprinkled with enigmas or parables, especially in a family setting. For example, when Joe asked nonchalantly for "Monsieur Herbert," he was referring to the Herbert brand of brown sugar. The matter-of-fact inquiry "Shall we go into the sitting room for tea?" meant he wanted to be served. The family calls this kind of talk "speaking in Laflamme." Joe also liked to give nicknames to Gogama locals. He called Gérard Jean, a boarder who did odd jobs around the place and played music, "*Ti-Jean L'Acadie.*" Even his wife received a nickname: "*la p'tite femme*" stuck with her for a long time. The couple's Christmas cards to the family were always signed "*Télesphore et p'tite femme.*"

While his family says Joe loved to joke around, especially with his brother Joseph, for many locals Joe was a serious man who seldom laughed and was not given to polite greetings. He usually returned a polite hello with a gruff "Euh!" Children usually got more grunting than actual speaking. Nonetheless, most agree, despite the fact that his size and pets commanded respect, Joe LaFlamme talked to everybody, was known for his dancing parties, and had a generous heart. He was always ready to help someone in need. Through the years, many a tramp found shelter and work at Joe's. In fact, several tran-

Lillie LaFlamme and Dave Ranger, dressed up for a masquerade party at the LaFlamme home in Gogama, circa 1930. Photo courtesy of Eunice Belisle.

sients—along with penniless locals—contributed to making his two-storey house the largest one in Gogama.

Schoolboys often escaped the boredom of the classroom by hiding at LaFlamme's house, where he always had a place for them at his table. Eight-year-old Ernest (Dubby) Turcotte much preferred visiting Joe LaFlamme to going to school. His fondest memories remain about Joe's heart-warming cabbage soup. Indeed, the Wolf Man was as skilful with pots and pans as he was with his long whip. Little did Ernest know, though, that Joe's secret ingredient was most likely whisky, a tradition among some of the Laflammes. A little shot of the hard liquor in the soup was enough to make the taste—and the boys—

linger. That is when Joe's whip came in handy; a little crack of the whip near the youngsters' ears was enough to shoo them away, either from the house or from the animals' cages.

Another Gogama resident may have wished for a similar power over her neighbour, though she might not have used it, given Joe's generosity. Often, attracted by the smell of freshly baked bread, Joe would knock three times on the door of Yvonne Nadeau (Ernest Turcotte's future mother-in-law), open it, say a polite "*Bonjour, madame,*" put 25 cents on the table, and walk away with a loaf of bread—without asking permission! At 25 cents a loaf, who could say no when, in the early 1940s, a loaf of bread sold for about 8 cents?

The dark side of Joe's personality

Like day and night, all personalities have two sides: a good side that we tend to show in public and a dark side which we often try to hide. According to Debbie Ford, "the more we try to suppress the aspects of our personality that we deem unacceptable, the more they find mischievous ways of expressing themselves." One malicious expression of Joe's dark side was evident in the way he sometimes treated his wife, especially when she meddled in his soup pot. Locals report that he kicked her in the behind or threw her down the stairs. He once dipped Lillie's arm in a boiling stew, causing severe burns that required hospital treatment. Luckily, Elzéar came to the rescue. He stopped the train, then boarded it with Lillie to accompany her to the hospital in Sudbury. He always kept a close watch over her after this nasty display of his brother's temper.

On summer days, when the windows were open, locals often heard Joe and Lillie yelling at each other; there was no mistaking *la p'tite femme*'s shrill voice. There are rumors that both Joe and Lillie drank heavily at times. Furthermore, the two were rarely seen together in public. There were apparently difficulties in the relationship, but Lillie never complained about it to her neighbours. She had the reputation of being smart and tough. In any case, Lillie and Joe stuck it out and remained together until the end.

Elzéar Laflamme

As for Elzéar, who was nine years younger than Joe, he stayed with his brother's family for a while after coming to Gogama, probably in the mid 1930s. He was deaf; hence his French nickname *"le sourd à LaFlamme"* (LaFlamme's deaf brother). Elzéar had left his work as a shoemaker and turned to his older brother for employment. Eventually, he moved into an old house on Poupore Street. He remained there until his death at the Sudbury General Hospital, on August 7, 1958, long after Joe had left Gogama. The 60-year-old Elzéar Laflamme was buried in a Roman Catholic cemetery in Sudbury. Joe surprised everyone when he appeared for the funeral in Sudbury and went for a subsequent visit to Gogama. Indeed, it was Joe's death, rather than his brother's, that had been mistakenly reported in some newspapers, including the *Sudbury Star*. Joe LaFlamme took that lightheartedly: "Don't you worry about that. Twice before I've been reported dead in papers all over Canada and the United States," he said, adding, "I'm in the best of health, and it is good to be back here in the North for a while again."

LaFlamme's "hotel"

Joe always knew how to create work for the jobless and the transients. Managing and maintaining his boarding house was a feat in itself, the more so because it doubled as a bootlegging business, or what one might call a "hotel." Although there is no proof that the boarding house was also a brothel, rumours are numerous.

Nonetheless, even in 1925, LaFlamme's boarding house was a busy place with a constant flow of railway workers, prospectors, and miners needing room and board in Gogama. To accommodate the flow, Joe expanded the house. By 1930 there were 10 or 12 bedrooms, each of them identified with a metal number on the door. The LaFlammes' sleeping quarters were on the main floor. With so many boarders, the owners needed all the help they could get to run the business, including a girl to help with domestic chores. Lillie also paid her neighbour Bertha Duguay to do washing and ironing.

Both Joe and Lillie cooked for the boarders and were excellent at it. The Wolf Man was proud of his wife's ability in the kitchen, especially when she was preparing a large meal or banquet: "When that woman gets near a stove, she is like she-bear.... 'Red my stove,' she hollers, meaning she wants her stove red hot, and then she throws us all out. Whoosh!" As for LaFlamme himself, twins Alfred and Roland Secord attested to his ability in the kitchen since they occasionally ate breakfast there. They were treated to a hearty serving of scrumptious milk curd pancakes, sausages, and eggs, in the company of Morris, LaFlamme's only son. Roland especially liked the rich cream stored in the kitchen porch. Occasionally, he would sneak in and drink some of it. Occasionally, Joe would catch him and holler, "You, cream drinker, I don't want you there anymore!"

To feed large groups on a daily basis required a well-stocked pantry. In addition to gardening and raising wild and domestic animals on his property, Joe also raised pigs on an island across Minisinakwa Lake. The piece of Crown land on the right of the train bridge was dubbed "Pig Island" because LaFlamme would bring his piglets there in the spring and round them up in the fall after they had fattened on wild plants and berries. Locals reported seeing Joe walk from his house to the local grocer, C.D. Payette and Sons, carrying a freshly killed pig across his bare shoulders. The giant Wolf Man was off to the market either to sell his meat or to have it cut up.

What groceries the LaFlammes could not buy locally, they ordered from Pianosi's butcher shop, in Copper Cliff, near Sudbury, just as other Gogama residents did. They placed an order by mail, and it later arrived by train. The supplies were then delivered either by horse and sleigh in winter or by three-quarter-ton truck in summer.

To manage his boarding house well, Joe LaFlamme needed a good measure of resourcefulness and business sense. Furthermore, he knew how to adapt to the circumstances that came his way.

14

Evolving into a "Joe of all Trades"

By the 1940s the LaFlammes' boarding house had expanded into a tourist lodge. Joe's letterhead promised a lot:

Moose Lodge

Ideal spot for your Big Game Hunting

Fishing—Pickerel, Trout and Northern Pike

Main water route leading to James Bay. Canoe Trips Anywhere

J. T. LaFlamme, Proprietor

P. O. Drawer 106, Gogama, Ontario, Canada.

This was just one version of his letterhead, which appeared in numerous forms. Admittedly, with Joe's expert knowledge of the area and of canoe handling, this canoe trip business seemed like a good fit.

In December 1930, while in Toronto, Joe announced his first camping parties to James Bay the following summer. The starting point of the proposed 400 mile (700 km) trek to Moose Factory would be Minisinakwa Lake, in Gogama. From there, the parties would paddle from Mattagami Lake to the Mattagami River, then downriver to the Moose River, which flows into James Bay. The trip would be undertaken in 18 foot (5.5 m) canvas-covered cedar canoes. One has to wonder if Joe built them himself, since he professed to be a canoe builder. If not, perhaps he bought some while in Toronto. If he did, he most likely got them at a bargain price given his powers of persuasion and his ready tongue. This ability to speak effortlessly was a talent he often put to good use, as was the case in February 1930, when he was a guest speaker at a farewell banquet for Roy Jessup, manager of Cochrane Lumber Company in Gogama.

In the meantime, the Wolf Man continued to raise mink and huskies. In an effort to instill courage and endurance in the dog breed, he tried mixing it with wolf strains. He succeeded in breeding three female huskies with wolves, but his attempts at breeding female wolves with huskies all failed. He trained the young animals for sled racing. He also continued to trap and train wolves to harness for races and exhibitions, though by 1930 he had only five wolves. In addition to wolves, he trapped fox, otter, and other small fur-bearing animals, whose pelts he traded at the local Hudson's Bay Company store. Prices fluctuated through the years, but as an example, on December 24, 1932, a fox pelt sold for $5.50, almost as much as mink; marten went for $9.33; ermine for 27 cents (as strange as that may sound); and fisher for $36.50.

Civil service at the local, provincial, and federal levels

In his spare time, LaFlamme attended the meetings of the Gogama Board of Trade. The first record of his membership in this organization dates back to June 18, 1929. Through the years, until March 17, 1946, he was active in the organization and often proposed motions. As much a go-getter as Joe was, it is surprising that he never became president of the board. Obviously, he was content being a leader of wolves rather than of men. Perhaps administration and politics were not his cup of tea, though in 1945 he did a short stint with the Progressive Conservative Party of Ontario. He apparently ran for MPP (Member of Provincial Parliament) for the riding of Sudbury, promising to press for a road to Gogama. Even though he was not elected, he represented Gogama as a voting delegate at the PC convention in Sudbury that year. All told, it is a wonder he joined the blue party when he grew up in a family of hardcore Liberals.

With time, Joe LaFlamme finally proclaimed himself "mayor" of his town. One reporter had an explanation for Joe's claim to mayoralty: "He still is about the largest human in Gogama, and when he announced…that he was now His Worship, Mayor Joseph T. Laflamme, no one disputed his claim." But as Gogama was not a municipality, the designation was never official. Whether he was mayor or not, as resident Ernest Turcotte reflected, Joe LaFlamme has certainly put Gogama "on the map."

Joe did indeed place Gogama in the limelight everywhere he went, including his travels to 21 Northern Ontario townships where he worked as a federal census worker collecting data for at least one (perhaps all) of the 1921, 1931, and 1941 censuses. He also occasionally guided hunters and fishermen for the Ontario Department of Game and Fisheries, though most of the time he did it on his own. In the 1940s, he worked for the Ontario Department of Lands and Forests as a forest firefighter, earning, for example, $462 in the fiscal year 1946-1947. It was in this capacity that LaFlamme was cast in a 19-minute documentary on controlling forest fires, titled *The Forest Commandos*.

In the movies

The script for *The Forest Commandos* was written by Glenn Ireton, Warner Brothers' publicist in Canada. Van Campen Heilner directed the filming and Gordon Hollingshead produced it, with the cooperation of the Forest Protection Service of the Ontario Department of Lands and Forests. Narrated by Knox Manning, it cast, in their real-life roles, Bill McCormick, George Phillips and Joe LaFlamme. The original footage featured a scene with LaFlamme hand-feeding his two pet moose. Another scene focused on firefighter Joe hauling heavy equipment from site to site and lifting a 150 lb (68 kg) water pump as if it was a mere feather.

In another scene, Joe's house was supposedly on fire and he had to climb down the ladder from a second-storey window. The moment "his ample derriere" straddled the sill to reach the first rung, the window fell and hit the back of his head. He took it all in stride, like the good comedian he was.

When interviewed about the falling window, LaFlamme said to the reporter, "I just laugh like I'm crazy." Joe obviously relished being a celebrity: "Thees movie business, she is all right." He was not a great fan of Hollywood movies, having seen only a few, which, for the most part, he did not like—

except for Bette Davis's films. Not so for his own film, though, as he told a reporter, "Stories are no good. But when you get pictures that are true, like this forest fire one, that's fine. Very educational. Very valuable."

Released by Warner Brothers Pictures in 1945, the Technicolor documentary was filmed—probably the previous summer—in Gogama and at Shining Tree Lake, 51 miles (82 km) south. When the movie company arrived in Gogama, Lillie LaFlamme showed off her culinary and organizational skills by throwing a banquet for the whole crew. For the occasion, she killed, cleaned, cooked, and served 23 hens. *La p'tite femme* was indeed a good match for Joe. Her man displayed just as much generosity, later giving Ireton a black bear cub for his young son Gabriel in Toronto. Not surprisingly the pet was named "Forest Commando."

On March 20, 1945, Joe attended the "rushes" of the film in Toronto. For the special event, he wore his lumberjack breeches, knee boots, a sweater coat over a flannel shirt, and a peaked cap. The 56-year-old woodsman had the cha-

Charlotte Batcher cuddles bear cub and Joe LaFlamme who was in Toronto, in March 1945, to see the preview of Warner Brothers' film *The Forest Commandos*, in which he is featured. Photo courtesy of *Toronto Star*/GetStock.com #2086200452

risma of a movie star and attracted female admirers, despite his long white hair and beard. It must have been the lure of his northern outfit and his fame as a tamer of wild animals that made pretty girls fall for him, as was evident in a photograph in the *Toronto Daily Star*. Joe also had female followers in his town—but whether or not the Gogama girls were admirers, they were often teased or pinched, willy-nilly, by LaFlamme.

The Forest Commandos was not Joe's first film. In 1925, he was featured in a short documentary filmed by the Ontario Motion Picture Bureau called *Transport in the North*. He was portrayed as a trapper travelling with his wolf team in the northern bush, as well as a wolf tamer caring for a sick wolf.

This dabbling in filmmaking probably gave Joe the incentive to buy himself a movie projector and show the public some silent movies at his home. Gordon Miller remembers that when he was a young boy in the 1930s he saw a quite disturbing war film in a large room at the LaFlammes'. According to him, Joe was the first to show black-and-white silent movies in Gogama.

Now that Joe had gotten a taste of Hollywood, his next step was to get a good movie camera to produce his own films. *Toronto Daily Star* reporter Jack Karr, who interviewed Joe at the time, reported, "When it was all over and done with, he bought himself a 16 mm movie camera—and now all he wants is somebody to show him how in tarnation the danged thing works."

The camera was only an upgrade for LaFlamme, who was a self-taught photographer. The *Sudbury Star* of April 2, 1932, featured three photographs relating to a tragic house fire in Gogama. The photo caption ended, "All photographs by courtesy of Joe Laflamme, Gogama." In the *Globe and Mail* of November 2, 1938, photos of bow and arrow hunters were also snapped by Joe, who was quick to grab his gun to join the hunt, as seen in the *Sudbury Star* of the same date.

In his travels as a tamer, Joe always carried a supply of postcards with black-and-white photos of himself with his wolves or moose. Though he was not the photographer, obviously, he was involved in their composition. The Gogama Heritage Museum collection has some photos of Joe, or taken by Joe, which are stamped on the back: "J. T. LAFLAMME, PUBLICITY PHOTOGRAPHER, Gogama, Ontario, Canada." The subject matter of the photographs varied from men in the bush to Joe's son Morris, of whom he was quite proud.

15

Raising Joe's Morrisson *and Lillie's* Petit Maurice

Morris Joseph LaFlamme, Joe's only son, was born in Gogama on Friday, April 26, 1929, nine years after his parents moved to Northern Ontario. The only record regarding the brown-haired, hazel-eyed boy's birthplace is an application for border crossing at Detroit in April 1948. There is also no record of Morris being baptized in the Catholic tradition. However, he did have a godfather, Dave Ranger, who, as mentioned before, was living with the LaFlammes at the time, so there must have been some kind of baptism ceremony. Both his parents were practising Catholics in their earlier years in Gogama, until the parish priest discovered that Joe and Lillie were living under common law and not legally married. At the time, according to the Catholic Church, this was a serious and mortal sin.

Father Achille Cournoyer did not take it lightly that some of his parishioners were living in sin. In fact, from then on, Joe and the parish priest did not get along—all the more because Joe was a bootlegger. Not feeling welcome in church, the Wolf Man abandoned religious practice, but not before setting fire to the building. Luckily, the fire was caught on time and the church did not burn down. The cleric must have been tempted to wish that one day this renegade Catholic would burn in hell—with his wolves. This would have taken care of the competition the priest encountered every time he rang the church bell and had to put up with a chorus of the infamous "singers."

The wolves' howling and yelping prevented not only the parish priest from sleeping at night, but other Gogama residents as well. The baying of wolves across the lake was, and still is today, a common occurrence in the small town nestled in the heart of the boreal forest. But a pack of wolves howling at one's door was another matter. For years, residents of Gogama put up with the blood-curdling howls of Joe LaFlamme's pets. However, there was no section of the Criminal Code which allowed the OPP to put an end to it. Constable Robert Van Norman had searched all law books, but to no avail.

Several pioneers remember the howling sessions triggered by barking dogs or the periodic ringing of the church bell. The lead wolf started and then the whole pack joined in the chorus. Like it or not, each day the town was serenaded with several raucous 15-minute concerts. Nowadays, tourists travel great distances to Ontario's Algonquin Park for a chance to hear wolves howl—with no guarantees. Young Morris grew up with the sound of wolves as if it were perfectly normal.

Morris obviously did not attend the Catholic school, Notre-Dame-du-Rosaire, just a hop and a skip from his home. Instead, he walked across the railroad tracks to the English Gogama Public School. The school was located near St. Mary's Anglican Church, a parish where Joe was actively involved as an elected officer, at least in 1935. In early June of that year, he was also elected delegate to the Anglican synod in Timmins. LaFlamme, who was described by school board members as "the most famous character out of the past in Gogama" was elected trustee in July 1939.

As earlier records for the local Anglican parish have been lost, so was the information—including the name—relating to the LaFlammes' second child, a girl who died in early infancy. She passed away so young, in fact, that hardly anyone in town had actually seen her. The cause and time of her death are also unknown, but locals remember where she was buried in the Anglican cemetery. They also remember Lillie visiting the cemetery and decorating her daughter's burial place with flowers. Both the white wooden cross and picket fence surrounding the plot succumbed to the great fire that ravaged the town in 1941.

Morris—or *mon petit Maurice* as Lillie affectionately called him—remained an only child, and a spoiled one at that, who did not know how to handle his pet bear cub properly. He was still quite young when he learned to ride. Joe bought him a small brown and white pinto equipped with a beautiful saddle. Morris enjoyed riding the pony along the track, following the train as far as he could. Joe was obviously proud of his son, but when he bought him all kinds of things, was he trying to give the boy what he himself had always dreamed of having as a young lad?

Morris also had an adventurous streak. In the *Toronto Star Weekly* of February 18, 1933, the four-year-old boy posed in his snowshoes and winter gear, complete with balaclava and snow goggles. The caption, titled "I'm a Gogama gold-getter and I'm tough, see!" described how Morris faced sub-zero weather and howling wolves, and was ready to follow his prospecting dad. It ended, "They're a hardy lot, these LaFlammes." Morris likely tagged along on some of his father's many treks across lakes and forests. The camaraderie between Joe and his Morrisson, as he called him, would be tested during adolescence. Nonetheless, Morris continued to help his dad run the "Gogama Zoo."

Morris LaFlamme, four-year-old prospector in training, in Gogama, winter 1933. Photo courtesy of *Toronto Star/GetStock.com* #2086200451

16
Running the Gogama Zoo

Give animal enthusiast Joe LaFlamme half an acre (2 ha) of land and you could bet he would turn it into a zoo, home to an ever-changing array of domestic and wild animals. Through the years, Joe and Lillie tended to chickens, canaries, pigeons, cows, pigs, a pony, huskies, a variety of other dogs, wolves, mink and other small fur-bearers, a bear or two, deer, and in the 1940s, several moose and a badger named Geraldine. Joe was quite proud of his pet badger, which was as playful as a dog, especially when she raided the cupboard for food. Anyone who tried to stop her would be swatted with her paw. There were also Lillie's pet skunks and foxes. The latter, she explained, were as easy to tame as cats, and they were especially fond of women, affectionately licking Lillie's face. One has to wonder why she enjoyed fox collarets so much.

Like Lillie, Joe loved his animals, especially his wolf pack. But he did not like to tie them up since they would waste away. At first, he kept the wolves in two partly covered cages, then later in several cages spread fan-like around his property, with the moose's pen at the back. Built with posts and chicken wire, the cages were 16 square ft (5 m^2) in area and 10 ft (3 m) high. The height was needed to prevent the wolves from escaping. According to Joe, when they were jumping for a piece of cake, they would climb up one side and down the other.

More than likely LaFlamme kept the female wolves separate from the males to curb the size of his chorus as well as to prevent trouble, which he said jealous females tended to cause. But wolves being wolves, besides pacing the perimeter of their pens, they occasionally escaped and ran through the village streets. Three or four of the braver teenage boys in town would volunteer to bring them back in chains. One of them, Roger (Ti-Pit) Carrière, now older and wiser, admitted they were not really aware of the risks back then, and that he would not do it today, not even for $100.

Several Gogama residents would have agreed that wandering wolves were dangerous. One Sunday morning in the mid-1930s, Elzire Dupuis—later Mrs. Wilfrid Charbonneau—and her older brother Hermas went to church, taking the back lane bordering LaFlamme's yard. Suddenly, they came face to face with one of Joe's timber wolves. Someone had cut the wire fence on its pen and the wolf had escaped. Probably surprised by the encounter, the wolf jumped at Elzire's throat. Since the six-year-old girl was wearing a scarf, the wolf had no hold on her, so he went for her leg and bit it severely. He then attacked the young boy. Luckily, Father Cournoyer heard the commotion, came out with a poker, and managed to scare the wolf away, though not before it had severely wounded the boy's right hand. Dr. Benjamin Susman was immediately available to treat both the children. As a result of her wounds, Elzire was bedridden for six months, and the damage on Hermas's hand was so extensive that it would later prevent him from joining the army. Very worried about the children's health, Lillie visited them every day to check on their recovery.

Needless to say, the villagers were quite concerned by these two incidents with the four-legged beast. For them, wolves were untamable and would always retain their wild instincts. Joe himself would agree that wolves could not be tamed. In fact, some of the wolves were hard to read. Such was the case with Pete, whom the trapper caught as a pup around 1924. When younger than two years old, the wolf was docile and even slept in his master's bed. As an adult, however, Pete showed his nasty side. Joe needed his thorough knowledge of wolf psychology and tremendous strength to get the upper hand.

One *Toronto Daily Star* reporter caught a glimpse, up close, of Pete's ferocity: "[H]e was then seventy lbs [32 kg] of fanged, fury, snarling, snapping, scratching [wolf], with hateful, bloodshot eyes, and body vibrating with viciousness and malignance. He had, of course, a muzzle on." Despite Pete's display of wolfishness, the curious reporter asked Joe what would happen if the wolf's muzzle were taken off. With his flair for drama, the Wolf Man answered, "You think he would not attack you, eh? All right, I'll take his muzzle off, and then I'll go away, and if you are still alive when I come back I'll give the wolf to what is left of you." LaFlamme's offer quickly stifled the reporter's curiosity.

Joe continued to explain, relating an incident with Pete: "Wolves are like that. They take on a certain steady look and then, bingo, they jump for you. No man can ever tame a wolf, no matter how long he might try. If Pete really made a jump at me and had his muzzle on, he'd hit me so hard that it would make his nose bleed. And then I wouldn't be able to stop him as long as there was any fight left in him. Once when he sprang at me and bit me, I choked him with a whip until he fell down. He lay there for five minutes, and then up he jumped at my throat again."

From experience, Joe admitted that three things were possible if you met a wolf in the woods. The animal could trot along without

JOE LA FLAMME AND "PETE"

POSTCARD: Joe LaFlamme and his wolf Pete, circa 1930. Photo courtesy of Gerry Talbot.

you even being aware of its presence; or it could sit down and look at you. But if it happened to be hungry or in a man-killing mood, it could tear you limb from limb. You might stand a chance, Joe explained, if you were up against a lone wolf and had arms powerful enough to choke it. But if there were two, the rear one would "tear you apart like a piece of toast."

Joe claimed that, contrary to popular belief, the idea that one could build a fire to deter a pack of wolves was a myth. It was not fires but light that they feared most. He had seen wolves lie down at night close to a hunter's fire, almost close enough to search his coat pockets. He himself had caught a wolf by mesmerizing him with a flashlight. It was then easy to put a chain around the confused animal's neck.

The wolf tamer had to be alert and constantly aware of his wolves' some-times destructive moods. He also needed to be physically fit and strong—and he was. This had earned the Wolf Man another nickname: the Strong Man of the North. The LaFlammes were known to be very strong, and Joe lived up to the reputation well past midlife. As an example of his herculean strength, once in the late 1920s he put his 200 lb (91 kg) tool chest on a sleigh and told Dave Ranger to get on it as well. Then, with the tips of his index fingers, he pushed the load over a distance of 1,500 ft (457 m).

In 1944, the 55-year-old Joe participated in a wrestling match against D. McLaren, a Timmins resident. The show was held on the stage of Gogama's silent-movie theatre, owned by Armidas Chenier. Supporters staked a $500 side bet on the contestants—and the Strong Man of the North won. He had not lost the stamina of his younger days as a champion wrestler because he had never stopped training. Indeed, the strapping former policeman wrestled a couple of wolves every morning before breakfast—just to whet his appetite. He bore many "battle" scars on his arms and legs because, according to him, wolves played more "brutal" than dogs.

Feeding all these carnivores must have been a feat in itself—and a full-time job. The daily ration of a working wolf or dog consisted of 5 to 7 lbs. (2-3 kg) of raw horsemeat or fish. On days when the animal was idle, it was either fish or oatmeal mush. As Joe could not rely on canned food or dry kibble at the time, he counted on dead cows and horses. He would cut the carcasses into large chunks and keep them on blocks of ice.

As for the moose, they ate mainly branches—a lot of branches: 33-44 lbs. (15-20 kg) per day in winter and more in summer. Joe paid young boys $2 per

Joe LaFlamme trains his moose in Gogama, circa mid-1940s. Photo courtesy of Gerry Talbot.

sleigh-load to gather the branches along the road to the dump. Young Roger Carrière, who was always willing to help, considered Joe generous. After all, during LaFlamme's moose days back in the 1940s, a package of 20 wieners cost about 10 cents. Two dollars was a lot of wiener roasts. Candies sold for a penny or two at the Hudson's Bay store and 15 cents would give you admission to the silent cinema.

LaFlamme did have a propensity for generosity, but when he smelled an opportunity to make money or a show, he snatched it. As moose needed to drink a lot of water in the summertime, Joe often sent local boys to the lake with the moose tethered by the neck. Alfred Secord recalls regularly taking a bull moose, a cow, and her calf to the lake across the railway tracks. The animals followed obediently, somewhat like cows, he says. Walking the moose was a lucrative business for the lad. When the train made its 15-minute stops in the village, tourists gave him 50 cents to take photos with the moose. But, when Alfred talked to Joe about it, he immediately lost his job. Joe started going to the lake himself. In fact, "Joe…living but a stone's throw from the railway, hardly even misses meeting a train in the hope there will be a fast sale of something or other to a hurried traveler." In the 1940s, three trains stopped in Gogama every day.

Other boys also took some of the moose, one at a time, into the woods behind the Department of Lands and Forests buildings, also across the tracks. Sometimes it would take three or four boys to pull an animal by its long rope. Once in the bush, they would tie the moose to a tree and let it feed on branches and alders for the day. They would return to pick up the beast before supper-time. When the boys wanted to play with the moose, they only had to go to Joe's with leafy branches. This was their ticket to the Gogama Zoo—excluding the wolves. These were out of bounds for everybody but Joe, who continuously spoke to them in French, English, and Ojibway. He knew how to handle them without ever using the stick on them, though at times he did have to grab them by the neck and throw them on the ground. Otherwise, he would have been the one who was thrown around. Over the years, he had several narrow escapes.

One incident happened in the winter of 1926. After he came back from New York, LaFlamme started training his first pure-blooded wolf team. One day, despite the minus fifty degree weather, he headed out on the trapline with his wolves. Feeling adventurous, he drove the team farther out in the bush than usual. Suddenly, the team stopped in the middle of a frozen lake. Had they heard wolves howling in the distance? This was Joe's first thought until Pete, who was leading the team, turned and stared at him. Then, coming from the left, Pete circled back on Joe. The eight other wolves rushed him from behind. The snow was deep, and the trapper did not have his snowshoes. There was no where he could have gotten the team tangled among the trees. So he tried the popular musher's trick to control lawless dogs: getting the team all coiled around the sleigh. The wolves then started to growl and come at him faster. Moving to the other side of the sleigh, he attempted to dissuade them with his whip. He knew that he had no chance of escaping: "I was sure scared plenty as I was up over my knees in snow…then 'Pete' for some reason got his eyes riveted on the pack on the sled where I had some food…all the wolves then turned on the pack and I never saw such a fight and tangle of traces and fur and fangs…I felt pretty sick, 'cause I knew my only chance of getting back to Gogama was to get the wolves to take me back."

By the time the wolves had finished snacking on Joe's lunch, as well as three beavers and the packsack, it was getting dark. The animals were restless. Carefully, Joe walked back to the sleigh, on the side opposite where Pete lay. "All I could say, my throat was so dry, was 'Mush, Pete,' and he started away." Joe credited the wolves' sudden attention to the food pack for saving his life. "If they had decided to make a meal out of me, then I was sure a goner. No one can tell me that timber wolves won't turn on a man," he asserted.

Another winter day in the late 1920s, LaFlamme was skidding logs with his team. He was turning the sleigh, when Pete suddenly lunged at him. Luckily, Joe was protected from the bite by his mitts, which were in his sweater pockets; only his stomach was grazed. He then grabbed a jack pine and pulled away from the wolf, shouting to his companion to fetch his whip. Joe knocked out the wolf, hitting him three times over the head with the butt of the whip. He felt sorry that he had to kill Pete—but five minutes later, Pete came to his feet. Joe immediately commanded the team to head for Gogama. "I never went near him and shortly after that he became tame and I could even let him run loose, and he come to me on command," said Joe.

The Wolf Man had a theory about wolves, explaining that they acted on impulse and that their instinct to kill could flare up without warning. But if their attention could be diverted to something else, then they would unleash their wild anger on this new target.

Similarly, in the 1930s, Joe LaFlamme would divert his own attention from his zoo to a new interest: prospecting.

17

Digging for Gold

The 1932 rush

"Around big bend in water." As the legend goes, this was the answer a Native hunter gave to a hotel owner in Chapleau, Ontario, who asked him where he had found his large chunk of gold ore. Ever since, prospectors had been searching every curve of the numerous lakes in the Swayze area, along a strip of inhospitable land roughly 100 miles long by 15 miles wide (160 by 24 km), southwest of Gogama. Nine years later, in the fall of 1931, brothers Jay and Jack Kenty finally came to the right spot. They discovered the motherlode near Brett Lake. All told, they staked 16 claims.

The summer of 1932 marked the beginning of a prospecting frenzy akin to the California and Klondike gold rushes of the nineteenth century. More than 300 hopeful prospectors from all over the continent homed in, making Gogama in the east and Chapleau in the west the hubs of a twentieth-century gold rush.

In this world of first to come, first to claim, lucky prospectors had to protect their claims until their mining potential had been determined. As most prospecting activities came to a halt when the cold season settled in, bushmen

The Gogama prospectors are, from left to right: George Simard, Joe LaFlamme, Dave Ranger and possibly Albert (King) Roy. The photo was taken circa 1930-1932. Photo courtesy of Eunice Belisle.

had no choice but to wait out the winter. Some 60 new log cabins were therefore built in the middle of nowhere. A few brave ones even faced the bitterly cold winter in canvas tents heated with small stoves. All were eager to see the first gold mine operating in the area.

Joe LaFlamme was also eager to take part in all this action. Being his usual "Joe of all trades," he flew to the different camps, delivering mail and newspapers. He also earned money as a prospector's guide—few men knew the bush as well as he did. Joe also did some prospecting of his own. With a nose for opportunity, Joe had obtained his prospector's license even before the rush, in June 1929, the year his son was born. He faithfully renewed his license annually, up to and including the year 1948-49.

Joe scoured the region so thoroughly that he did eventually strike gold. On a trail between Beaver and Bagsverd Lakes stood a balsam tree featuring a wide blaze on its trunk, on which was written: "Trail to Tom Hall and Joe LaFlamme's Klondyke [sic] vein. Assay $200 per ton in gold. Witnessed by Howard J. Brennan and Jim MacKenzie, September 1932." Brennan and MacKenzie were also prospectors. A vein bringing in $200 of gold per ton was quite lucrative, since the average hovered between $12 and $16 per ton.

LaFlamme later sold the gold claim to a large mining company. Despite all the money he made with this transaction, he did not get the chance to buy jewelry for his mother. Marie Théoret died on December 3, 1932, in Montreal. Neither Joe, Lillie, nor Morris attended the funeral service, which was held in February 1933 at Ste-Élizabeth-du-Portugal church; their names were not mentioned in the list of people at the ceremony. Travelling from Gogama to Montreal in winter was a long trip.

Winter or not, Joe and little "gold-getter" Morris kept busy prospecting—and when Joe was not out in the bush with a pick and hammer, he enjoyed a good game of stud poker with other prospectors.

The 1938 rush and the silk-stocking prospector

The buzzing activities of the 1932 gold rush had gradually petered out, but the excitement picked up again in July 1938 when nine claims were staked by prospector Bert Jerome on behalf of the Mining Corporation of Canada, in Osway Township, a few kilometres south of the Swayze gold area. Again, Gogama became the centre of northern prospecting.

This new rush generated much talk and speculation on the street, in all the drinking places, and of course at the LaFlammes' boarding house. Lillie must have eavesdropped on the lively conversations as she served coffee— or liquor—to her clients. Her curiosity about this new goldfield was quickly aroused. On Wednesday, August 3, when Gogama guide Omer Gagnon dared her to fly to Osway Township and do a little prospecting of her own, she took up the challenge. "I really had no intention of going in, but when he dared me, well I just went," *la p'tite femme* explained. Adventurous at heart, Lillie got her prospector's license that same day, packed up her gear, and flew to the gold field with Austin Airways pilot Phil Sauvé, Gagnon at her side. She set up camp on Opeepeesway Lake, her home base until Saturday. The site was bustling with activity since it was also home base for many other prospectors.

Lillie travelled the area by canoe wearing a dress, since pants were not yet popular with women. The weather was hot and stuffy, and the black flies horrible. To prevent the little beasts from biting her, the prospector wrapped newspaper around her legs, underneath her silk stockings.

The former Parisian woman worked diligently and, within a couple of days, she found real gold quartz: "small, true, but real gold." Lillie staked three claims near the original claim site, in a district that was so wild there were no birds or flowers. On Saturday, August 6, the silk-stocking prospector flew back to Gogama and then to Sudbury to record her claims. Among the first prospectors to stake claims in the area, she laughingly remarked, "That was once that I beat Joe to the draw." LaFlamme had to agree since he had no claims in the area yet.

But the Wolf Man's claim to fame did not rest on gold but on his great strength and his ability to handle wild animals. Aware of this, prospector Archie Burton asked the hefty bushman to hog-tie his two 700-lb (318 kg) ponies before flying them to his camp near Opeepeesway Lake. There they would spend the winter hauling wood and moving the diamond drill. The animals had to be shackled to prevent their hooves from tearing through the fabric fuselage of the Austin Airways plane. Joe was the only man around who could perform such a feat. The following day, for the benefit of reporters and prospectors swarming the town for the gold rush, LaFlamme gave a demonstration of how he broke timber wolves to harness.

These two Northern Ontario gold rushes of the 1930s differed from others in terms of transportation. Canoe travelling in summer and dog-sledding in winter would have been very slow, if not impossible, given the heavy goods needing transportation. What would normally have taken two to three days by conventional means, the modern seaplane covered in 40 minutes, with canoes strapped to its floats. Since Gogama served as a rallying point for prospectors, its air base enjoyed a flurry of activities during these years. Joe LaFlamme was a frequent user of the air service, but, in the fall of 1938, he took the plane almost one time too many.

Joe LaFlamme with two of his wolves and some local boys at the Minisinakwa Lake dock in Gogama, late 1938. Photo courtesy of Helen Schruder.

18

Diving In—with the Pike!

Friday afternoon, October 14, 1938

Shortly before 3 p.m., pilot Phil Sauvé checked his Waco VKS-7, a four-seater biplane used for light transportation during the 1930s and 1940s. The aircraft's fuselage was constructed out of welded chrome tubing with light wooden ribs to give it shape. The body was covered with canvas. The smaller bottom wing was fastened directly to the fuselage while the larger top wing was attached on top and linked to the fuselage and the lower wing with steel struts.

Sauvé was teamed up with Chuck Austin, a fellow pilot who was also president of Austin Airways in Sudbury. The two pilots were doing alternate runs to the Opeepeesway Lake gold rush area, each spending a week operating out of the Gogama air base. It was Phil's turn to return home to Sudbury. He left Gogama at 3 p.m., having picked up supplies and a single passenger, Joe LaFlamme. The plane made a stopover at the Ronda Gold Mine, near Shining Tree, a mere 25 minutes due south. At 4:15 p.m., Sauvé took off with two more Sudbury passengers, who settled in the back: salesman Donald T. Groom, of Cochrane-Dunlop Hardware Limited, and Leslie L.W. Ashcroft, manager for the Canadian General Electric Company.

At 5 p.m., the aircraft was flying at an altitude of 5,000 ft (1,539 m) and was two-thirds of the way to its destination when Sauvé heard a loud noise. The veteran muskeg pilot instinctively recognized the sound—the crankshaft had broken! Now loose, the propeller flew off to the right, hitting the lower wing. The rudderless plane bumped and jolted. Sauvé advised the men to fasten their seatbelts. Assessing their predicament, he turned off the engine. LaFlamme's immediate response was "Did we hit a goose?" Groom answered negatively, and Joe remarked, "Well, it could be worse. We could have lost a wing." Don added, "Hell, the wing's tearing off right now!" Seeing the damaged wing shredding to pieces under the force of the wind, Joe hoarsely told the pilot, "The wing is gone!" "How far?" Phil asked. "From the end into the strut," answered Joe. Phil craned his neck to check it out for himself. Even the tip of the upper wing was curved downward.

The plane lurched from side to side. It was losing altitude. The trees appeared closer and bigger. Questions erupted from the excited passengers. Needing to focus, Sauvé held his hand up, silencing his worried companions. Sitting taut, the pilot's face was emotionless, his nerves like steel, and his adrenals in overdrive. He knew they did not stand a chance of surviving this ordeal, but he did not tell the travellers. It was a long shot, but the very least he could do now was to try landing the plane.

With no propeller and the right wings damaged, the wobbling plane was hard to control. Carefully holding the control column, he leaned to the left, searching for the best place to land. Among several very small lakes, he spotted a larger one, five miles (eight km) to the east. Trying to keep the plane from going into a spin, he steered toward this lake. The passengers were in for the longest glide they would ever experience.

Three minutes of floating in the air like a kite seemed like eternity. The plane's speed made it vibrate, tearing off pieces of fabric, ribs, and spars. Phil feared losing the other half of the broken wing. Finally, at 200 ft (62 m) over the lake, still cruising at 80 miles per hour (144 kph) yet unable to reduce speed, Phil took a sharp and short dive for the water. When the floats hit the surface, the plane swayed one last time, stabilized, and then sped along over the water until the pilot finally managed to stop it, not far from shore. Sauvé collapsed over the controls, his nerves shot. "I do not think it would have held together for another 1,000 ft [300 m]," he later reported. As for Joe's version of the landing, it was characteristic of his deadpan humour: "Away goes our wing and down into the water go four honest men. With the pike."

After taking a minute to recover, Sauvé got out of the plane and waded ashore, plane in tow. The three unharmed men, pale but relieved, took off their shoes, got out of the aircraft, and busied themselves setting up camp before nightfall. Though it was only about 5:15 p.m., it would be dark soon since this was October.

Marooned on a small, nameless lake in the dense forest of Fraleck Township, some 35 miles (56 km) north of Sudbury, the men were glad the plane was equipped for emergencies. The basic survival kit included four down sleeping bags, four blankets, tools, and food rations. Joe had also brought a supply of moose meat he was delivering to Sudbury. The men cleared a camping spot and got a fire going. They were lucky the nights were not too cold yet. After eating a light dinner, they snuggled up in their makeshift beds and went to sleep under the stars. Whether they slept or not is another matter. It shouldn't have been a problem for Joe, who was used to roughing it, and perhaps not for Phil, who flew regularly over the boreal forests and muskeg. As for Don and Les, still dressed in their business suits, they must have at least loosened up their ties.

Saturday, October 15, 1938

Back at the Austin Airways base, Chuck Austin was worried because Sauvé had not reported in on Friday afternoon. The Gogama base confirmed the pilot had indeed left Ronda Mine at about 4 p.m. the day before. Not taking any chances, Austin sent out three planes to check out all the lakes on Sauvé's regular course. With no sign of the missing party by noon, Austin organized a search party, calling in seven planes: three from his own company, two from Algoma Air Transport in South Porcupine, and two others from Biscotasing's Ontario Forestry Branch. They followed the Waco's flight pattern all afternoon, to no avail. Visibility was considerably reduced by heavy smoke blowing east from a forest fire near Foleyet. All planes flew back to base as darkness set in.

Meanwhile, the stranded men kept their campfire going all day, hoping some plane would spot the smoke signals. In the afternoon, they heard one of the search planes in the distance. But since Sauvé had landed his plane about 10 miles (16 km) east of his course, the searchers could not see them. With plenty of food and warm sleeping bags, the men's main worry was that their loved ones did not know they were safe.

Sunday afternoon, October 16, 1938

At dawn, the seven planes resumed what would be one of the most extensive aerial searches in Northern Ontario history. At noon, three of the seven planes came back to base to refuel.

At the lake, Pilot Sauvé and his companions knew they definitely had to signal their location to the search team. It was their only chance of survival. Joe insisted that the best alert was a bush fire. Not wanting to set the whole forest on fire, the men decided the best place to start the fire was on a small island, far enough from shore to contain the blaze. To get there, they built a raft. Soon after, the fire was burning, releasing two thin columns of smoke. This was what finally alerted Chuck Austin. His pilot's instinct had led him to fly off course on the way back to Sudbury, still searching. Spotting the smoke, Austin flew low over the lake to investigate the fire. Sighting the plane on shore, he landed and was met by four happy men. He returned to the base with Groom and Ashcroft. Before landing in Sudbury, he signalled the crew and about 100 bystanders of his success by swooping over the company office and dipping his wings. Shortly after, Toronto pilot Jimmy Bell and mechanic Red McCrea left to rescue Sauvé and LaFlamme.

The passengers' safe arrival was greeted by a cheerful crowd and curious journalists. Groom and Ashcroft both admitted they had been terrified, and that the experience was one they would not care to relive. As for Joe, when asked if he was scared, he replied nonchalantly, "Ho, no, nobody was scared, just weak from hunger, or something."

All three rescued passengers had nothing but praise and admiration for their pilot's extraordinary skill and courage. Joe summed it up: "It was one of the greatest feats of Northern aviation, and I don't mean maybe. If you had been in that plane 5,000 ft [1500 m] in the air and had the propeller fall off, the wing struts cut, and parts of the wing fabric falling in chunks, you would have agreed that Sauvé is without a doubt the best pilot in the North to have done what he did. He surely saved our lives." Groom added, "Only one pilot in a thousand could have done what he did. They don't make them any better."

This skillful maneuver was not the former Michigan pilot's first. Among several mercy flights, one of the most heroic had happened in 1933, in Chapleau, where he landed a plane full of dynamite on ice, on one ski. During this latest ordeal in Fraleck Township, in addition to all the worries about meeting his maker and landing a crippled plane, Phil had had the forethought to choose a lake big enough to fly the plane out once it was repaired. Several days later, he flew it out himself.

Forty-four years after the accident, Leslie Ashcroft declared to author Larry Milberry that LaFlamme sure kept things humming: "Actually we had fun out there. We had nice warm blankets and kept a good fire going. The wolf man commented several times, 'No need for my wife to worry about me, but I sure hope she's feeding my wolves.'"

In fact, LaFlamme needed his 11 timber wolves to be healthy because he had made arrangements to exhibit them next winter at the New York and Boston sportsmen's shows, with planned stopovers in Sudbury and Montreal on the first leg of the tour.

19
Wishing He Had a Gun!

Building the best wolf team

LaFlamme so thoroughly enjoyed his 1926 trip to New York that he planned to return in the winter of 1939. This time, he would bring a team entirely made up of wild timber wolves. His first wolf team had been dispersed. Three of the wolves were sold to a Hollywood movie company at $75 each, in 1928. At the time, Joe was in financial straits and could not refuse. After that, he was too busy prospecting to train another team. Around 1937, however, he sold his lucrative gold claim and placed an order for a dozen wolves from the Hudson's Bay Company, each costing between $35 and $50 F.O.B. (Free On Board), meaning that there was no charge for their transportation. Joe knew that trapping so many live wolves would take a while, and for the team to be ready for 1939 winter sports shows, he had to start training as early as the summer of 1938.

He also had to negotiate his participation at these shows. In June 1938, he headed for Montreal to meet Albert C. Rau, manager of the New York and Boston winter shows, at the office of C.K. Howard, tourism manager at Canadian National. Joe promised Rau he would mush in the streets of Boston and New York with a fresh team of wolves.

One of the first adult wolves he obtained was a large female he named Calgary. He spent all summer convincing the wolf that he meant her no harm. It took another four months to train her to lead the team. Meanwhile, in August, one or two at a time, the other wolves slowly started coming in from Quebec, Saskatchewan, and Manitoba. Most were pups that Joe immediately started training.

Joe was convinced that he now had the best pure-wolf team ever: "I believe that this team I have now will always pull a load for me." His 1939 team, from the leader down the gangline to the rear dogs, included Calgary, four years old; Shownia (silver) and Mok-uman (jacknife), both yearlings; Wolf, 19 months; and Muckoos (bear cub), Maheegan (wolf), Nigig (otter), Wagoosh (fox), Ojeek (fisher), Wabsehech (marten), and Weeweepe (flash) who were all 11 months old. Joe liked to get his wolves used to city lights and traffic while they were young, so they would be easier to handle. This was also the reason he gave most of them Ojibway names. If people in a crowd heard their names, they would not be able to grasp them clearly enough to call the animals and distract them while they were mushing.

Joe's pride and joy in this wolf pack was undoubtedly Wolf, a powerful, 110 lb (15 kg) snarling grey beast with piercing yellow eyes, a sullen temper, and an uncanny ability to read people's minds. It took Joe two months just to be able to approach him and pat him on the head without danger of losing an arm. Even Lillie and Morris could now get close to him without danger. While Wolf sometimes needed a couple of hours of coaxing to get him to leave his cage, Joe never let him win. He had a strategy for the successful handling of wolves: kindness, with a lot of persuasion in French, Ojibway, and English. He explained to a reporter, "I've handled wolves for a long time, and cruelty will never get you anywhere, although a good licking is essential now and again."

On Tuesday, January 24, 1939, the day before leaving for Sudbury, Joe gave his team a trial run with his new 12 foot (3.5 m) sleigh. Custom made in Joliette, Quebec, by ALP Paquin & Fils, it was a long-distance touring sleigh, with a bed that measured 8 ft (2.5 m) long. From experience, Joe realized that larger teams required longer metal-lined runners and wider beds to provide stability and allow greater freight capacity. Mostly likely made of white ash, the wood traditionally used for dogsleds, Joe's two-stanchion sleigh had a curved brush bow and a comfortable 42 inch (1 m) high driving bow with long handles and footboards. Metal "pig feet brakes" stopped the sleigh when pressure was applied to the large wooden break mat. It was truly a sleigh made for the giant musher, one he would use for several years.

On test day, the thermometer read -20°F (-28°C). Sudbury's temperature was similar, a plus for the wolves. Starting from home, LaFlamme mushed past the train station, heading to the local air base. Curious children ran around them, trying to follow the musher. This distracted Calgary, causing her to stray away from her course. Joe brought her back with a firm command: "Heigh, Calgary!" On the way to the air base, the team faced a brisk wind, but it did not deter the wolves and they continued pulling the long sleigh with ease. The

POSTCARD: Joe LaFlamme and his lead female wolf Calgary, probably in Gogama, in January 1939. Photo courtesy of the Gogama Chamber of Commerce, circa late 1990s.

two-hour workout reassured Joe. Finally satisfied with their training, he got his team ready to travel to the big cities.

When, in October 1938, a *Toronto Daily Star* journalist asked LaFlamme how he was planning to bring his wolves to New York, Joe replied in a matter-of-fact tone: "Oh, I'll pile them into the baggage car and stay there with them myself." Not convinced this was a good idea, the reporter questioned Joe as to whether the wolves could turn on him in such a situation. Joe replied, "Well, if that happened, I guess I wouldn't be around to tell you the story, but I'm not worried about that. It won't happen." The Wolf Man knew his wolves.

Wolves in the air

Joe also knew that, at -38°F (-38°C), a long and cold train ride to Sudbury would not be healthy for the wolves. At the last minute, he decided to buy airplane tickets for his 25-year-old assistant George Thibodeau, himself, and his 11 wolves. This was the first time in Canadian aviation history that wolves flew as paying passengers—and Joe made history again. In the afternoon of Wednesday, January 25, 1939, with tickets and transportation permit in hand,

Joe LaFlamme (left), Morris LaFlamme, an unidentified man, Austin Airways pilot Jimmy Bell, another unidentified man, and probably assistant George Thibodeau in front of the airplane which will fly LaFlamme's team of wolves from Gogama to Sudbury, on January 25, 1939. Photo courtesy of Gerry Talbot.

LaFlamme and his party headed for the winter air base on Minisinakwa Lake. His wolves were already harnessed and ready to be hitched to the sleigh as soon as they arrived in Sudbury.

But for a wolf even getting near a plane was scary. Three wolves had already boarded, when the leash on one of Joe's two prized black wolves suddenly came loose. Now free, Muckoos made a dash for the bush across the lake.

"He was off like a flash and in a minute he was just a black speck on the snow-covered lake," Joe later explained to a reporter. "Before we even got

Joe LaFlamme with his black wolf in Gogama, circa 1938. Photo courtesy of Gerry Talbot.

started after him he was two miles [three km] away."

Wanting his rare black wolf back, the Wolf Man quickly put together a search party. As several of his friends had come to see him off, he assigned them the duty of guarding the shore. Joe and Austin Airways pilot Jimmy Bell—the same man who had rescued him from the plane crash—chased the wolf by plane, circling the lake to force the animal to head for the northern shore. When the wolf's running was hindered by deep snow, Bell cornered him close to shore. The pilot then landed, jumped out, waded through deep snow—thank goodness for his long legs—and threw his arms around the fugitive. Joe got his wolf back.

But as soon LaFlamme's back was turned, an annoyed Wolf lashed at Mokuman's throat with his long fangs. Badly mangled, the yearling was left to heal in Gogama. Joe thought he might even die. Wolf was muzzled, as was Calgary, as a precaution.

In retrospect, LaFlamme knew he shouldn't have hurried the wolves. But the pilot, afraid of flying in the dark with a pack of wolves, kept pleading with Joe to get the wolves into the plane so they could leave. Joe explained, "The more you hurry with wolves the less speed you make.... Now wolves are the most contrary creatures on earth and seemed to sense that I was rushing them, and the result was that they were more difficult to handle than if we had taken everything as a matter of course."

Finally, Canada's first all-wolf team was loaded in the light six-passenger Fairchild plane and the 40-minute flight to Sudbury began. So did Joe's most hectic episode in his 16 years as a wolf tamer. As soon as the aircraft started to move, the wolves became uneasy. This was normal given that the wolves were not used to this mode of transportation. On takeoff, things took a turn for the worse. Some wolves stood up on their hind legs, fighting. They clawed at the windows trying to escape. Suddenly, all ten wolves were fighting with each other and scratching the walls. Joe and George pushed them back. In a tangled mess of fangs, fur, and claws, the beasts charged again. Joe yelled to his assistant to push them back again. George hit one with his fist. Another wolf jumped on top of LaFlamme. Joe tossed it to the back of the plane. The animal came at him again. The battle continued, with the wolves tearing up the fuselage's interior walls. In the process, they also shredded Joe's new mukluks.

As the plane leveled to its regular cruising altitude, however, the ride was smoother and the wolves relaxed a bit and lay down on their bellies, sniffing the floor. Joe opened a window to cool them off a bit. With a little more time on his hands, the pilot turned around and asked Joe how the wolves were faring. The Wolf Man answered that the animals had not moved an inch. He was convinced that, if Jimmy had seen what had happened in the back, he would have dropped off the wolves at the first lake available to land on.

In any case, the trip to Sudbury was made in record time. Joe had an explanation: "I think we must have had a tail wind or else that plane wanted to get rid of its cargo of wolves." He added, tongue in cheek, "This time we arrived with the propeller on the front of the plane."

LaFlamme must have regretted not having tied the wolves in the plane. He had feared that they might get all tangled up and choke. He later confided to a reporter that this flight had been the most thrilling one he had ever made. He was sure the wolves were going to jump off the plane, adding that "it was the first time since I have been handling wolves that I wished I had a gun with me."

Once at the Sudbury air base, the wolves took a whiff of the -25°F (-32°C) bracing cold weather, and decided the plane was comfortable after all. It took Joe and his helper over an hour to coax them all out. Calgary and two others were already outside when a local dog passed by. Intent on pursuing their prey, the wolves got all tangled up underneath the plane. Crawling on his back, Joe mustered every wrestling technique he knew to untangle the excited wolves and dissuade his huge lead wolf from her canine hunt. Then, as the other wolves were taken out and hooked to their harnesses, they kept twisting their tug lines around the gangline. Despite all the commotion, LaFlamme still believed this wolf team was the best he ever had.

Joe LaFlamme takes one of his wolves from the Austin Airways plane at the Sudbury air base, on January 25, 1939. Photo courtesy of *Toronto Star*/GetStock. com #2086200444

20

Whipping up the Crowd in Sudbury

After their first plane ride and their first exposure to bright city lights, the wolves were more than happy to take refuge in a big barn in the west end of the city. The barn stood behind the warehouse belonging to the Sudbury Brewing and Malting Company Ltd., which was sponsoring the Wolf Man's visit. Joe and his assistant also camped out in the barn for the first two nights. They all needed a rest before making their first public appearance on the following day, a trial run for the American shows. Sudbury, also known as the Nickel Capital of the World, was the first city in Canada, and likely the world, to see an all-wolf team in harness.

It was Thursday, January 26, 1939, and Joe LaFlamme skipped shaving. Usually clean-shaven, the Wolf Man had grown a beard for the exhibition tour. He had done so ever since his first trip to New York in 1926; it gave him a more authentic musher's look. This time, Joe's black whiskers were streaked with grey, common enough at 50 years old. Joe had also gained weight, now tipping the scale, pot-bellied, at 250 lbs (114 kg). He dressed in his traditional show suit: green fur-trimmed parka with Voyageur sash, cone-shaped fur hat, elbow-length Indian mitts, bear grease-smelling shoepacks, and his 24-foot (7 m) moose-thong whip.

At midday, the thermometer had hit the -30°F (-35°C) mark. The snow-covered streets were lined with people, four to five deep. A crowd of 5,000 was feverishly waiting for the wolves and their colourful musher. Hundreds of school kids had been there for several hours. The schools were half-empty and many a meal was getting cold on the dinner table. As one teacher remarked to the *Sudbury Star*, "After all,…you don't get to see timber wolves running through city streets every day."

Meanwhile, Joe was preparing for his historic race through the city. He and George were harnessing the wolves, saving the leader for last because Calgary tired easily. As she was still very timid, he handled her gently. But gentle was not the reaction he got from the rest of his harnessed wolves. They stared angrily at the onlookers. Joe and George kept their cool, even among the keyed-up crowds. The northern outfit was itching to go. However, to give his team some leg room, the musher asked the curious bystanders to leave the brewery yard. Most did, except a small group who got to see a sideshow when Wolf's nasty temper suddenly flared up at the entrance of the barn.

The huge animal refused to listen to his master's commands, regardless of the language used. Wolf kept snapping at Joe's thick leather mitts, all the while slobbering and glaring defiantly. His growling was a warning that the tamer heeded none too soon. Joe stepped back and retaliated quickly. He grabbed Wolf's right front paw and flipped him over to expose the beast's vulnerable underside. Before long, Wolf submitted, his anger spent. Knowing his charge, Joe did not beat the wolf, but muzzled him—just in case. Given his young age, the wolf's wild instinct was still fresh in his mind, so he could not be trusted around people, particularly in such a new situation where the wild animal had no reference point. This suspense-filled episode caused the musher to leave his hitching post on Lorne Street about 45 minutes late. Joe had an explanation for the waiting crowd: "You can't hurry a wolf."

Nor could you hurry a wolf cavalcade, especially when they were continually pressed by excited bystanders. Consequently, Joe arrived downtown well after 1 p.m. The team's pace through the city traffic and crowds slowed down considerably. There was nothing Joe could do about it because he could not risk cracking his whip in case he hit someone. People, children especially, seemed oblivious to the fact that the nervous animals were indeed wild and unpredictable. Joe had to resort to another strategy to prevent a mishap. As he stood at the back of the sleigh controlling the brake, George walked in front of the wolf team to keep them focused on their task. Holding the chain on Calgary's collar, he kept a watchful eye on youngsters who might have been tempted to pet the wolves.

This did not stop one bystander from commenting that the timber wolves looked tame enough. Joe quickly responded with an invitation: "If anyone thinks he can tickle a timber wolf under the chin and get away with it, then he can stay in this barn with Wolf." He pointed at the large leering wolf.

No volunteers

Nonetheless, the children continued to approach the team. At first, Joe could not help but smile as he noticed: "Sudbury's got a lot of kids."

The team slowly proceeded east to Elm Street, then south to Durham. The downtown crowd became increasingly more dense, the traffic jams broke records, and no police officers were anywhere in sight. At one point, the lead wolf could not even move forward through the crowd. Calgary became scared. She spotted a way out—a nearby shed—and dashed for it, with team and sleigh in tow.

Joe shouted to warn the crowd: "Those who want to feed the wolves stay where they are, and we won't have to buy any meat. If you don't want to feed the wolves, get back." But the excited crowd kept pressing on. Joe had no choice. He uncurled his whip and cracked it at the legs of the curious bystanders who scattered quickly—and came back just as fast.

Joe and his wolves proved an irresistible attraction for the children, even to LaFlamme's ten-year-old son. When not riding in the sleigh, Morris was part of the crowd of children closing in on the cavalcade. Excited, he called out each wolf by name, including his favourite, Shownia. Thrilled by his father's performance, the boy declared, "When I grow up I want to drive wolves like my dad." Indeed, grown-up Morris did end up driving, not wolves but taxis in Montreal and, later, transport trucks.

The animals did not take to the city well. Bothered by the car fumes, they were constantly on the lookout for vacant lots and deep white snow. So George and Joe ran with them. A lot of time was wasted dragging the wolves from underneath freight cars, automobiles, and verandas. Downtown mushing proved to be a harrowing experience. But wolves cannot be hurried—still less when their leader shows signs of fatigue. In the Central School yard on Station Street, Joe replaced Calgary with the less experienced Wolf: "He hasn't got any harness sense to make a good lead yet, but if you let him get a look at a dog he's after it like a flash."

True enough, Wolf was a slow lead on city streets, among people and traffic. But as soon as they turned at the corner of John and Elizabeth streets, the crowds diminished and so did the traffic. Policemen had arrived. Then, at the sight of the wide-open space, the team sped down the hill, heading straight for Ramsey Lake. Imagine Wolf's thrill when he spotted a dog team on the lake. He led his team to it, and soon both teams were racing side by side. Here too, Thibodeau ran next to Wolf, holding his leash to prevent the wolves from tangling with the dogs. This was mushing as the Gogama residents knew it. After the competition, LaFlamme commanded the wolves to head home to the barn. The return trip was quick and easy, a welcome ending to LaFlamme's first lap in his two-country exhibition tour.

In addition to downtown mushing, Joe had one more demonstration in Sudbury and that was to show off Wolf's incredible strength. Though the location of this side show is unknown, we know that Wolf pulled a seven-passenger automobile for a distance of 50 ft (15 m) through the snow. The animal probably would have pulled over a longer distance but his harness snapped when one of the tires hit a hole.

Parting with Muckoos

Two days after the race on Sudbury streets, Joe parted with Muckoos. Having just met Nettie Madger, a *Toronto Daily Star* reporter, he asked her if she wanted a wolf. When she replied that she would not know what to do with one, he prodded, "Ho, you can do anything you like with this one. If you want her, she is yours." He continued his sales pitch: "She is Muckoos. She is kind. She is a woman, and a real lady. She's not like most wolves. She won't bite your hand off. But she doesn't like lights. She won't be any good in New York, so I'll have to ship her back to Gogama, unless you help me out. Take her off my hands and she's yours." Aware that LaFlamme had helped many reporters through the years, Nettie succumbed. So Joe brought her to the warehouse where his wolves were now chained.

On arrival, LaFlamme realized that things were not as he had left them: "Well, I'll be a son of a gun. Sonja [Shownia] got free and fed the others." Indeed, witty Shownia had gotten another wolf to chew her leather collar until it fell off. Once she was free, she had walked to a huge box of meat and dragged it around from wolf to wolf. None of them needed coaxing to indulge.

When Joe patted Muckoos on the head and asked her if she would like a new master, she looked at Nettie with agreeable eyes and licked her hand. "If she's that fond of me, Joe, it will be a pleasure to take her off your hands," said Nettie. And she did, leaving with Muckoos, all the while wondering what she would do with her: "After all, we are taking her away from a royal wolf household when we take her away from Joe's care," Nettie reported to the *Toronto Daily Star*.

Between Saturday and Monday, however, Nettie had a change of heart, and rightly so. Keeping Muckoos made the journalist liable to four different charges under the Ontario Game and Fish Act, including a jail term for possessing a wolf without a permit. She contacted Joe, who sent a telegram to Gogama asking that a special crate be shipped to Nellie. She was to send the wolf to the Belle Isle Zoo, near Detroit. Although she was sad to part with the gentle wolf, Nettie admitted, "I wouldn't like to be in Joe LaFlamme's place with ten wolves. My one Muckoos has given me headaches enough."

This meant that the Wolf Man had one less wolf to worry about on his tour. While Muckoos would be leaving for Detroit on Tuesday, January 31, Joe would be trucking his nine other wolves to Montreal on Monday night, January 30. But before leaving, he had one last visit to make in Sudbury.

21
Snarling Live at the Opera

C ast

Joe LaFlamme, the wolf tamer from Gogama
George Thibodeau, the tamer's assistant
Wolf, the 110 lb (50 kg) timber wolf
Mr. CKSO Announcer (whose name remains a mystery)
Barney Gloster, the *Sudbury Star* photographer

Background

CKSO, a Sudbury radio station, published a weekly newsletter targeting a southern Ontario audience. The newsletter's cover photo usually depicted a Northern Ontario theme or scene. On Thursday, January 26, 1939, the day he mushed through the city, Joe LaFlamme was also a guest on the radio, talking about his experience as a wolf tamer. This interview was to be the subject matter for the next newsletter, and Joe and one of his wolves were invited to come back to the station two days later to have photographs taken.

On the afternoon of Saturday, January 28, George, Joe, and his nasty wolf paraded down Elm Street on their way to the radio station. With the allure of a large police dog, Wolf impressed both the crowds and the dogs, which avoided him like the plague.

Once at the station, Joe was advised that his appointment had been delayed. As Wolf found the studio a bit warm, the two men took him outside. A crowd was gathering and Wolf, chained to a tree, started to feel uncomfortable. As he revealed his long fangs in frustration, George took out the muzzle. Joe worked a good five minutes to get the contraption on. When Wolf had finally calmed down, they brought him into the studio for the photo shoot.

Act I

Protesting, Wolf was lifted off his feet onto a table between his master and the announcer.

"Now we'll take his muzzle off," said Joe. "It will make a better picture."

The announcer and photographer both resisted: "It won't make any difference whether he has a muzzle on or not."

Joe did not listen and removed the muzzle, asking, "How can Wolf talk with a muzzle on?" Feeling the snarling fangs too close for comfort, the announcer gradually slid away from Wolf, who was still loosely chained. Joe reassured the announcer, "Don't worry. He's mad at me, not at you."

Wolf shook his head and jerked back, setting himself free of the chain. The photographer quickly hid behind the piano. The announcer, who was now watching close to the studio entrance, stepped out discreetly and closed the door.

Act II

Wanting to regain control of his charge, Joe made a long loop in the chain and went in Wolf's direction. Wolf made a jump for an open window at the back of the room. It was heavily screened. He then headed for the entrance. It was closed. Angry, he gashed the door with his huge paw. Joe followed Wolf closely, trying to approach him gently. Wolf glared at his master. Joe got closer. The wild beast lunged and slashed at him. Joe stepped back, avoiding the fangs. Wolf dashed to the other end of the studio.

Needing more freedom of movement, LaFlamme took off his exhibition parka and sash, and traded his fur hat for a beret. He and George then each grabbed a metal chair. Each holding a chair before him like a lion tamer, the two men finally cornered Wolf near the studio door. Chair still in hand, Joe held the loop of the chain above the wolf's head and slid it over his neck.

Witnessing all the excitement, somebody exclaimed, "This should have been broadcast." Somebody else shouted back, "Well, it's not over yet." Seeing that the situation was somewhat under control, the announcer returned to the studio.

INTERMISSION

On Saturdays, CKSO broadcast live operas from New York's Metropolitan Opera House. It was now the intermission of the matinee performance of *Louise*, by Gustave Charpentier.

Act III

The announcer turned on the microphone but had no time to explain to the listeners what was happening in the studio. Wolf, now chained to the door, snarled savagely, yapped, and rattled his chain—on the air. All this commotion interrupted the Metropolitan announcer. Joe commanded Wolf to "Get down, get down." Excited, the announcer tried to explain how the situation came about. He followed up by giving a detailed account of the battle of the giants.

In the meantime, Wolf lunged toward Joe again. He slashed at his master several times, almost tearing his heavy sweater coat and wool pants. Wolf kept jumping at the tamer. Each time, Joe slapped him over the head with his tam-o'-shanter. This continued for several minutes. Being in the corner, Wolf had the advantage of seeing his master coming. He refused to submit.

Taking the offensive, Joe unhooked Wolf from the door and handed the chain to George. He then tried to approach Wolf from behind. The beast wheeled at him, snarling and snapping. Joe distracted Wolf by dangling the muzzle in front of him. He then quickly straddled him and applied a scissor hold, restraining the wolf in a headlock with his right arm. He then proceeded to slip the muzzle on him. While Joe kept the animal close to his body, George grabbed one of Wolf's front paws and tightened up the muzzle. Wolf finally submitted to the muzzling. His ears lay flat. He was unhappy about having lost the battle.

Act IV

Unnervingly calm, Joe put his exhibition suit back on. This gave Wolf a few moments to settle down after the 25-minute duel. It was now time for the photo shoot. Gloster composed the photo: Joe stood and held Wolf by the chain while the announcer bent down to put the microphone near the animal's jaws. Wary about his pet's emotions, LaFlamme watched Wolf carefully for unexpected moves.

Once the shoot was over, Joe and George headed for their quarters with memories of the epic battle floating in their heads. As for Wolf, he fell sick after his presentation at the opera and would remain so for some time.

22

The Wolf Man's Last Tour

LaFlamme's main challenge in doing the 1939 exhibition tour was transportation. To get from Sudbury to Boston, he would normally take the CPR. But the railway company insisted that, because wolves were considered dangerous, Joe would have to lock them in iron cages. Joe saw things differently: "I want to transport them as a theatrical troupe." Since he did not own nine iron cages with locks, the train was not an option, and he wondered how he would get the animals from Sudbury to Montreal, then to the Boston show. He would worry about New York later.

Of a generous nature, Joe had always been willing to help people. It was now payback time. A kind-hearted Sudbury man by the name of Dick Fee offered him a small panel truck and a driver. Romeo Elie would drive the "troupe" all the way to Montreal and Boston. En route, they passed through North Bay where Joe wanted to show a reporter how tame his wolves were. To do so, he opened the rear doors of the truck. Several pairs of slanting yellow eyes blinked in the bright light. Even though all the wolves but Wolf were loose, none of them moved as Joe climbed on top of the duffel bags in his sleigh. So the wolves were indeed tame. But what about the rips and tears in the musher's clothes?

Suzanne F. Charron

The troupe's next stop was Montreal. There, Joe demonstrated to Montrealers what mushing with wolves was all about. Then, on Thursday, February 2, they headed for Boston. Joe did not anticipate any problem crossing the US border with his wolves since he held a transportation permit from the Ontario Department of Game and Fisheries.

The Boston Sportsman's and Boat Show was held February 4-12, 1939, in the Mechanics Hall in the heart of the city. The organizers had put a lot of effort into creating a wilderness atmosphere. Deer roamed in large pens, trout swam in real streams, and hunting and fishing guides mingled with the public. Joe, the "wonder-man" of Canada, fit right in. He attracted a lot of attention with his wolves, not only at the show but as he paraded with them through the streets of Boston. Reporter John F. Kenney and his guide Floyd Bell were looking over the wolves with basketball player Foster Browning when they exclaimed, "Can you imagine a guy living among a pack of wolves?" Browning responded cynically, "Aren't we all?" Few, though, could walk in Joe LaFlamme's boots. It took a great deal of strength, stamina, patience, and courage to travel great distances with a pack of unpredictable wolves.

Next they were on to the National Sportsmen's Show at the Grand Central Palace, in New York. Joe put in long days since the show ran from 11 a.m. to 11 p.m., February 18-25. It was attended by several thousand outdoor enthusiasts. Adult admission was 75 cents and a mere 35 cents for children.

The show featured Canadian exhibits from New Brunswick, Nova Scotia, Newfoundland, and British Columbia. LaFlamme seems to have been the only Ontario exhibitor, as he probably had been in 1926 as well. The "Bad Wolf Man from the North," as organizers at Campbell-Fairbanks Expositions liked to call one of their main attractions, had set up Camp LaFlamme on the Palace's mezzanine floor. The camp featured a realistic northern bush setting, complete with a Native trapper's hut made of birch bark and bound with spruce roots. Joe's wolves were not fooled by the decor, however. Kept indoors, they became enervated. Joe explained to the media that his wolves "feel best when the temperature is 40 to 45 degrees below freezing and begin to get soft when the weather is 'off.'" Not on their best behaviour, they snarled at reporters and visitors, some of whom would probably have loved to see them snap at Joe or

Joe LaFlamme walks his wolves on 47th Street, off Park Avenue, in New York, on February 16, 1939. Photo courtesy of AP/The Canadian Press.

George. But the cunning wolves were docile when spectators brought them ice cream cones, or when they were sleeping near the block of ice in their enclosure.

After the New York show, LaFlamme and his "troupe" headed to Indianapolis, Indiana, for the Hoosier State-Wide Sportsmen's Show, held at the Manufacturers Building, on the State Fair Grounds, March 4-12. It was Joe's first time at the Indianapolis show.

The last show of Joe's 1939 tour was at the Coliseum, on the State Fair Grounds in Detroit. The second annual Michigan Sportsmen's Show ran the first week of April. As Joe's transportation permit expired March 31, one has to wonder if he had applied for an extension, or if he was travelling with his wolves without permission.

On his way home, Joe LaFlamme stopped over in southern Ontario. On April 11, he brought his whole team of timber wolves onto the stage at the Windsor's Empire Theatre. He was well received by the public: "We know Joe, and we recognize his stunt to be one of the most unusual in show business. He's a great attraction, and ought to follow in the footsteps of Grey Owl, Jack Miner, [and] Ernest T. Seton." His last stop was in Hamilton where he paraded through the streets with his wolf team as hundreds of curious bystanders kept a safe distance.

As much as LaFlamme loved wolves, he always had a healthy respect for them. Even though he could anticipate most of their moods and moves, he still had to be constantly on the alert for unsuspected actions and quick to resolve problems as they arose. His knowledge of wolves opposed the theories held by Jim Curran, editor of the *Sault Daily Star*. Curran was of the opinion that wolves never attacked humans. He had the backing of the United States Biological Survey, which stated that there were no known cases of wolves having attacked people. Confident in this statistic, the editor offered, on behalf of the newspaper, a reward of $100 to anyone who could provide proof of a wolf attack. The tamer saw wolves differently: "I wouldn't take a chance on any wolf, no matter what the United States biology survey says. I've had thirteen years' experience with wolves and believe me, I know something about the critters.... On many occasions my wolves have attempted to attack me." He added, "Wolves will attack humans and have attacked them; they are not so all-fired scared of us as some people think." Luckily, the *Sault Daily Star* never had to give away the reward.

Two sad events

Usually a VIP attractor, LaFlamme missed out on one very special occasion. King George VI and Queen Elizabeth were travelling by train across Ontario and were scheduled for a seven-minute stop in Gogama on Monday, June 5, 1939. A public holiday was declared in Gogama and the surrounding communities along the CNR route. This would allow residents, including school children, to join in the reception festivities organized by local businesses. The Board of Trade had even appointed, as mayoress for the day, Emma Poupore, wife of Michael J. (Joe) Poupore, owner of Gogama's first lumber mill. This meant that Joe LaFlamme, self-appointed mayor of Gogama, would not even have a chance to perform his duty at the event. What upset Joe the most was that he would not be able to show his famous wolves to the royals. The railway police forbade the animals from attending the ceremonies. Joe was one disappointed man.

The other sad event was the sudden death of the LaFlammes' cherished lead dog Billy. The 15-year-old blind police dog was hit by a train. Joe was heartbroken. After this tragic event, for whatever reason, his wolf team was dispersed—but it was not long before Joe found other pets to train. The Wolf Man was about to become the Moose Man.

Joe LaFlamme and his wolf in the office of D.J. Taylor, Deputy Minister of the Ontario Department of Game and Fisheries, at Queen's Park, Toronto, in 1939. Photo courtesy of City of Toronto Archives, Fonds 1257, Series 1057, Item 3328.

23

The Moose Man's First Tour

Joe LaFlamme was a true animal lover who simply was not happy if he did not have pets of one kind or another to care for. He had now obtained two young moose. The two-and-a-half-year old, named Quebec, was captured near Senneterre, Quebec. She was smaller and smarter than eight-month-old Moosenose, who had been caught by Joe himself, near Gogama. Both were full of tricks and attached to their master. They liked to play with him—perhaps a little too roughly at times. With the help of "Mrs. Joe," who was by default second trainer for all her husband's pets, Joe had succeeded in house-training the huge animals. Now that they could even climb the steps to the LaFlamme home, they joined the family at the breakfast table, eating their own bowl of bran mush.

On one occasion, the mush was not only in the bowl, as Leo A. Landreville, then a young Sudbury lawyer who often represented Joe in court, once observed. LaFlamme was bragging to his visitor about his moose's obedience: "By gar, that moose I have, she do anything I tell her. See those stairs, she even climb them. Watch, you see." Landreville did watch as Joe coaxed his moose up the creaky stairs to the upper level. That was easy enough—and the climb

Joe LaFlamme trains his moose to climb the stairs to the balcony of his house in Gogama, circa early 1940s. Photo courtesy of Gerry Talbot.

down was even easier. The upstairs was heated with a Quebec heater that, at the time, happened to be red hot—and the clumsy moose bumped into it. Landreville reported, "Need we say more...except that Joe's house was never the same."

Joe's oversize pets were less vicious and easier to handle and train than his wild wolves, but the moose still had a knack for keeping him on his toes. In early October 1939, Joe had temporarily placed his two protégés on an island on Minisinakwa Lake. When a storm broke out, the animals either got scared or lonely. They swam to shore, searching for their master. Some local cottager must have spotted the loose moose and advised Joe. It was not long before he was out on their trail with a search party consisting of three Natives and a husky. The moose were found, and they were brought home. Joe later commented to the *Toronto Daily Star* that his moose were very glad to be back, because Joe was the only one who treated them like pets. Perhaps it was Joe who was the happiest, seeing them safe and sound at home. But they would not be home for long.

By the end of November, Joe had already announced that he would be attending the New York Sportsmen's Show, February 17-25, 1940. His two moose had now been trained to harness too. In fact, the moose would be participating in their first sportsmen show in Boston, two weeks prior to the New York show. Before crossing the border, the moose needed a medical check-up, as required by US federal law. On Saturday, January 27, Joe, Quebec, and Moosenose boarded the train to Montreal, where a veterinarian Joe knew would examine his pets. Luckily for Joe, the moose were both given a clean bill of health.

Then, it was off to Boston, the first leg of a three-month tour of the United States. LaFlamme foresaw the reaction of many show visitors at the sight of his two moose: "A lot of moose hunters who never even saw a moose are going to have itchy fingers when they see these two fellows close up." As a precautionary measure, Joe was going to ask the show committees to ensure all guns on display were unloaded.

As he had in 1939, Joe then moved on to the New York show, held at the Grand Central Palace. When he arrived by train at the Pennsylvania Station, Joe created a great photo opportunity for the media. He got Quebec, the smaller moose, to climb into a taxi for her ride to the Palace. No photo of this moose ride was found in the newspapers, but one can picture the back seat covered with moose from door to door, assuming the animal was lying down on the bench. If she was not, then she must have been sitting down on her rump, with the four lanky legs crisscrossed over the front seat—just like in the cartoons.

On Friday, February 16, 1940, on the eve of the Sportsmen's Show, Joe and one of his moose had a special errand to run. Len Hugues, president of the Northern Ontario tourist brigade, handed Joe an envelope. The Moose Man attached it to the moose's back. Then he and his pet climbed the steps to City Hall and delivered the message for Mayor Fiorello LaGuardia. The mayor of North Bay, Arthur Beattie, was inviting his American counterpart to visit the northern city and the world-famous Dionne quintuplets—five girls born in May 1934. Whether Joe was paid or not for this "moose mail" delivery is not known.

However, the New York Sportsmen's Association, sponsor of the show, was paying him about $400 a week to exhibit his moose. This may seem like a lot of money for that time, but Joe was not making a fortune, considering the costs of transportation, veterinary services, exhibition permits, set decor, post-cards, food and lodging for moose and men—though there is no mention of an assistant for this tour—and time spent en route between the various shows. But he was earning a living doing what he loved best. He was also meeting people from all walks of life, something he undoubtedly found very rewarding.

On this tour, LaFlamme did things differently. He joined forces with the Northern Ontario Tourist Association, which was intent on putting up a really good show to attract more tourists. Instead of exhibiting on his own, Joe set up camp with Moosenose and Ontie within the immense Ontario section. In a burst of political correctness, Joe had changed Quebec's name to Ontie, most likely because the Province of Quebec also had an exhibit at the show. LaFlamme's presence with his two moulting moose helped the Northern Ontario exhibit steal the show from many other popular exhibits.

With all this attention, Joe took the opportunity to do some public relations for Canada. Since the outbreak of World War II, some American publications were warning anglers and hunters who intended to visit the Dominion that the Canadian government could seize their guns and equipment. Furthermore, they stood a chance of being conscripted to serve in the army. As these statements were completely false, Americans had to be reassured that Canada would not impose more restrictions than it did before the war. With his convincing talk and his great love of the northland, LaFlamme was evidently one of Ontario's, and Canada's, best ambassadors.

After the New York show, Joe and his animals had a week to get to Detroit's Sportsmen's Show, which was held March 4-10, 1940. They continuously attracted crowds of curious visitors to the Convention Hall. The Moose Man must have visited other shows after Detroit since he was supposedly on tour until April. In all likelihood, Joe ended his tour in Buffalo since he presented his moose to the Buffalo municipal zoo, which was expanding and in need of exotic animals. This came about during the week of the exhibition when Joe met the curator of the zoo, Marlin Perkins, at a sportsmen's banquet.

In the middle of the banquet, the master of ceremonies suddenly directed the diners' attention to the entrance of the hall which was located on the eighth floor of the building. Appearing in the doorway was Moosenose, standing two metres at the shoulder. Walking calmly behind her was Ontie, herself followed by LaFlamme wearing his trapper's garb. The crowd was thunderstruck. Once over their shock, the diners started feeding the docile moose some lettuce—a change from their regular tour menu of brushwood, hay, oats, and cow feed.

Finding the moose easy to handle, the curator approached LaFlamme regarding the possibility of acquiring the sleigh-pulling moose at the end of his tour. With Joe, anything was possible. In any case, as the moose had been touring in warmer weather than in Northern Ontario, they had lost their winter coats. Since it was still cold up north, they could have died from exposure. As he cared for his pets, Joe thought it was best not to bring them back to Gogama. A testimony to the Moose Man's love of his animals later came in a letter from Jim M. Taylor, District Forester in Gogama: "I have personally observed the care given these animals by Mr. Laflamme … and feel that nothing further could be desired in this respect." However, let us hope that Joe's two moose outlived the species' three-year life expectancy in a zoo. According to Dr. J.A. Campbell, who was once in charge of Toronto zoos, the feet of moose often got sore for lack of marshy soil. Since they could not relieve their pain in woodland streams as they would do in the wild, they died.

It was now April 11, 1940, and time for Joe to head home to the northern wilderness. Passing through Toronto, he decided to pay another visit to Queen's Park, most likely to lobby for who-knows-what cause. When a *Toronto Daily Star* reporter found out that Joe had given away the moose, he asked him about his plans for the following year. Surprisingly, the animal tamer talked about getting another team of wolves, all black this time. He already had four at home. Why would Joe go back to wolves? He admitted, "Wolves are most popular. … So I get me a few more black wolves and really have team to make tourists' eyes stick out."

Wolf fatigue at 52

The only evidence that Joe followed through with this plan was his own testimony to a *Toronto Daily Star* reporter in 1945: "I come back from the sportsmen's show in New York in 1941 with my wolves, and my blood pressure is low. The doctor tells me I'm overweight and I must reduce slowly. But

I reduce so fast, I get sick, am no match for wolves. I still get along fine with wolves, but they are like women. You can never really tame them." This last comment was one Joe often made during his career as a wolf tamer. He never really did explain how he knew so much about women.

LaFlamme probably didn't undertake an exhibition tour in the US after Pearl Harbour. It would have been difficult to cross the border given wartime travel restrictions. Joe might have attended the North Bay winter carnival, from February 4 to 9, 1946. The *Toronto Daily Star* of January 22 reported that LaFlamme was expected there with the two moose he had trained to plow his farm in Gogama. Oddly, there was no mention in the local *North Bay Nugget* of Joe's attendance before, during, or after the carnival. Given his widespread popularity, he surely would have been mentioned if he had attended.

By this time, Joe LaFlamme had indeed become an international celebrity. His name had gone down in history and folklore, as was evident in newspaper articles such as the *Montreal Gazette*'s story about the plight of Montrealers facing their first heavy snowfall of the season: "If anyone wants to hear sleigh bells he may go to the Laurentian villages and enjoy the chimes to his heart's content. He may even take a dogsleigh ride around a lake, with a local Joe Laflamme shouting 'mush' at the baleful-eyed huskies."

Joe's reputation had spread far and wide, not only in Canada but in the United States as well. In a 1955 newsletter titled *Lost Battalion Survivors*, Raymond Flynn, a former member of the American Co. E. 308th Infantry, reported that, from 1932 to 1935, he had acted the part of Joe LaFlamme in the French-Canadian dialect team of *Joe and Bateese*, a radio program originating from Station WBZ in Boston. Unfortunately, no transcripts of this program could be found.

When, in the 1950s, CBC radio entered an international frog-jumping contest in California and suffered a major defeat, the CBC announcer invoked Joe's fame. Who could prove to the world that Northern Ontario's bullfrogs could out-jump the best? Why, the one and only Joe LaFlamme, wolf tamer extraordinaire, of course.

According to "Tall Tales from the North," in a February 1962 edition of the *Toronto Star Weekly*, animal trainer Joe LaFlamme was able to carry by himself a 23 foot (seven-metre) freight canoe, called a "three-moose" canoe. According to the tale, it usually took two Indians—or four white men—to portage it. But the Strong Man of the North could do it solo.

What was the legendary Moose Man up to, now that he had no more animals to train? According to the dictates of his health, he continued trapping and dabbled in prospecting and even movie-acting, as seen with Warner Brothers' *The Forest Commandos*. He also hosted radio talk shows on CBC, where he related his experience with wild animals and his observations of nature. Then, CKRC radio announced, in the *Winnipeg Free Press* of April 26, 1945, that Joe LaFlamme would be one of five guests on the *Canadian Cavalcade*, at 8:30 that evening. Lorne Greene would be the narrator and Cy Mack, the interviewer. The advertisement presented LaFlamme as a prospector, trapper, dog derby winner, and internationally famous mayor of Gogama. It targeted women listeners: the title under Joe's photo read, "Girls, he tames wolves." There was at least one woman who would have tuned in to the program—if, of course, she had broadband on her battery-operated radio—and that was the wolf tamer's wife. Lillie was a big fan of the radio: "No go to bed till one, two o'clock—got beautiful concert or some t'ing interesting ever night."

24

Catching the Tour Bug Again

In the fall of 1946, Joe LaFlamme was approached by Campbell-Fairbanks Expositions Inc., based in Boston, to appear with his wild animals, mainly moose and deer, in several sportsmen's shows in the United States the following winter. General Shows, from Minneapolis, had also requested his presence at shows in St. Louis, Chicago, Minneapolis, San Francisco, and Portland. Consequently, Joe had to apply for a renewal of the transportation permit granted to him in 1940 by the Department of Lands and Forests. The Moose Man offered to put up an exhibit for the department at the various shows.

It would have been unreasonable for the department's Division of Fish and Wildlife not to give him the permit. In district forester Taylor's own words, "I…feel that the publicity gained through the exhibition of these animals is probably greater than any amount of written propaganda that might be put forth by our publicity agency." But it was not only the animal exhibitions that contributed to this public relations effort. Wherever he travelled, Joe distributed free postcards and brochures depicting the North's best assets. He always travelled with a good supply of them. He strongly believed in Northern Ontario's untapped potential as a prime tourist destination.

Off to Toronto

Joe's wards for the upcoming tour were three moose and a deer. Eighteen-year-old Morris would also accompany him. Leaving Gogama on Thursday, January 23, 1947, the 57-year-old Moose Man, his son and his four "children," as he called his pets, all travelled together in the CNR express car. The group arrived in Toronto the next morning, their visit announced by several telegrams that Joe sent to reporters. Through the years, LaFlamme had entertained many journalists in his home, thus building a solid network of media contacts.

Invited to Toronto by the Carling Conservation Club, Joe and his moose visited several schools in the poorer section of the city, which proved a worthwhile experience for youngsters who might not have had another chance to see the huge animals. It was also a perfect opportunity for Joe to mingle with children, whom he loved dearly. They loved him too, and because of his long greyish-white flowing hair and beard, he undoubtedly passed for Santa Claus's double and, in fact, was often mistaken for the jolly fellow.

While in Toronto, Joe and one of his bigger moose attended a Rotary Club luncheon at the Royal York Hotel, at the time the largest hotel in the

British Commonwealth. No detailed account has been found of this fabulous appearance in the posh dining room.

Joe was unable to reach Toronto Mayor Robert Saunders for an appointment. He had intend-

Joe LaFlamme and his moose enter the Royal York, in Toronto, during a Rotary Club luncheon at the end of January 1947. On the left are his son Morris and Dr. J.A. Campbell, from the Toronto zoo. Photo courtesy of *Toronto Star*/GetStock.com # 2086200454

ed to visit with one of his moose, climbing the stairs at City Hall. Nonetheless, a *Globe and Mail* reporter had these encouraging words for the moose tamer: "It is believed if his worship extends the customary courtesy he extends to mayors of other municipalities, he will not overlook Gogama." In the meantime, Joe lodged his moose and deer at the Dufferin Race Track over the weekend.

A presentation to Bette Davis

Before leaving Toronto, LaFlamme wanted to pay tribute to his favourite movie star, Bette Davis. In January 1947, she was pregnant and not making movies, but Joe wanted her to get back to acting as quickly as possible once the baby arrived. To help her out, he presented her with a Native baby carrier. Accepting the gift on behalf of Bette Davis was Warner Brothers' public relations representative Glenn Ireton—the same man who had written the script for *The Forest Commandos* a few years before. The used carrier was made of a rectangular board on which was fastened cloth bedding, with lacing to secure the baby and straps for mother. At the head of the board was a metal support

Joe LaFlamme presents a papoose carrier as a gift to Bette Davis, his favourite actress. Accepting the gift for Ms. Davis is Glenn Ireton, Canadian public relations representative for Warner Brothers. The presentation takes place in Toronto probably during the last week of January 1947. Photo courtesy of the City of Toronto Archives, Fonds 1257, Series 1057, Item 3327.

for a blanket to protect the child from the elements. The crude gift came with a large note: "To Betty Davis with devotion. Joe LaFlamme, the Wolf Man." Accompanying the present was a letter from Joe, written in very broken English:

> Dear Bette Davis:
>
> I did just see now your pretty picture outside Canadian liberty magasine. Yesterday or so hear you gone to have little papoose. Good. This also very good winter north Canada plenty moose, coon, beaver. Hear you never seen these things in Hollywood. Maybe good idea. About papoose I send soon you papoose carrier chief squaw wear on back as carry 23 papoose. Squaw 75 summers no more use papoose carrier, so send you Bette Davis. Think this is good idea. Also good idea use papoose carrier so lose no time and hurry back Hollywood and make more Warner picture. Maybe papoose on back all time. I like you Bette Davis also Indians too.
>
> (Signed) Joe LaFlamme
>
> Honor White Chief "Miganinvinna" Ojibway Indians

Joe presented himself as an honorary chief of the Ojibway, bearing the name "Miganinvinna," which means "leader of animals and men." As the Mattagami Indian Reserve was only a few kilometres north of Gogama, it is evident that Joe had some rapport with the community, especially given the fact that he had learned to speak some Ojibway. In giving him this title, the Ojibway may have wanted to recognize either his taming of wild animals or his efforts to raise wildlife awareness, or perhaps some form of help Joe may have given them. In any case, the "continent's most novel trainer of native wild animals" retained his title—and now wore glasses.

Next stops: Montreal and Boston

Before crossing the border to the United States, Joe travelled to Montreal, again by express car, to take his pets for a check-up at the end of January 1947. Afterwards, they headed to the New England Sportsmen's and Boat Show, held from February 1 to 9, in Boston.

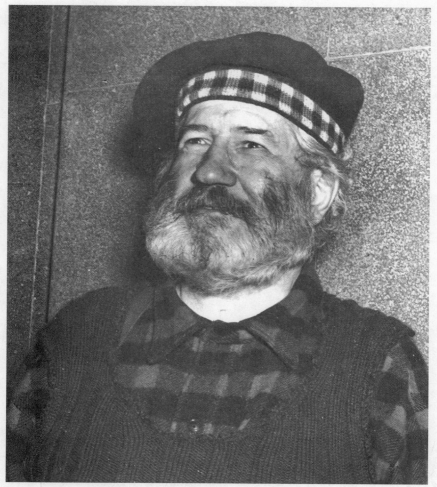

Joe LaFlamme at 57 years old, probably in Montreal in January 1947. Photo courtesy of Canada Science and Technology Museum / Musée des sciences et de la technologie du Canada.

New York again

Joe decided to transport his three moose and the buck deer from Boston to New York in a plane from the Bruning company, making history again as it was the first time that moose were flown. All three moose got airsick during the trip! The bushwhacker had to muster all his ingenuity and animal-training skills to stay on top of the situation. Once they landed at LaGuardia airfield, the moose, like the wolves in 1939, decided they did not want to

Joe LaFlamme (left) and his son Morris with three moose and a deer on board a Bruning airline plane at LaGuardia Field, in New York. The team arrives from Boston on February 13, 1947. Photo courtesy of the Associated Press, New York.

leave the aircraft. With help, Joe dragged the moose, one at a time, on a ramp padded with patchwork blankets. With some ropes and a lot of human labour, he finally pulled the beasts out of the plane. All this pushing and pulling was strenuous work when you consider that a moose can weigh up to 1,300 lbs (600 kg) and can have, according to Joe, the strength of 10 horses. All in all, flying with moose proved as adventure-filled as travelling with wolves.

The 1947 show, once gain held at the Grand Central Palace, was the first since the US had entered the Second World War in 1941. From February 17 to 23, a record 300,000 people flocked to the Palace to see the latest in hunting, fishing, and other outdoor paraphernalia. Joe was in New York when baseball hero Babe Ruth left the hospital after an 82-day stay: Ruth was greeted by a crowd of fans outside the French Hospital whereas LaFlamme was welcomed by crowds of fans inside the Palace.

Over the week, he put on a sensational act with one of his moose, most likely his favourite, Muskeg. Pointing to the moose, Big Joe—who had regained a lot of weight—told onlookers that the animal was so strong he could butt his way through the building if he put his mind to it. Well trained, at Joe's cue, the moose rumbled. Joe walked up to him and put his face against the moose's head, declaring that the animal wanted to tell him something. What message Joe conveyed on the moose's behalf is anyone's guess. Knowing his sense of humour and showmanship, the message was probably tailored to the group of onlookers present at the time.

One day, LaFlamme decided to walk downtown New York with Muskeg in tow. The crowd of curious bystanders grew so large that man and moose created a traffic jam on Fifth Avenue. Joe was happily mingling with the trendy downtown crowd, sporting wool breeches, sweater coat, and long boots. As for his usual fur hat, he must have retired it along with his parka because photos from that period on showed him wearing a tam-o'-shanter with a checked band. Imagine the anachronistic scene: a burly and bearded northern trapper, wearing a Scottish beret, strolling down busy Fifth Avenue with a Canadian moose on leash.

When not performing with his moose, Joe entertained the crowds with his "fabulous fund of stories." He had a knack for telling jokes, not only about bush men visiting the city—*à la Crocodile Dundee*—but also about city dwellers going into the woods. As one reporter recalled, "There isn't a city slicker around Grand Central Palace who can match the yarns that the trapper from Gogama, Ont., tells in his quaint Quebec English, spiced with an odd Indian word here and there." But was the joker only a façade? Photos of that era reveal a lot of sadness in the Moose Man's eyes.

Wrapping up the 1947 winter tour

While at the Philadelphia Sportsmen's Show, during the first week of March, self-appointed Gogama mayor Joe LaFlamme took the opportunity to pay a visit to Mayor Bernard Samuel at City Hall. Of course, Joe always brought along his "political attaché," in this case, Ti-Moose (French for "Little Moose"). Also on the agenda were appearances on four radio programs. He and Morris had been very busy since leaving New York. The Moose Man's popularity followed him like a shadow wherever he went.

After this show, LaFlamme returned to Buffalo, but he did not leave his moose behind this year. He still had other shows to do further west. It is likely that after the Buffalo exhibition Joe participated in sportsmen's shows in St. Louis, Chicago, Minneapolis, San Francisco, and Portland. He then travelled to the National Sportsmen's Show of Canada, held at the Ottawa Coliseum from April 21 to 26. As usual, Joe and his moose became the centre of attention at the Ottawa Fish and Game Association display.

After wrapping up these shows, Joe was homeward bound, where he would stay at least until the coming summer. However, he did visit Sudbury with his pet badger, Geraldine, although we are not exactly sure of the date this trip took place.

25

Finding His Way to Columbus, Ohio

In the summer of 1947, smelling money, Joe answered an invitation he heard on international radio. He wired a telegraph to Columbus, Ohio: "I hear on radio that somebody in Columbus, Ohio, wants moose to go to meetings. I, Joe LaFlamme, have only moose in whole North country that will go to meetings. You tell these people in Columbus, Ohio, that Joe LaFlamme and moose leaving right away. Where is Columbus, Ohio, anyhow? Signed, Joe LaFlamme."

Joe would soon find out. He wanted to collect the $1,000 reward offered by the Loyal Order of Moose to anyone who would deliver a pair of live moose to the international convention in Columbus, almost 600 miles (1,000 km) away. The only hitch was that the moose had to arrive on time for the meeting scheduled to start on August 17, 1947. Otherwise J. Jack Stoehr, regional director of the Moose for Ohio, Pennsylvania, and West Virginia, would keep the money. Apparently, Stoehr himself took up the challenge and succeeded in bringing live moose to the convention site, on the Statehouse grounds. Unfortunately, for some reason, the moose died before he got them into the meeting hall.

In the meantime, on Saturday, August 9, the "bes' tam' woodsman in

Canada, by gar!" was heading for the Gogama railway station with two moose. Together, the three were to board the evening train for Toronto—or so thought Joe. His moose had other plans, which quickly became obvious when Joe tried coaxing them up the ramp to the baggage car. As the train whistled, Muskeg, the more rebellious of the two animals, suddenly turned around and jumped off the ramp. Keeping his cool, Joe studied the moose's reactions, all the while adjusting the suspenders over his bare chest and leveling his straw hat with his fingertips. Then, like a true lion tamer, the Moose Man slowly picked up a rope, his eyes never leaving Muskeg. Carefully, he approached the beast.

Pretending to ignore his approaching master, the bull moose dropped his head, one hoof slowly digging in the coal cinders. Joe grasped his chance and pounced on the short antlers. At the same time, Muskeg quickly lifted his head, catching Joe in the process. A wrestling match ensued, with moose and man tangled. Finally, Joe succeeded in putting a lasso around Muskeg's neck. Undefeated, the Strong Man of the North proudly reset his straw hat, oblivious to his sooty and bloody chest. The moose had deeply gashed Joe's neck and shoulder with his left front hoof. The tamer finally got the moose on board. Thirty minutes late, the train left Gogama, its passengers having enjoyed an extraordinary side show.

When he arrived in Toronto the next morning, LaFlamme was weak from loss of blood and was admitted to the hospital. As for Muskeg, off to the zoo he went. The other moose had died from heat exhaustion at the beginning of the trip. When released from the hospital on Wednesday, an eager moose tamer declared: "Joe LaFlamme get dat moose money soon, by gar!" Joe was on his way to Ohio. And so was moody Muskeg—in a refrigerator truck. Joe was taking precautions as a heat wave was currently hitting the eastern states. So Dew the Mover Ltd., of Toronto, was en route to Columbus, Ohio, to the Moose national convention—and every load was insured, as the publicity on the truck stated. Geared to LaFlamme's venture, the advertisement seemed to have been painted on tarps that were tied over the truck's refrigerated box.

After a stopover in Hamilton, to the pleasure of local sportsmen, LaFlamme and a docile Muskeg crossed the International Bridge into Buffalo on Friday night, August 15, 1947. They arrived at the Moose convention under heavy

Muskeg and Joe LaFlamme, probably on Joe's release from the hospital in Toronto, on August 14, 1947. Photo courtesy of the City of Toronto Archives, Fonds 1257, Series 1057, Item 3316.

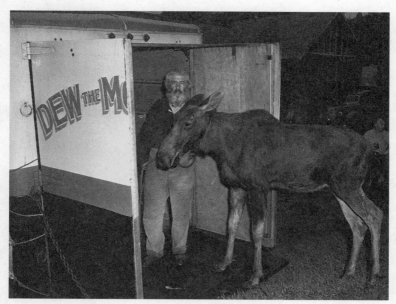

Joe LaFlamme loads his moose Muskeg into a refrigerated truck from Dew the Mover Ltd., in Toronto, heading to the Moose convention in Columbus, Ohio. Photo courtesy of the City of Toronto Archives, Fonds 1257, Series 1057, Item 3321.

rain. Twenty-five thousand Moose members enthusiastically welcomed their four-legged counterpart and his master: "We've got to elect Muskeg supreme governor."

Joe received his $1,000 prize money at a public ceremony the following night. Proud of his success, as he was one of five to have taken up the challenge, Joe softly praised the 500 lb (227 kg) Muskeg: "Nice leetle moose. Sweet leetle moose." But Muskeg had no inclination to be a nice little moose for much longer. When Joe walked him across the street to the State Capitol yard for a photo shoot, the moose slipped out of his halter and headed for High Street. Unfazed, Big Joe halted traffic, and in a mixture of English and Ojibway, commanded Muskeg to him. It was time to go home, now, "nice leetle moose."

26

Influencing a Canadian Icon

At Toronto's CNE

Toronto's popular Canadian National Exhibition (CNE), commonly known as "the Ex," was also opening its doors after the war. About three million visitors were expected at the 1947 show, and Joe LaFlamme wanted to be part of the action. A thinner Joe LaFlamme set up his own display with Moosie. They would remain there from August 22 to September 8. Occasionally, the Moose Man took a break and walked Moosie around the CNE grounds, in search of something to eat. But Moosie was not a big fan of fast food, not even hamburgers. The tea booth was more her cup of tea. In one sitting, the moose could drink a full gallon (4 l) of the brew.

While at the Ex, Joe got another chance to play movie star. The National Film Board prepared a short film—*Johnny at the Fair*—about a young boy who gets lost at the Ex and who, in searching for his parents, meets various celebrities: Canadian prime minister William Lyon Mackenzie King, skater Barbara Ann Scott, boxing champion Joe Louis. In one shot, four-year-old actor Charles Pachter is seen with Joe, petting Moosie. Pachter, now an art icon in Canada and renowned for his moose paintings, clearly remembers the pungent smell

Joe LaFlamme (58 years old) holds four-year-old Charles Pachter who pets Joe's moose at the Canadian National Exhibition (CNE) in Toronto, in August 1947. Photo courtesy of Charles Pachter.

of the hide of the female moose lying beside Joe on the sawdust-covered floor. He also recalls the supple chamois feel of LaFlamme's doeskin outfit. He still chuckles at the thought: "And of course I thought Joe had stepped right out of the Bible!"

In 2010, Pachter explained in an email that the scene shot with Joe hadn't made it to the final cut; nonetheless, the clip was used for publicity activities. He then added, "And as an artist who has made the moose famous, I trace my initial inspiration to that long-ago encounter with Joe Laflamme and his pet moose." It is amazing how much influence the Wolf Man/Moose Man, or the Animal Man as he was known at the CNE, has had over the years. And perhaps Joe should have been nicknamed the Bear Man, since he had recently started taming bears as well.

On September 4, LaFlamme brought to the Ex a six-month old black bear cub. Louise caused quite a stir for all journalists hoping to take a photo of her before she left for Sydney, Australia. Donated by Joe, the bear cub had been chosen to represent the Toronto Press Club at the Sydney Journalists' Club By-Line Ball in October. She would go as an exchange for Bluey, the kangaroo, sent earlier that spring on behalf of the Sydney reporters. The intent was to raise money for the children of journalists who had lost their lives in World War II.

But mischievous Miss Byline of 1947 was none too enchanted with the whole business, whether the cause was worthy or not. As the cub arrived at the women's building, she was taken aback by the crowd and climbed the spruce tree on a homemaker's set. The tree fell down and a perplexed Louise with it. She then tried the rocking chair, after knocking down the butter churn. She must have felt like a bare bear in front of all those camera-carrying onlookers. Looking for a safe place, she ducked under a bed, just in time to avoid a hatchet falling off a shelf. Only after much coaxing was Joe able to get her out of hiding and take her home until her scheduled flight to Australia.

When they found out about Louise's imminent plane trip to their country, Australian government officials almost sparked an international feud. They insisted that animals had to be imported by ship, rather than by plane, thus allowing any disease to manifest itself before the arrival. But if Louise could not fly to Sydney, she would not make it in time for the By-Line Ball. She waited out the diplomatic furor in LaFlamme's menagerie. The Canadian naturalist, as the *Lethbridge Herald* reporter called Joe, confided that Louise would very much like to travel with a male companion of her species. Could it be he had another bear to give away… since he himself was about to have to run away to avoid going to court?

Living like a fugitive

LaFlamme probably wanted the 1947 Ex to last forever—then he would have been safe from the police. In July 1947, Joe had again been convicted of illegal possession of liquor. But since he had a commitment with the CNE until early September, his case was held over until the following month. On October 17, Joe was sentenced to spend three months in the Sudbury jail. As he knew it was coming, Joe had already started to take animals to his brother's farm in St. Zotique, Quebec. His brother Joseph was not keen to have wild animals share the stable with his cows, but Joe insisted so adamantly that his older sibling gave in, much to the pleasure of neighbours who would get to see some unusual wild animals up close. In addition to welcoming visitors to his brother's farm, Joe often trucked the animals from farm to farm and entertained the curious bystanders. He enjoyed making Muskeg talk into a microphone or even giving moose rides to the youngsters, especially his nieces and nephews.

The family suspected Joe, or rather Télesphore, was again hiding from the law. Unless he wanted to be behind bars for a few months, the Moose Man could not return to Ontario. Although there is no proof, it is possible that Joe was able to obtain a conditional discharge allowing him to return to Ontario for a few days at a time, which he did according to some Gogama locals.

In any case, for the next few months LaFlamme travelled between the two provinces, but Lillie stayed in Gogama for another year. The couple communicated by letter or telegram, most likely, as the town had only a short-distance telephone system.

Touring with a menagerie in 1948

The sentence did not deter LaFlamme from planning other exhibition tours. Before undertaking his 1948 American tour, he took Muskeg to Montreal for a check-up. On January 29, he and Morris arrived by train at the Central Station. Joe knew he had time to get the exam done before the next train to Boston.

The Moose Man crossed the station concourse with his full menagerie: a moose, a badger, a wolf, and a bear cub. He was heading for the Railway Express Agency where he would check in all animals except the moose. Then he walked out of Central Station with moose in tow. The downtown Montreal crowds were wide-eyed at the unusual sight. This did not bother Joe or the moose, who were heading to the office of veterinarian George Etienne, on Drummond Street. The examination confirmed that the moose was healthy despite the fact that he ate the doctor's model sailing ship and a pot of shamrocks. Joe thought nothing of his moose's extravagant taste: "He eats almost every kind of wood—without indigestion." After the visit, Joe and Muskeg

Joe LaFlamme and his moose Muskeg walk downtown Montreal as they head to the office of veterinarian George Etienne, on January 29, 1948. Photo courtesy of *The Montreal Herald* Fonds/*The (Montreal) Gazette* photo archives. (Photographer: Richard Arless)

walked back up Ste. Catherine Street and south to the train station. The moose tamer then met his son, collected his other pets, and together they boarded the train, en route to the Boston sportsmen's show.

The next exhibition was in New York in mid-February 1948. Among the highlights of the visit to the Big Apple were Muskeg's and the wolf's guest appearances on the *Nancy Craig Show*, an ABC radio talk show about vacations. The visit was probably sponsored by LaFlamme's close friend, Glenn Ireton. Joe took the elevator up to the Radio City studio with the 700 lb (318 kg) moose and the heavily chained timber wolf. The animals took it in stride. Muskeg then performed a superb interview with Joe as the main interviewer who talked to the moose in Ojibway, then translated for the audience:

Joe LaFlamme (centre) takes his moose and his wolf out of the elevator at the Radio City building in New York, sometime in mid-February 1948. Photo courtesy of *LIFE*, March 15, 1948, p. 61.

LaFlamme: *"Would you like to say something to the radio
   audience, Mushkeg?"*
Mushkeg: *"Bra-a-a-a-h."*
LaFlamme: *"He says he would be glad to. Now Mushkeg,
   let's have a weather report for the people. Will it be a
   fine day tomorrow or is it going to rain?"*
Mushkeg: *"Bra-a—. Uh."*
LaFlamme: *"Mushkeg says it is going to be fine."*
Craig: *"Thank you very much!"*

Other members of the audience were not so keen on thanking Muskeg,
especially the female press agent who got nibbled on by the moose while
Muskeg was waiting for his cue. Included in the moose's buffet were also some
vacation brochures, gum, and even the foliage on Nancy Craig's hat.

Everything went well at the sportsmen's show but, towards the end, the
veteran woodsman, who had never liked the city much, had had, in one reporter's words, "just about enough of civilization…and [was] ready to go back to
his cabin and traps." *New York Times* reporter Raymond Camp obviously did
not know that LaFlamme owned the largest house in Gogama—by no means
a cabin.

Although no evidence has been found that LaFlamme attended other
American shows in March, he must have stayed in the States until March 29.
That day, *La Presse* reports that the Moose Man and his moose passed through
customs with inspector Marcel Bonin, at Central Station in Montreal. From
there, Joe and his menagerie were expected at the upcoming Sportsman's Exhibition in the 17th Hussars Armory, on Côte-des-Neiges Road. The proceeds of
the early April show would be given to an organization supporting the conservation of wildlife in the Province of Quebec—a cause dear to Joe's heart.

The wildlife exhibitor's next destination was the Convention Hall in
Detroit, Michigan. On April 15, he and his son applied for border crossing.
On the applications, Joe's occupation was listed as being a hunter and Morris's
as a photographer. Both men gave Gogama as their home address, but Joe's
departure point was Niagara Falls, Ontario, whereas Morris left from Lacolle,
Quebec.

Customs officer Marcel Bonin (right) clears travellers Joe LaFlamme and his moose Muskeg at the Central Station in Montreal, on March 29, 1948. Photo courtesy of *La Presse* Archives.

On that same day, Gogama District Forester Jim M. Taylor wrote a letter to Joe, regarding the renewal of his "authority to capture any animals that you might require for live exhibits." Taylor also mentioned that Lillie had come to his office that day. The letter was sent to Joe via the Campbell-Fairbanks Sportsmen Show, which means that Joe and Morris were still touring for a few weeks. The 1948 show season was winding down and so was Joe's last tour in the United States. Major changes were ahead for the LaFlammes.

27

Turning into a True Conservationist

None of the Gogama locals remember exactly when or how Joe and Lillie LaFlamme permanently moved out of the community. There are rumours that Morris had left first to find work in Montreal, most likely in 1946 or 1947. Ever since the fire of 1941 destroyed the lumber mills, business had been slowing down and people were moving out, often abandoning their property. Between the lagging local economy, the pending prison charge, and the fact that he was nearing 60, Joe had enough reasons to return to Montreal with his wife. Furthermore, his chronic low blood pressure required medical attention. He must have caught a few wild animals before leaving in 1948, however, since he had just renewed his permit to do so. He clearly intended to continue working with animals.

Joe seems to have caught several black bears before the summer of 1948. The *Montreal Gazette* of August 4 reports that Joe LaFlamme had gone to Dorval airport the day before to check his nine bears prior to their long flight overseas. Their cages had been placed in the cabin behind the seat of the Trans-Canada Air Lines pilot. Crew members had been given dog biscuits to feed the animals on their way to London, England, and from there to the

Chipperfield Circus at Pontypridd, in South Wales. According to the *Gazette*, LaFlamme had captured the animals in the Gogama area and had tamed them at his Belmont Park animal showplace. This amusement park was located on the bank of Rivière des Prairies, in the Montreal neighbourhood of Cartierville.

As Joe LaFlamme's name was not listed in the *Montreal Directory* before 1952, it is possible that Joe and Lillie were subletting from relatives or friends in the area, perhaps close to the park and the animals. As for his main property in Gogama, three of the four lots were sold in 1951. The lot at the south end of the yard was sold four years later to the same person.

Even in the big city, LaFlamme continued to do what was close to his heart: give the public a chance to see wild animals live and to get to know them better. Thanks to the initiative of the Anglers Association of Montreal, Joe took his menagerie on a tour of Quebec to raise awareness about conservation. The tour also received backing from various fish and game protection groups that committed the tour's receipts to conservation work in their local areas.

LaFlamme's first stop was in Trois-Rivières, during the last week of August 1948. About 100,000 visitors were expected at the fair. The acts performed by Joe's animals again proved to be a popular attraction. Maheegan the wolf wrestled Louis the bear, no holds barred! This was not their first fight nor their last: through the years, they regularly practised in their cage. Muskeg, the only moose to have been on the radio, took up the microphone again, ending his interviews with an 18-point love call. Moose mating season was, after all, just around the corner. Joe, a recognized showman, put on an exhibition that truly delighted children, though a few of them thought nothing of kicking at the cages and making the animals nervous, something which would have annoyed LaFlamme.

The travelling zoo was then exhibited in Shawinigan Falls, Sherbrooke, and Quebec City. At every stop, Joe explained the importance and the activities of wildlife conservation. He illustrated his talks with the help of three dozen wild specimens: his own animals, including Muskeg, Maheegan, and Louis the bear; and some on loan from the Charlesbourg Zoo near Quebec City, including a wildcat, beavers, coyotes, porcupines, wild ducks, and owls. And what better prop than Muskeg to drive home the value of moose conservation? Observing the dwindling moose population, Joe had always been an avid spokesman for

Joe LaFlamme shows his moose Muskeg to an unidentified couple, circa 1948. Photo courtesy of Gerry Talbot.

proper management. Now there was urgency in his voice, especially when it came to the issue of poaching: "Very few people are poachers at heart. The trouble is they take the instinctive attitude that protective laws are passed to antagonize. They only need to be told the reasons behind it all and to realize the dangers and most of them will cooperate." At least, that was what Joe was hoping would happen.

The associations that sponsored the tour were pleased with the public's response to LaFlamme's conservation message. Leo Cassidy, the president of the Quebec Federation of Fish and Game Associations, had nothing but praise for his work: "If such an example had more imitators, all Quebecers would get to know the full meaning of conservation, and we might then go to work managing our great outdoors before it is too late."

Joe had always been a wildlife conservationist at heart, even in his role as the Wolf Man. In *Wolves: Behavior, Ecology, and Conservation*, considered by many professionals to be the academic standard on the species, Luigi Boitani states that by 1930 the wolf population had disappeared from almost all of the 48 contiguous states, and even from Yellowstone National Park. In Canada and Alaska, they were doing well in most of their original range. But massive campaigns to eradicate them caused the Canadian wolf population to reach an all-time low in southern Quebec and Ontario by that year as well. Something had to be done to ensure the wolf's survival.

Because "popular information about wolves is often biased or inaccurate," public education was imperative if informed decisions were to be made to ensure the species' survival. Joe LaFlamme was therefore ahead of his time because he was already using, as early as 1925, several of the educational approaches recommended and adopted decades later: extensive travelling exhibits with his "ambassador" wolves, and public lectures on the radio, in schools, and at his Montreal zoo.

Granted, LaFlamme's activities might not have been part of a focused and well-planned wolf education campaign. But, through his presence at sportsmen's shows in Canada and the United States, he had come into contact with hundreds of thousands of people, many of them children and adolescents. His great love of nature and wildlife, especially wolves, might well have positively influenced a whole generation of young minds, many of whom later became teachers and possibly even decision-makers regarding wolf management. In 2006, biologists L. David Mech and Luigi Boitani concur that, looking back 60 years, "both scientific knowledge of wolf biology and human attitudes toward the wolf have improved tremendously... and most of the changes occurred in urban populations." This happened after LaFlamme's many exhibition tours with his wolves.

All things considered, one could therefore consider Joe LaFlamme (b. 1889) to be an embryonic Canadian version of conservationist Aldo Leopold (b. 1887), one of the first Americans to speak in defense of the wolf. In any case, LaFlamme had a great passion for the wilderness and had his own way of conveying that passion to the public. He succeeded in getting his message across, as Jim M. Taylor made evident: "Since 1920, J.T. Laflamme of Gogama has been interested in the training of wild animals for exhibition purposes, particularly wolves and moose. Press dispatches, photographs, and the continued demand by sportsmen shows for these exhibitions attest to his success in this line and value as a publicity agent for tourism and possibly wildlife conservation."

As he had done for many years while in Ontario, LaFlamme continued to exhibit animals in his home province of Quebec. According to family members, Joe had participated in at least one Montreal sports show. The *Gazette* reported that, in 1949, the wildlife expert, already well known throughout North America, showed a moose (Muskeg), a black bear, a badger, a raccoon, two otters, and three wolves. The night before the exhibition, the latter were mistaken for beautiful big dogs by unsuspecting reporter-in-training Jerry Williams, who reported that LaFlamme had accepted news editor Gerald Fitzgerald's invitation to visit the office. He was to give a preview of Muskeg's performance at the show. The Moose Man arrived at 1000 St. Antoine Street, driving his "rattling old cage-packed flatbed truck" right up to the door of the *Gazette*'s building. He had the "friendly horse with antlers" go down the truck ramp and then inside, up the freight elevator to the fourth floor.

Meanwhile, the young journalist was assigned to keep an eye on the rest of LaFlamme's menagerie. Having never been close to wild animals before, the lad circled the flatbed, in awe of the magnificent dogs whose eyes "reflected the yellow glow of the corner street lights." He talked to them through the cage's wire mesh. They responded with a faint mournful sound as they pushed against the side of the cage. Williams then proceeded to widen the mesh enough to get his hand inside. The animals nuzzled his fingers. He then patted and scratched their necks, as they pushed one another. The cub reporter felt quite proud, thinking the "dogs" were seeking his attention.

This got the attention of the editor, who opened his office window and yelled at the boy, "Get your hand out of there, you damned fool. Those are wolves!"

Though Williams slowly withdrew his hand from the cage, he felt no fear—only wonder. He could now explain the animals' glowing yellow eyes. He also realized, as "the amazement of it all permeated [his] brain," that he had petted real wolves. The incident surely made for a vivid souvenir of the Moose Man's visit.

28

Standing at the Crossroads

Since his final move to Quebec in 1948, Joe LaFlamme had owned and operated a zoo at 7450 Décarie Boulevard, near the Namur metro station, just in front of the Blue Bonnets Raceway (the former Hippodrome de Montréal). In the small, fort-like zoo, the "zoo keeper" looked after several species of animals: a moose, a wildcat, a ferret, some wolves, a 500 lb (227 kg) bear, and two horrible-looking crocodiles.

"Those I leave alone," Joe admitted to a reporter. "Impossible to reason with them like with wolves!"

LaFlamme sometimes invited children to the zoo for lectures on wild animals. One former youngster clearly remembers an incident that happened on one of her Sunday visits. As LaFlamme was hand-feeding the wolves, one of them accidently bit his finger: "Joe had a very emotional 'talk' with the wolf—after which the wolf lowered his head and cried," Sarah Hartt-Snowbell recalls.

In addition to keeping a menagerie, LaFlamme worked for an indefinite amount of time as a night watchman on the Montreal docks. He was also employed as a school-crossing guard for the Montreal Police Service, a job he held until he turned 61, in 1950. That summer, he found work at the Waumbek

Louis the bear affectionately kisses his master Joe LaFlamme, on September 18, 1950. The animal is probably in his enclosure at the Joe LaFlamme Zoo, in Montreal. Photo courtesy of the Charles Laflamme family.

Hotel, a tourist resort in Jefferson, New Hampshire, about 120 miles (200 km) southeast of Montreal. Then, as the Randolph Mountain Club was in need of help, the owner of the hotel sent Joe to blaze trails in the bush. Weighing in at 265 lbs (121 kg), Joe still had stamina for his age: he could portage, over a quarter of a mile (400 m), a 300 lb (136 kg) load on his back.

Suzanne F. Charron

When Joe returned to Montreal in August 1950, he experienced problems with his wolf Maheegan, who escaped from his enclosure twice within in a couple of weeks. The second time, Maheegan was not given another chance: the police put the wolf down. Needless to say, Joe was heartbroken. He had done several shows with this Saskatchewan-born timber wolf, who was residing, until his death, at the Joe LaFlamme Zoo.

In the summer of 1951, Joe returned to blazing trails for the Randolph Mountain Club, but the job was too demanding at his age, and this was his last year. The following winter, according to the Laflamme family, Joe loaded his favourite moose Muskeg, along with some other animals, in the back of his 1950 red panel Dodge truck. He headed for South Carolina with Lillie, Morris, and a little monkey in the front seat, though it is not known which sportsmen's shows he attended. In the warm weather of the south, the moose moulted. As a result, in February 1952, Muskeg caught a cold after his return to Montreal's subzero weather. The animal died a few weeks later and was buried on the family farm on concession road St. Thomas, in St. Zotique.

For the second time in 18 months, LaFlamme suffered the loss of a long-time animal friend. He had taken in the baby moose after the mother had abandoned Muskeg several years earlier, in the Gogama area. The moose, who grew up in the village, followed Joe everywhere, even when he went to the local stores for supplies. In fact, Muskeg had been caught several times munching on bushels of apple outside Muriel Cooke's general store. Joe and his pet also visited Albert Giroux's hotel together. The moose did not mind climbing the stairs to the local pub, his reward being a bottle of beer. Come fall, Joe would let the moose loose in the woods because Muskeg had a better chance of surviving the cold season there. In spring, the Moose Man put a half-tamed wolf on his trail, and unfailingly, the moose was found.

After Muskeg's death, Joe completely retired from the animal business. He and Lillie made a move to apartment life in Westmount. As of 1952, Joe's name appears for several consecutive years in the *Montreal Directory*, listed as a tenant at 2300 Souvenir Street, near the former Montreal Forum. The local papers were fairly quiet about the sportsman's-show hero during that period. Still, in 1953 he was quoted on an invasion of coyotes in New York State: "Pound per pound he

Joe LaFlamme and two unidentified men saw up a tree trunk at the LaFlammes' home, 2300 Souvenir Street, Montreal, circa mid-1950s. Photo courtesy of the Charles Laflamme family.

Joe LaFlamme measures the diameter of the tree trunk cut at his home in Montreal, circa mid-1950s. Photo courtesy of the Charles Laflamme family.

can hold his own with anything alive in battle," declared Joe, who no doubt had met several of these creatures in his many rambles through the northern bush.

But what kind of creatures was he meeting now as a special guard with the Barnes Investigation Bureau in Montreal? The business was run by a former policeman and friend who had been in the force at the same time as LaFlamme—over four decades earlier, since Joe was now in his mid sixties. This was likely his last job before officially retiring.

From left to right are Morris LaFlamme, most likely Auguste Haigneré, as well as Lillie et Joe LaFlamme. Auguste was Lillie's young brother, visiting the LaFlammes in Montreal, circa late 1950s. Photo courtesy of the Charles Laflamme family.

To continue bringing in after-retirement income, Joe and Lillie sublet rooms in their apartment. One of their long-time tenants was a Veteran Taxi driver. In early April 1964, the 42-year-old Tony Ladansky was stabbed to death while on his shift. This was a terrible blow for LaFlamme, who considered Ladansky a close friend. When interviewed by a *Nouveau Samedi* reporter, Joe's only comment was, "There are humans who are more ferocious than the most ferocious of the wolves I have tamed." Otherwise, Joe had a lot of anecdotes to tell the reporter about his days as the Wolf Man. His memory was sound, even though painful joints were limiting his activities.

According to relatives, in his last few years Joe lived a very secluded life, hardly going out of the apartment other than to let out his wife's two dachshunds. "Go make war," he would order the pets. When they barked to get back in, he would open the door, declaring, "The war is over." It's odd that he used war as a metaphor in his later years, when he had so adamantly refused to go to war as a young man.

Joe LaFlamme (right) with his older brother Joseph Laflamme in St. Zotique, Quebec, circa 1956. Photo courtesy of the Charles Laflamme family.

Lillie and Joe LaFlamme (left) with friends Paul Giroux and Aldéa Laflamme, Joe's sister, probably in Montreal, in the early 1960s. Photo courtesy of the Charles Laflamme family.

Suzanne F. Charron

Another contrast with LaFlamme's younger days was his regard for clothing. When he was touring with his animals, he loved to dress for show, wearing the same signature outfit, whereas now he spent most of his days in his undershirt and long underwear or pajamas, if not totally naked. When relatives would visit, they were sometimes greeted by a man who was not decently attired. Some great-nieces and great-nephews remember their great-uncle Télesphore's retort when their father would say to him, "By the way, uncle…" Joe would promptly answer, "I'm not naked—I have my slippers on." His ankles were indeed well covered with his big sheepskin slippers. This habit was not totally new: Joe had occasionally taken air baths on his high veranda in Gogama as well. Always close to nature and as uninhibited as his wolves, perhaps he felt constrained in his clothes and needed, once in a while, to feel the breeze on his bare skin.

After Ladansky's death, Joe and Lillie moved to a new neighbourhood, foregoing subletting to tenants. In the 1964-1965 *Montreal Directory*, Joe's name appears with Morris's at 8265 Baillargé Street, in Anjou. The memories and the absence of his friend were probably too painful to bear for a man who now had fewer social contacts. Furthermore, in addition to chronic low blood pressure, LaFlamme had been suffering from diabetes and was not getting any better. Lillie was also ailing.

Sometime in January 1965, LaFlamme was admitted to the Montreal General Hospital and he had a tough decision to make. His right leg was so badly infected below the knee that it needed to be amputated. But how was a man who had done so much footwork in his life supposed to accept losing a leg?

Joe's answer was an emphatic "No!" The doctors insisted that the operation had to be done as soon as possible. The answer was still no. Friends begged Joe to agree to the surgery: "No," again.

Then came W.G. (Bill) Power, manager of the Montreal sportsman's shows. He knew how to handle temperamental Joe, having dealt with him at the peak of his fame as an animal trainer. Power tried to change the Wolf Man's mind. The answer remained, definitely, no. Refusing to take no for an answer, Bill continued to urge Joe to listen to the doctors. "No," "No," and "No."

LaFlamme finally confided that he wanted to wait out winter before heading to a magic spring 150 miles (240 km) north of Quebec City. He was no doubt referring to the Ermitage Saint-Antoine, at Lac-Bouchette, 60 miles (100 km) west of Chicoutimi-Saguenay. The shrine has been renowned since 1912 for the healing properties of its spring. Joe was confident that bathing his infected leg in the miraculous water would cure it. Having been in close relationship with nature all his life, it was normal that the Wolf Man turned to her in times of need. But the spring season was still months away. His leg might not last that long. Was Joe really willing to sabotage his own existence?

In the meantime, the medical care was costing money and Lillie was running out of funds. Aware of LaFlamme's financial plight, Bill Power and Dick White—also involved in sportsman's shows in Joe's time—set up a trust fund to help out. Contributors were to make cheques payable to the "Joe Laflamme Fund."

Power's benevolence did not stop there. He frequently visited Joe at the hospital, continuing to beg him to give his consent for the operation. "Yes," Joe finally agreed.

But the next morning, Bill and a surgeon went to Joe's room to prepare him for the impending surgery. "No!" Joe had changed his mind overnight.

29

Mushing "Home"

Persistent, Power continued to beg Joe to allow the surgeon to amputate his leg. Finally, on Wednesday, February 3, to everyone's relief, Joe said, "Yes." Before he changed his mind again, he was scheduled for operation the very next day.

But his choice did not serve him well after all. Five minutes after leaving the hospital recovery room, Joe LaFlamme died, with Bill Power holding his hand. On Friday, February 5, 1965, newspapers announced the Wolf Man's passing.

The funeral service was held at 11 a.m., at the William Wray Chapel, on University Street, on Tuesday, February 9. Joe's final resting place is at the Hawthorn-Dale Cemetery, on Sherbrooke Street, at the east end of Montreal Island. It is a humble place. His grave remains unmarked—unlike his life with wolves and moose.

In the last moments of his life on earth, hovering between the anaesthesia and moments of lucidity, the Wolf Man may have revisited the event that had been the "thrill of his life" and made him a legend in his own lifetime: his first trip to New York...

Saturday, January 23, 1926, promised to be fair but cold, with strong northwest winds blowing over the city. The thermometer stood at 10°F (-12°C), perfect weather for mushing. The Wolf Man and his dog-and-wolf pack arrived at the Pennsylvania Station by train, then took a truck to 210th Street, in Queens. It was 11 a.m. The first moments were a bit overwhelming, but the tamer and his wolves adapted quickly to new situations.

Setting up their gear in a garage, Joe and his assistant Paul Giroux wasted no time preparing for the team's first mushing experience in downtown New York. The crowds would soon be lining Broadway in anticipation. The two men unloaded the eight dogs and the five wolves from the truck, and chained each to a separate post in the garage. Joe gave each dog and each wolf a reassuring pat on the head. They were excited by the new sights, smells, and sounds of the second largest city in the world. A deafening chorus of barks, yelps, and snarls resonated in the building. Undoubtedly, the animals could also feel their master's excitement. Joe put on his green fur-trimmed parka, Voyageur sash, and fur hat. His bushy black beard gave a note of authenticity. He would don leather Indian mittens just before leaving.

After unloading the gear from the truck, the men extended the chain gangline in front of the sleigh, which was tied to a post with the snubline. Then they started the harnessing procedure. Joe began with Billy, his lead dog on this tour. Then he and Paul harnessed the point dogs and wolves, swiftly slipping the webbing collar over each head, careful not to get their fingers snapped. Next, they lifted each animal's right front leg, guiding it through the canvas harness loop. After repeating the procedure with the other leg, they could now fasten the belly belt and tie each animal's tugline to the main gangline. Next came the swing dogs and wolves.

Joe and Paul worked fast and could barely hear themselves talk with the clamour of the animals, all eager to run. Lunging forward and from side to side, the dogs and wolves wove themselves in and over the chain gangline. A little untangling would be necessary when the men finished harnessing the wheel or rear animals. Finally, the team was almost ready to leave, with the wolves in their strategic positions on the line.

Giroux now went to the front of the team and held Billy to keep the gangline taut. LaFlamme took his place on the footboards at the back of the sleigh. He tested his brake mat, put on his mittens, and bent to grab his long whip from the sleigh, holding the driving bow with one hand. Signalling to Paul, he then released the snubline and cracked his whip, shouting, "Mush, Billy!"

Off went the team, with heads bobbing, tongues lolling, tails up and swaying, and snow flying from all 52 paws!

Only a short time later, he cried, "Gee!" and the lead dog turned right onto Broadway. The street was slightly snow-covered and provided a perfect glide. Excited, Joe took it all in: buildings, people, and traffic. Vehicles stopped or gave the musher and his train a wide berth.

That day's itinerary was a 14 mile (22 km) run on Broadway, from 210th Street right down to City Hall Park, where Joe intended to call on Mayor James J. Walker. Depending on traffic and road conditions on the busier southern section of Broadway, this would have taken from 90 minutes to two hours. So far, the going was good. The dogs and wolves were pulling well, using up the pent-up energy from the long journey. They soon settled into a steady stride. "Easy!" The command cautioned Billy against the nearby intersection. Then, "Heigh, Billy!" prompted him to increase his speed again.

Thousands of people stood in the streets cheering. Letting go of the driving bow, an elated Joe waved back at them. This was a dream come true!

But the dream hit a snag at Times Square, where the dense crowds pressed in, slowing down the cavalcade and causing a traffic jam several blocks long. The team's pace had slowed almost to a stop. Remaining calm, LaFlamme kept his dogs and wolves in check, hoping none would snap at onlookers. Fortunately, the traffic officers took control of the situation. Before long, Joe could order Billy to "Animoosh, quitch!" The team was trotting again. Joe must have been relieved, to say the least. The mushing went smoothly from then on, and the crowds kept on cheering. Joe would have been beaming with pride. After all, to this day, he was the only musher in the world to have driven a team of wolves down Broadway. Always an original, the Wolf Man did Broadway theatre—his way.

Now approaching City Hall Park, Joe slowed down. Once in the park, he put his foot on the brake mat and barked, "Whoa!" The team came to a full stop. He then returned the whip to the sleigh and stepped off the footboards. His head high, the musher walked up to his team, patting the head of each wolf and dog with pride. Certainly not your typical New York scene ... but truly Wolf Man Joe LaFlamme in all his glory.

Notes

Notes are divided by chapter, and each note is preceded by the number of the page to which it refers, as well as by a short phrase in **bold** type drawn from the page in question.

Notes to Preface

p. 13—**"Wolf Man" Joe LaFlamme**: Throughout the book, Joe's name is spelled "LaFlamme," with a capital "f," except in quotations from articles that wrote "Laflamme" without the capital "f." As a young man, Joe signed his name without the capital "f" as well, like all other members of his family. "LaFlamme" started appearing in newspaper articles as early as the mid-1920s, and all documents signed by Joe after that period had the capitalized "f." Joe probably changed the spelling of his name when he started climbing to fame as a wolf tamer.

Notes to Chapter 1

p. 17—**fresh air, exercise, snow, and work**: Rutherfoord Goodwin, "Wolves Race Dogs at A.G. Strong Farm; First Time Timber Beasts Ever Harnessed," *Rochester Times-Union*, Saturday Evening, February 20, 1926, p. 8.

p. 17—**Gogama, a Northern Ontario village**: See map on page 214.

p. 17—**young Alfred and Roland suddenly stumbled upon the loot**: Details of events in this chapter were related in interviews with Alfred (Médé) Secord on May 2, 2009 and March 28, 2011, and with Roland (Bidou) Secord on March 28, 2011.

p. 18—**Accessible only by train, plane, or boat**: Ontario Department of Lands and Forests, *A History of Gogama Forest District*, District History Series no. 11, Toronto: Queen's Printer, 1964, p. 37. Unless otherwise specified, information about Gogama throughout the book was taken from this publication.

Notes to Chapter 2

p. 20—**2,000 or so residents of Jumping Fish**: Lex Schrag, "Progress Rocks Northern Ontario Village," *Globe and Mail*, December 3, 1959, p. 25.

p. 22—**slab firewood**: Details of Joe's firewood and bootlegging business were related in an interview with Alfred (Médé) Secord on May 2, 2009.

p. 22—**330,750 acres (133,954 hectares)**: D.H. Burton, *The Gogama Fire of 1941*, Toronto: Ontario Department of Lands and Forests, Division of Research, 1949, p. 1. All measures are given in Imperial, with metric equivalents in brackets.

p. 22—**greenish-grey eyes**: Leslie Avery, "Joe and Wolves Reach New York for Sport Show," *Oshkosh Northwestern*, February 17, 1939, p. 7. Members of the Laflamme family remember Joe with greenish-brown eyes.

p. 22—**six feet two inches tall…225 lbs**: Gisèle Laflamme Lanthier, personal interview, May 21, 2010; *Sudbury Star*, "Joe Laflamme Out Again after Second Wolf Team," May 30, 1938, p. 6.

Notes to Chapter 3

p. 23—**one case in point**: Peter V. MacDonald, "Old Joseph Laflamme a Sudbury Lawyer's Dream," *Sudbury Star*, May 19, 1990, p. 16; all details about the hearing are from this article. According to MacDonald, Landreville and LaFlamme teamed up for the first time in 1947, a relationship that lasted for 10 years. This must have been an error, and the two must have teamed up in 1937, since Joe left Gogama unofficially at the end of 1947. Furthermore, as of 1947, court hearings in Gogama were held in the newly constructed courtroom. Before that, they were often held in the church/community hall, as was the case in 1937.

p. 23—**his deadpan humour**: Gisèle Laflamme Lanthier, personal interview, October 14, 2008.

p. 25—**"a tremendous lawyer"**: Peter V. MacDonald, "Old Joseph Laflamme a Sudbury Lawyer's Dream," *Sudbury Star*, May 19, 1990, p. 16.

p. 25—**His first offence**: *Toronto Daily Star*, "Northern Racer Fined," March 26, 1931.

p. 25—**defended his own case**: *Sudbury Star*, "Resort Keeper Sent to Jail: Three Months Term for Joe Laflamme, of Gogama," September 19, 1931, p. 1; *Sudbury Star*, "Judge Quashes L.C.A. Conviction on Wolf Tamer: Joe Laflamme Free; Evidence Conflicting," December 19, 1931, p. 1; *Evening Telegram*, "Liquor Term Is Cancelled: Gogama Man Turns in Appeal Against Second Conviction," December 19, 1931, p. 2.

pp. 25-26—**services to the provincial government**: Ontario Treasury Department, *Public Accounts 1931; Estimates, Supplementary Estimates 1932*, Toronto: Baptist Johnston, 1932, p. J17.

p. 26—**accused of stealing**: *Sudbury Star*, "Joe Laflamme Sent to Jail for 15

Days," October 16, 1936, p. 1; *Sudbury Star*, "Joe Laflamme's Sentence Boosted to Three Months," October 23, 1936, p. 1. The articles disagree on how much gasoline was stolen; the former article states four drums, the latter six.

p. 26—**to jail in his place**: Gisèle Laflamme Lanthier, personal interview, October 14, 2008. No proof of either Joe or Elzéar serving time is available, as correctional records are currently inaccessible under the Privacy Act. Gisèle also provided the information about the origins of the Laflamme family name.

p. 26—**accused of setting fire**: Details about the trial come from the following sources: *Sudbury Star*, "Jury Declares Mrs. Fortin Did Not Set Fire: Cross-Questioning of Joe Laflamme Is Feature," June 10, 1938, p. 5; *Sudbury Star*, "Laflamme's Reply Was a Boomerang," June 10, 1938, p. 5. Mrs. Fortin's first name is not given.

p. 27—**in need of a few dollars**: Rhéal Véronneau, personal interview, June 27, 2008.

p. 27—**given or sold beer**: *Standard-Freeholder*, "Bushman Who Wrestles Wolves to Whet Appetite in Toils at Gogama," October 5, 1938.

Notes to Chapter 4

p. 28—**bootlegging side**: Details about LaFlamme's business in this chapter come from personal interviews with the following: Roger (Ti-Pit) Carrière, May 12, 2009; Ernest (Dubby) Turcotte, May 2, 2009; Gordon Miller, August 5, 2011; Rhéal Véronneau, June 27, 2008; Gerry Talbot, April 29, 2011; Robert Laflamme, October 19, 2010; Alfred (Médé) Secord, May 2, 2009; and Gisèle Laflamme Lanthier (October 14, 2008).

p. 29—**two strategic summer jobs**: *Emmetsburg (Iowa) Democrat*, "Outdoors with G.K. Jr.," April 3, 1947, p. 2; *Sudbury Star*, "Jury Declares Mrs. Fortin Did Not Set Fire: Cross-Questioning of Joe Laflamme Is Feature," June 10, 1938, p. 5.

p. 29—**moonshine run**: Percy T. Cole, "'Wild Wolf Man of Gogama' Plans to Drive 10 Wolves into New York and Boston," *Evening Telegram*, September 22, 1938.

p. 29—**concoctions hidden**: LaFlamme must have planned this, since in those days most houses did not have a basement or a cellar.

p. 30—**the moonshine—and the evidence**: Gordon Miller, personal interview, August 5, 2011.

p. 30—**Joe started bootlegging**: Paul Michaud, letter to Gerry Talbot, June 26, 2004; Michaud had done some preliminary research on LaFlamme.

p. 30—**prohibition**: "Prohibition in Canada," *Wikipedia*, http://en.wikipedia.org/wiki; "Prohibition in the United States," *Wikipedia*, http://en.wikipedia.org/wiki; "Vermont Prohibition on the Sale of Intoxicating Liquor Act (1916)," *Ballotpedia*, http://ballotpedia.org/wiki/index.php/Vermont_Prohibition_on_the_Sale_of_Intoxicating_Liquor_Act_(1916).

Notes to Chapter 5

p. 31—**choose Gogama**: Maurice Desjardins, "Tous les sports: Avec Fernand dans la cage aux loups," *Photo-Journal*, August 17, 1950, p. 46; *Sudbury Star*, "'Wolfman of Gogama' Will Always Be Remembered Now," January 2, 1968, p. 7.

p. 31—**LaFlamme's origin**: *Historical Records: Census & Voter Lists—1901 Census of Canada*, Ancestry.com, http://search.ancestrylibrary.com. The information on the siblings who died early was obtained from the *Association des familles Laflamme inc.*, Chambly, QC.

p. 32—**Baptized**: "Extrait du registre des baptêmes: Laflamme Joseph Télesphore," Paroisse de St. Télesphore, QC, April 4, 2005; "Pope Telesphorus," *Wikipedia*, http://en.wikipedia.org/wiki/Pope_Telesphorus.

p. 32—**no desire to be drafted**: Gisèle Laflamme Lanthier, personal interview, November 12, 2008; Guy Laflamme, personal interview, October 14, 2008.

p. 32—**employed with the police force**: Julie Fontaine, Division de la gestion des documents, des archives et de l'accès à l'information, Montreal, email to author, April 27, 2011; Télesphore Laflamme's employee file may no longer exist, but in any case cannot be released until 100 years after leaving the force, i.e., 2016. See also *Montreal Directory* (*Annuaires Lovell*), Bibliothèque et archives nationales du Québec, http://bibnum2.banq.qc.ca/bna/lovell.

p. 33—**Training as a police officer**: Gisèle Laflamme Lanthier, personal communication, May 1, 2009; Jean-Marc de Nobile, Musée de la police, Montreal Police Service, telephone communication with author, July 8, 2010.

p. 33—**Laflamme was stationed**: Izaak Hunter, "Rod and Gun," *Montreal Gazette*, April 26, 1967, p. 24.

p. 33—**Jack Renault**: Serge Gaudreau, "Jack Renault," *Greb*, www.harrygreb.com/jackrenault.html. LaFlamme may also have been a traffic officer.

p. 33—**heavyweight wrestling championship**: *Globe and Mail*, "Gogama's 'Paul Bunyan' Bringing Moose to City," January 24, 1947, p. 3.

p. 34—**LaFlamme house**: Details about the house come from personal interviews with Gerry Talbot, June 7, 2010; Rhéal and Marguerite Véronneau, June 27, 2008; Alfred (Médé) Secord, May 2, 2009; and Violette Charbonneau, January 31, 2010. See the Sudbury (no. 53) Land Registry Office, roll #53ER12, parcel 7492, p. 458; roll #53ER16, parcel 10024, p. 773; roll #53ER18, parcel 11823, p. B1. See also Tom Dare, "'Stackie' Adds Thrills in Search for Santa," *Toledo News-Bee*, October 22, 1926, p. 1. Details about the later house come from photographs in Gerry Talbot's personal collection.

Notes to Chapter 6

p. 36—**distemper epidemic**: *Sudbury Star*, "'Wolfman of Gogama' Will Always Be Remembered Now," January 2, 1968, p. 7.

p. 36—**Dave Ranger**: *Sudbury Star*, "'Wolfman of Gogama' Will Always Be Remembered Now," January 2, 1968, p. 7.

p. 37—**Joe lured one**: *The Bee*, "Takes Wolf He Caught to Zoo Under his Arm," June 7, 1923, p. 3.

p. 37—**Toronto Zoo**: *The Bee*, "Takes Wolf He Caught to Zoo Under his Arm," June 7, 1923, p. 3.

p. 37—**he obtained his wolves**: Rhéal Véronneau, personal interview, July 18, 2002; *Sudbury Star*, "'Wolfman of Gogama' Will Always Be Remembered Now," January 2, 1968, p. 7. No evidence was found regarding the Hudson's Bay Company selling wolves. However, given LaFlamme's ease at forming connections, it was possible the local post manager or some other person in the company acted as intermediary between LaFlamme and the network of Canadian trappers.

p. 38—**trapping wolves humanely**: *Toronto Daily Star*, "Can't Wipe Out Wolves by Rifle, Says Trapper," January 19, 1925, p. 23; *Sudbury Star*, "Joe Laflamme Out Again After Second Wolf Team," May 30, 1938, p. 6.

p. 39—**training wolves**: Laurie York Erskine, "The Great Gray Wolf: Mighty Hunter of the Wilds," *Frontiers: A Magazine of Natural History*, December 1950, condensed version at *Stillwater Woods* [blog], http://stillwoods. blogspot.ca/2008/06/gray-wolf_18.html; *Toronto Daily Star*, "Can't Wipe Out Wolves by Rifle, Says Trapper," January 19, 1925, p. 23.

p. 39—**Joe's first sled**: See the photograph accompanying *Popular Science Monthly*, "Ontario Trapper Drives Team of Wolves," December 1924, p. 58. This was one of the earliest references about LaFlamme and his wolves.

p. 39—**chew the harness**: *Montreal Gazette*, "Uses Wild Wolves For Hauling Sled," June 25, 1938, p. 13; Geneviève Carbone, *Destination loups*, Paris: Éditions Solar, 2007, p. 38; Maurice Desjardins, "Tous les sports : Avec Fernand dans la cage aux loups," *Photo-Journal*, August 17, 1950, p. 46; *Sudbury Star*, "Joe Laflamme Out Again after Second Wolf Team," May 30, 1938, p. 6. Also Alfred (Médé) Secord, personal interview, May 2, 2009.

Notes to Chapter 7

p. 40—**Erskine**: *Toronto Daily Telegraph*, "The Wolf That Doesn't Whistle," January 18, 1951, p. 4.

p. 40—**February 9 event**: *Montreal Gazette*, "Wolf Tamer Stars as Court Witness," June 9, 1938, p. 31; *La Presse*, "Les chiens de Holt-Renfrew se classent bons premiers," February 11, 1924, p. 17; Leslie Avery. "Joe and Wolves Reach New York For Sport Show," *Oshkosh Northwestern*, February 17, 1939, p. 7; *Le Droit*, "Gogama, Ont.," February 20, 1924, p. 6; Jean Côté, "L'homme aux loups a perdu son seul ami," *Le Nouveau Samedi*, April 11, 1964, p. 5.

p. 41—**Dickens**: Peter V. Allingham, "Dickens in Montreal," *Victorian Web*, http://www.victorianweb.org./authors/dickens/montreal/montreal.html.

Notes to Chapter 8

p. 42—**Montreal**: "Metropolis: Montreal at Its Peak," *Wikipedia*, http:// en.wikipedia.org/wiki/History_of_cities_in_Canada.

p. 42—**Toronto**: Janet McNaughton, "Toronto in the 1920s," www.janet-mcnaughton.ca/Toronto,%201920s.html.

p. 42—**Isaac Lewis (William)**: There is a discrepancy regarding this person's name in various articles. Some call him Isaac Lewis, and others Isaac William.

p. 42—**1925 winter festival**: *Toronto Daily Star*, "Wolf-husky Cavalcade in Town as *Star*'s Guest," January 26, 1925, p. 1; *Toronto Daily Star*, "12 Below To-night, Predicts Weatherman," January 27, 1925, p. 1; *Toronto Daily Star*, "Wolves Will Run on Danforth and Other Streets To-morrow," January 27, 1925, p. 1; *Toronto Daily Star*, "Joe LaFlamme, Isaac Lewis, the Indian, and 'Tommy', a Wolf," January 28, 1925, p. 17; *Toronto Daily Star*, "Winter Sports Pow-wow Near Grenadier Pond on Saturday Afternoon," January 29, 1925, p. 19; *Toronto Daily Star*, "Wolf Captured after Half Day of Roaming," January 30, 1925, p. 9; *Toronto Daily Star*, "The Star's Gogama Wolves and Dogs on City Streets and Grenadier Pond," January 30, 1925, 2nd sec., p. 1; *Toronto Daily Star*, "Spend Night at Grenadier's with Wolves near Bedside," January 30, 1925, p. 2; *Toronto Daily Star*, "And Now Mrs. Joe LaFlamme and 'Sparky'," January 31, 1925, p. 1; *Toronto Daily Star*, "Eerily, High Park Hills Re-echo Wolf Pack's Howls," January 31, 1925, p. 4; *Toronto Daily Star*, "Dog Team Is Greeted by a Capacity Curb," January 31, 1925, p. 4; *Toronto Daily Star*, "Old and Young City Migrates High Parkwards," January 31, 1925, p. 17; *Toronto Daily Star*, "Joe Backs Wolves with $100 Offer," January 31, 1925, 2nd sec., p. 17; *Toronto Daily Star*, "Prefers Northern Life to Comforts of Paris," January 31, 1925, p. 18; *Toronto Daily Star*, "50,000 People Crowd Grenadier Pond and Hillsides at The Star's Winter Carnival," February 2, 1925, 2nd sec., p. 1; *Toronto Daily Star*, "Star's Wolves Captured in Long Trail over Hills," February 2,1925, p. 6; *Toronto Daily Star*, "Fun and Exercise in The Star's 'Wolf Hunt' at High Park," February 2, 1925, p. 24; *Toronto Daily Star*, "Crowds Saw Wolves Perform at High Park," February 2, 1925, p. 24; Tom Dare, "'Stackie' Adds Thrills in Search for Santa," *Toledo News-Bee*, October 22, 1926, p. 1; *Globe and Mail*, "Gogama's 'Paul Bunyan' Bringing Moose to City," January 24, 1947, p. 3.

p. 44—**Pete**: Some of the news articles claim that Pete was a dog, but of the ten dogs, none was named Pete; however, one of the adult wolves was.

p. 44—**"northern racial expressions"**: *Toronto Daily Star*, "Joe LaFlamme, Isaac Lewis, the Indian, and 'Tommy', a Wolf," January 28, 1925, p. 17.

p. 45—**dogsled train 65 feet long**: Marcelle Fressineau, *Le traîneau de la liberté: L'aventure extraordinaire d'une femme dans le Grand Nord*, Lausanne: Éditions Favre SA, 2004, p. 197.

p. 45—**mouthpiece**: *Sudbury Star*, "'Wolfman of Gogama' Will Always Be Remembered Now," January 2, 1968, p. 7.

p. 45—**signature costume**: The description of the costume comes from several photos of LaFlamme in the Gogama Heritage Museum collection, as well as the following articles: *Sudbury Star*, "Thousands See Wolves Run on City Streets," January 27, 1939, p. 6; Percy T. Cole, "'Wild Wolf Man of Gogama' Plans to Drive 10 Wolves into New York and Boston," *Evening Telegram*, September 22, 1938.

p. 46—**Grenadier Pond**: "High Park," *Wikipedia*, http://en.wikipedia.org /wiki/High_Park. It is named this because, according to one legend, British grenadiers (soldiers) drowned there during the War of 1812.

p. 46—**not the petting zoo variety**: *Toronto Daily Star*, "Joe LaFlamme, Isaac Lewis, the Indian, and 'Tommy', a Wolf," January 28, 1925, p. 17.

p. 47—**massive wolf expeditions**: *Sault Daily Star*, "100 Take Part in Bar River Wolf Hunt Today," December 9, 1924, p. 1.

p. 47—**"Toronto's Wall Street"**: *Toronto Daily Star*, "Spend Night at Grenadier's with Wolves near Bedside," January 30, 1925, p. 2.

p. 48—**"a Gogama, go-get-em dog"**: *Toronto Daily Star*, "Spend Night at Grenadier's with Wolves near Bedside," January 30, 1925, p. 2.

p. 49—**"guest of the *Star*"**: *Toronto Daily Star*, "The Star's Gogama Wolves and Dogs on City Streets and Grenadier Pond," January 30, 1925, 2nd sec., p. 1.

p. 50—**"sea of wolf fans"**: *Toronto Daily Star*, "Crowds Saw Wolves Perform at High Park," February 2, 1925, p. 24.

p. 51—**"Eskimo limousine"**: *Morning Leader*, "Toronto Agitated as Wolf in Musher Team Makes Getaway," January 30, 1925, p. 1.

p. 51—**"You move 'em"**: Tom Dare, "'Stackie' Adds Thrills in Search for Santa," *Toledo News-Bee*, October 22, 1926, p. 1.

p. 52—**"in first-rate shape"**: *Toronto Daily Star*, "Eerily, High Park Hills Re-echo Wolf Pack's Howls," January 31, 1925, p. 4.

p. 52—**Star reporter**: *Toronto Daily Star*, "Eerily, High Park Hills Re-echo Wolf Pack's Howls," January 31, 1925, p. 4.

p. 53—**the huskies**: One article mentioned Steffannsons, a heroic canine belonging to Joe. Counting Billy, there would be a total of 12 dogs on the team. Perhaps LaFlamme brought Steffannsons to Toronto to sell him. *Toronto Daily Star*, "Spend Night at Grenadier's with Wolves near Bedside," January 30, 1925, p. 2.

p. 53—**day six**: Details of the scene at Grenadier Pond come from *Toronto Daily Star*, "Crowds Saw Wolves Perform at High Park," February 2, 1925, p. 24.

p. 53—**cast a doubt**: *Toronto Daily Star*, "Joe Back Wolves with $100 Offer," January 31, 1925, 2nd sec., p. 17.

p. 54—**reporter commented**: *Toronto Daily Star*, "50,000 People Crowd Grenadier Pond and Hillsides at The Star's Winter Carnival," February 2, 1925, 2nd sec., p. 1. Details of Joe's clothing on day six come from photos in this article.

p. 56—**"wolf hunt"**: *Toronto Daily Star*, "Star's Wolves Captured in Long Trail over Hills," February 2, 1925, p. 6.

p. 56—**carved a place**: *Toronto Daily Star*, "Old and Young City Migrates High Parkwards," January 31, 1925, p. 17.

Notes to Chapter 9

p. 57—**Quebec City and Lake Placid**: *Border Cities Star*, "Toronto Gets Real "Mush" Thrill," January 26, 1925, p. 2.

p. 57—**Governor General**: *Toronto Daily Star*, "Lord and Lady Byng See Joe LaFlamme and Wolves," June 18, 1925, p. 7.

p. 57—**Mrs. LaFlamme's origin**: Details of Émilie's family origins come from *Étaples—État civil: tables décennales, 1893-1902* (3 E 6141), Archives départementales du Pas-de-Calais, France; Frédérique Desmet, email to author, July 10, 2010. Émilie's family tree was provided by the *Archives départementales du Pas-de-Calais*. However, there are discrepancies regarding the spelling of Émilie's surname: the decennial tables 3 E 614 show "Hagnéré" whereas the Archives spell it "Haigneré"; the records at Hawthorn Dale Cemetery,

Montreal, identify her as "Hagnere." There are further discrepancies regarding the rest of her name: her birth register has her under the name of Émilie Ernestine Hélène, while her baptism record shows Émilie Aristide Hélène. Aristide could be a misspelling of Ernestine, as the decennial tables list her as Émilie Ernestine; however, there her third given name is Julie.

p. 58—**petite auburn-haired lady**: *Toronto Daily Star*, "Finds Wolves Are Like Women 'Can Never Really Tame Them,'" March 20, 1945, p. 2; 1.3 metres' height sounds a bit short; the general consensus is that Émilie measured less than 1.5 metres (five feet). See also interviews with Huguette (Laflamme) Levac, October 14, 2008, and Gisèle Laflamme Lanthier, October 14, 2008.

p. 58—**"I haf so many t'ings nice"**: *Toronto Daily Star*, "Prefers Northern Life to Comforts of Paris," January 31, 1925, p. 18.

p. 60—**marriage to Florence May West**: *Quebec Vital and Church Records (Drouin Collection), 1621-1967*; *Historical Records: Birth, Marriage & Death, Ancestry.com*, http://search.ancestrylibrary.com; Institut Généalogique Drouin, *Répertoire alphabétique des mariages des Canadiens-Français, 1760-1935 : Ordre masculin*, vol. 49 (Veillette-Zyne), Ottawa: Institut Généalogique Drouin, 1990, v. "West-William"; "Florida Passenger Lists, 1898-1951," Ancestry.com, http://search.ancestrylibrary.com. The ages of the couple in the "Florida Passenger Lists" do not exactly match their true ages; Quebecer Joseph T. Laflamme is listed as being 31 years old, instead of the 26 he would have been in 1915, and his wife Florence, also a Quebecer, is listed as 25 years instead of 22.

p. 60—**godfather**: *Quebec Vital and Church Records (Drouin Collection), 1621-1967*; *Historical Records: Birth, Marriage & Death* and *Historical Records: Census & Voter Lists—1901 Census of Canada, Ancestry.com*, http://search.ancestrylibrary.com.

p. 60—**Joe and Émilie**: "Canadian Passenger Lists, 1865-1935," *Ancestry.com*, http://search.ancestrylibrary.com. The record of Émilie's passage from Liverpool is retrievable under "Emilie Haynes," even though the original handwritten entry on the passenger list shows "Émilie Haignere." See also Robert P. Swiernega, "Going to America: Travel Routes of Zeeland Emigrants," paper presented at the "Zeeland to America" conference, Roosevelt Studies Center,

Middelburg, Netherlands, September 5, 1997, http://www.swierenga.com/RSC_pap.html; "Saint John, New Brunswick: Maritime Activities," *Wikipedia*, http://en.wikipedia.org/wiki; "Acquisition of Canadian Citizenship at Birth or by Derivation through a Parent or Spouse," *The Ships List*, http://www.the-shipslist.com/Forms/CanCitAq_Natz.shtml. No naturalization record has been found for Émilie; she probably officially acquired her Canadian citizenship after January 1, 1947, since she was a British subject by default because she had been living under common law with Joe LaFlamme.

p. 61—**northern bush**: *Toronto Daily Star*, "Prefers Northern Life to Comforts of Paris," January 31, 1925, p. 18.

p. 61—**"billiard cue"**: Gogama Chamber of Commerce, "'Joe LaFlamme': Wolfman/Mooseman," *Crossing the High Portage: A Guide to the Gogama Area*, Sudbury: Journal Printing, c2000, p. 20.

p. 61—**cake platter**: Eunice Belisle, phone interview, September 3, 2010; the cake platter and lifter are now owned by Eunice Belisle, daughter of Dave and Simone Ranger.

p. 62—**good time**: *Toronto Daily Star*, "Prefers Northern Life to Comforts of Paris," January 31, 1925, p. 18.

Notes to Chapter 10

p. 63—**"Mushes 700 Miles"**: James P. Dawson, "Mushes 700 Miles with Dogs to See Hockey Here Tonight," *New York Times*, January 23, 1926, p. S11.

p. 63—**welcomed by thousands**: *Sudbury Star*, "Joe Laflamme Out Again after Second Wolf Team," May 30, 1938, p. 6.

p. 63—**dropping the puck**: James P. Dawson, "Mushes 700 Miles with Dogs to See Hockey Here Tonight," *New York Times*, January 23, 1926, p. S11; Harry Cross, "New York Six Ties with Boston Again," *New York Times*, January 24, 1926, p. 1.

p. 64—**other hockey matches**: *Democrat and Chronicle*, "Wolf Team to Be Shown on Golf Course," February 21, 1926, p. 25.

p. 64—**avid hockey fans**: Gisèle Laflamme Lanthier, personal interview, May 21, 2010.

p. 64—**second largest city**: *Sudbury Star*, "Timber Wolves to Visit City," January 23, 1939, p. 1.

p. 64—**seven million people**: "Rural and Urban Conflict: Congressional Reapportionment," *American Decades: 1920-1929*, ed. Vincent Tompkins, vol. 3, Gale Cengage, 1995, *eNotes.com*, http://www.enotes.com/1920-government-politics-american-decades/rural-urban-conflict-congressional-reapportionment.

p. 64—**Al Greene**: Leslie Avery, "Joe and Wolves Reach New York for Sport Show," *Oshkosh Northwestern*, February 17, 1939, p. 7.

p. 64—**George Lewis "Tex" Rickard**: "Tex Rickard," *Wikipedia*, http://en.wikipedia.org/wiki/Tex_Rickard.

p. 64—**dog show**: *New York Times*, "2,000 at Winter Fete," February 8, 1926, p. 16; *New York Evening Graphic*, "Dangerous Dogs," February 2, 1926; *Evening Independent*, "Canadian Trapper Prefers Wolves to Dogs," March 15, 1939, p. 10.

Notes to Chapter 11

p. 66—**Strong's country estate**: Information about Alvah, the family, and the estate was provided by Griff Mangan, personal interview, June 19, 2008; "Alasa Farms," *Wikipedia*, http://en.wikipedia.org/wiki/Alasa_Farms; and "History of Kodak Milestones—Chronology 1878-1929," *Kodak* website, http://www.kodak.com/global/en/corp/historyOfKodak/1878.jhtml. The events of February 18-29, 1926, were reconstructed from photos donated by the Alasa Farms/Strong family and the following newspaper articles: *Democrat and Chronicle*, "Team of Timber Wolves to Be Shown at Strong Country Home," February 19, 1926, p. 19; Rutherford Goodwin, "Wolves Race Dogs at A.G. Strong Farm; First Time Timber Beasts Ever Harnessed," *Rochester Times-Union*, February 20, 1926, evening ed., p. 8; *Sodus Record*, "Sodus Residents Get Thrill from Timber Wolves," February 26, 1926, p. 1; *Democrat and Chronicle*, "Timber Wolves and Huskies Give Exhibition," February 21, 1926, p. 25; *Democrat and Chronicle*, "Wolf Team to Be Shown on Golf Course," February 21, 1926, p. 25; *Democrat and Chronicle*, "Wolf and Dog Teams to Race Here Tomorrow and Thursday," February 23, 1926, p. 17; *Democrat and Chronicle*, "Seen and Heard," February 24, 1926, p. 27; *Democrat and Chron-*

icle, "Thousands See Wolf Team Dash through Streets," February 25, 1926, pp. 17, 24; *Rochester Herald*, "Thousands See Wolf Team in Races at Oak Hill and on Trip through Streets," February 25, 1926, p. 7; *Democrat and Chronicle*, "Timber Wolves to 'Mush' To-Day," February 26, 1926, p. 17.

p. 67—**375-mile trip**: Rutherfoord Goodwin, "Wolves Race Dogs at A.G. Strong Farm; First Time Timber Beasts Ever Harnessed," *Rochester Times-Union*, February 20, 1926, evening ed., p. 8.

p. 67—**Approximately 300 people**: Accounts in the papers vary: from 200 to 400 people.

p. 68—**"wolves is about"**: *Democrat and Chronicle*, "Seen and Heard," February 24, 1926, p. 27.

p. 68—**"absurd"**: Rutherfoord Goodwin, "Wolves Race Dogs at A.G. Strong Farm; First Time Timber Beasts Ever Harnessed," *Rochester Times-Union*, February 20, 1926, evening ed., p. 8.

p. 69—**first man in the world**: *Emmetsburg (Iowa) Democrat*, "Outdoors with G.K. Jr.," April 3, 1947, p. 2.

p. 70—**first-aid stations**: *Transport in the North*, Trenton (Ontario), ISN #185638, Trenton: Ontario Motion Picture Bureau, 1925, part 1; *Emmetsburg (Iowa) Democrat*, "Outdoors with G.K. Jr.," April 3, 1947, p. 2. These sources provided many of this chapter's details about travelling with the wolves by sled or toboggan. Part one of the film *Transport in the North* depicts care for sick wolves.

p. 71—**working with sled wolves**: *Toronto Daily Star*, "Can't Wipe Out Wolves by Rifle, Says Trapper," January 19, 1925, p. 23.

p. 71—**"sick like dogs"**: Leslie Avery, "Joe and Wolves Reach New York for Sport Show," *Oshkosh Northwestern*, February 17, 1939, p. 7.

p. 71—**Ford automobile**: "Model T Facts," *Ford* website, http://media. ford.com.

Notes to Chapter 12

p. 73—**trip to Rochester**: Details of Joe LaFlamme's visit to Rochester in February1926 were taken from the following newspaper articles: *Democrat and Chronicle*, "Wolf Team to Be Shown on Golf Course," February 21, 1926,

p. 25; *Democrat and Chronicle*, "Wolf and Dog Teams to Race Here Tomorrow and Thursday," February 23, 1926, p. 17; *Democrat and Chronicle*, "Thousands See Wolf Team Dash through Streets," February 25, 1926, pp. 17, 24; *Rochester Herald*, "Thousands See Wolf Team in Races at Oak Hill and on Trip through Streets," February 25, 1926, p. 7; *Democrat and Chronicle*, "Timber Wolves to 'Mush' To-Day," February 26, 1926, p. 17.

p. 73—**"I have been told"**: *Democrat and Chronicle*, "Wolf Team to Be Shown on Golf Course," February 21, 1926, p. 25.

Notes to Chapter 13

p. 76—**an Ontario mink rancher**: E. Rendle Bowness, "Ontario," in *History of the Early Mink People in Canada*, n.p.: Canada Mink Breeders Association, 1980, http://www.jkcc.com/minkpeople/ontario.html.

p. 76—**LaFlamme's fur farm**: *Sudbury Star*, "'Wolfman of Gogama' Will Always Be Remembered Now," January 2, 1968, p. 7.

p. 76—**Hodgson**: Hodgson and Johnston's visit to Gogama is described in Robert G. Hodgson, *Let's Go Fur Farming*, Toronto: Fur Trade Journal of Canada, 1953, pp.158-160; E. Rendle Bowness, "Ontario," in *History of the Early Mink People in Canada*, n.p.: Canada Mink Breeders Association, 1980, pp. 54-70. http://www.jkcc.com/minkpeople/ontario.html.

p. 77—**"a real character of the north"**: Robert G. Hodgson, *Let's Go Fur Farming*, Toronto: Fur Trade Journal of Canada, 1953, pp. 157-158.

p. 77—**LaFlamme's everyday speech**: Gisèle Laflamme Lanthier, personal interview, October 14, 2008; Rhéal and Marguerite Véronneau, personal interview, June 27, 2008; Ernest (Dubby) Turcotte, personal interview, May 2, 2009; Alfred (Médé) Secord, personal interview, November 10, 2009. Translations provided by the author.

p. 77—**help someone in need**: Cécile Turcotte, personal interview, May 2, 2009; Rhéal Véronneau, personal interview, June 27, 2008.

p. 78—**cabbage soup**: Ernest (Dubby) Turcotte, personal interview, May 2, 2009; Gisèle Laflamme Lanthier, personal interview, May 21, 2010.

p. 79—**freshly baked bread**: Cécile Turcotte, personal interview.

May 2, 2009; "How much did a basic loaf of bread cost in 1940, 1943, and 1967?" *Yahoo Answers,* http://answers.yahoo.com/question/index?qid= 20070128021723AAUwPqX.

p. 79—**Debbie Ford**: Deepak Chopra, Debbie Ford, and Marianne Williamson, *The Shadow Effect: Illuminating the Hidden Power of Your True Self,* New York: Harper Collins Publishers, 2010, p. 112.

p. 80—**Elzéar Laflamme**: Marguerite Véronneau, personal interview, June 27, 2008; Robert Laflamme, personal interview, October 19, 2010; *Sudbury Star,* "Joe Laflamme Dies in Sudbury," August 7, 1958, p. 1; *Sudbury Star,* "Obituaries: Mooseman," August 7, 1958, p. 3.

p. 80—**"good to be back"**: *Sudbury Star,* "Been Reported Dead Twice Before but Joe Laflamme in Best of Health," August 8, 1958, p. 1.

p. 80—**LaFlamme's "hotel"**: Details about the hotel's layout and operation also from the following personal interviews: Roland (Bidou) Secord, March 28, 2011; Simone Talbot, November 15, 2008; Alfred (Médé) Secord, November 10, 2008; Gordon Miller, August 5, 2011; Raoul and Reina Véronneau, November 15, 2008. See also *Toronto Daily Star,* "Prefers Northern Life to Comforts of Paris," January 31, 1925, p. 18; *Gogama Community News,* "The End of an Era." November 1996, p. 1.

p. 81—**"Red my stove"**: *Toronto Daily Star,* "Finds Wolves Are Like Women 'Can Never Really Tame Them,'" March 20, 1945, p. 2.

Notes to Chapter 14

p. 82—**letterhead**: Joe and Morris LaFlamme, letter to Jim M. Taylor, District Forester, Ontario Department of Lands and Forests, Gogama, March 3, 1947; *Globe and Mail,* "Gogama's 'Paul Bunyan' Bringing Moose to City," January 24, 1947, p. 3.

p. 82—**camping parties**: *Toronto Daily Star,* "Wolf Team Driver Joe LaFlamme, Here," December 5, 1930, p. 10; *Emmetsburg (Iowa) Democrat,* "Outdoors with G.K. Jr." April 3, 1947, p. 2.

p. 83—**guest speaker**: *Toronto Daily Star,* "Lumberman Honored," February 8, 1930, p. 34.

p. 83—**wolf strains**: *Transport in the North,* Trenton (Ontario), ISN

#185638, Ontario Motion Picture Bureau, 1925, part 1; *Sudbury Star*, "Joe Laflamme Out Again after Second Wolf Team," May 30, 1938, p. 6.

p. 83—**only five**: *Toronto Daily Star*, "Wolf Team Driver Joe LaFlamme, Here," December 5, 1930, p. 10.

p. 83—**he trapped**: Tom Dare, "'Stackie' Adds Thrills in Search for Santa," *Toledo News-Bee*, October 22, 1926, p. 1; Hudson's Bay Company, *Gogama Post 1932-1933: Journal of Events*, December 1932, sheet no. 30, Reference B.415/a/1-2: Post journals, microfilm IMA27, Hudson's Bay Company Archives.

p. 83—**Gogama Board of Trade**: Gogama Board of Trade, Minutes, 1929-1946, private collection.

p. 83—**ran for MPP**: Nicole Kivi, Nickel Belt Community Office, email to author, June 7, 2013; Dieter K. Buse and Graeme S. Mount, *Come On Over! Northeastern Ontario A to Z*. Sudbury: Scrivener Press, 2011, p. 159.

p. 83—**PC convention**: *Sudbury Star*, "Moose, Badger, Wolves, Elk and Bears 'Friends' of the Mooseman of Gogama," February 8, 1965, p. 3; Gisèle Laflamme Lanthier, personal interview, October 14, 2008.

p. 83—**"mayor"**: *Globe and Mail*, "Gogama's 'Paul Bunyan' Bringing Moose to City." January 24, 1947, p. 3.

p. 84—**"on the map"**: Ernest (Dubby) Turcotte, personal interview, May 2, 2009.

p. 84—**census worker**: *Emmetsburg (Iowa) Democrat*, "Outdoors with G.K. Jr." April 3, 1947, p. 2.

p. 84—**forest firefighter**: Ontario Treasury Department, *Public Accounts 1947; Estimates 1948*, Toronto: Baptist Johnston, 1947, p. I15; "*The Forest Commandos* (1946)," *IMDb*, http://www.imdb.com/title/tt0164030/.

p. 84—*The Forest Commandos*: *The Forest Commandos*, by Glenn Ireton, dir. Van Campen Heilner, Warner Bros., 1946; *Boxoffice*, "Joe Laflamme Featured," 26 April 1947, p. 114, http://www.boxoffice.com/the_vault/issue_page?issue_id=1947-4-26&page_no=128#page_start; "*The Forest Commandos* (1946)," *IMDb*, http://www.imdb.com/title/tt0164030/. "The Legend of Joe Laflamme—Mooseman/Wolfman of Gogama, Ontario," *Gogama* [website], http://www.gogama.ca/joelaflamme_2.html; Jack Karr, "Movie-Go-Round,"

Toronto Daily Star, March 21, 1945, p. 11. Joe's comments on the filming experience come from the *Toronto Daily Star*, "Finds Wolves Are Like Women 'Can Never Really Tame Them,'" March 20, 1945, p. 2.

p. 85—**black bear cub**: Gabriel Ireton, emails to Gerry Talbot, December 13 and 20, 2007.

p. 85—**attended the "rushes"**: *Toronto Daily Star*, "Finds Wolves Are Like Women 'Can Never Really Tame Them," March 20, 1945, p. 2; *Toronto Daily Star*, "Pretty Girls, Bear Cubs—Joe Laflamme," April 27, 1945, p. 2.

p. 86—**female followers**: Marguerite Véronneau, personal interview, June 27, 2008.

p. 86—*Transport in the North*: *Transport in the North*, Trenton (Ontario), ISN # 185638, Trenton: Ontario Motion Picture Bureau, 1925.

p. 86—**movie projector**: Gordon Miller, personal interview, August 5, 2011.

p. 86—**16 mm movie camera**: Jack Karr, "Movie-Go-Round," *Toronto Daily Star*, March 21, 1945, p. 11.

p. 86—**self-taught photographer**: *Sudbury Star*, "Gogama Tragedy," April 2, 1932, p. 11; *Globe and Mail*, "They Prefer Arrows to Bullets," November 2, 1938, p. 3. *Sudbury Star*, "And They Pulled Many a Stout Bow," November 2, 1938, p. 6.

Notes to Chapter 15

p. 87—**Morris Joseph LaFlamme**: Details of Morris's life and relationship with his family come from *Detroit Border Crossings and Passenger and Crew Lists, 1905-1957, Ancestry.com*, http://search.ancestrylibrary.com; and from personal interviews with Cécile Turcotte, May 2, 2009; Edelta Turgeon, November 12, 2008; Rhéal Véronneau, June 27, 2008; Rhéo Beauchamp, June 27, 2008; Alfred (Médé) Secord, May 2, 2009; and Gisèle Laflamme Lanthier, October 19, 2010.

p. 87—**practising Catholics**: For the LaFlammes' relationship with the church in Gogama, see interviews with Rhéal Véronneau, June 27, 2008; Marguerite Véronneau, June 27, 2008.

p. 88—**wolves' howling**: *Toronto Daily Star*, "Howling Lupi Disturb

Gogama People's Sleep: But There's Little Danger; They Are Tied Up," October 26, 1938, p. 24.

p. 88—**Gogama Public School**: Wivine Bruneau, personal interview, November 15, 2008.

p. 88—**elected**: "Gogama Anglicans Elect 1935 Officers." *Sudbury Star*, February 17, 1935, 2nd sec., p. 8; P.S.S. #1 Noble/Gogama Public School, "Events and Changes to the School," 1939 records, private collection.

p. 89—**"Gogama Zoo"**: *Globe and Mail*, "Gogama's 'Paul Bunyan' Bringing Moose to City," January 24, 1947, p. 3.

Notes to Chapter 16

p. 90—**pet badger**: *Sudbury Star*, "Moose, Badger, Wolves, Elk and Bears 'Friends' of the Mooseman of Gogama," February 8, 1965, p. 3.

p. 90—**Lillie's pet skunks**: *Toronto Daily Star*, "Prefers Northern Life to Comforts of Paris," January 31, 1925, p. 18.

p. 90—**his wolf pack**: Leslie Avery, "Joe and Wolves Reach New York for Sport Show," *Oshkosh Northwestern*, February 17, 1939, p. 7; William Kinmond, "Joe Has Wife and Wolves and Says They Are Alike," *Toronto Daily Star*, October 26, 1938, sec. 2, p. 1; Simone Talbot, personal interview, November 15, 2008; *Toronto Daily Star*, "Wolf Team Driver Joe LaFlamme, Here," December 5, 1930, p. 10.

p. 91—**jealous females**: Leslie Avery, "Joe and Wolves Reach New York for Sport Show," *Oshkosh Northwestern*, February 17, 1939, p. 7.

p. 91—**not even for $100.**: Roger (Ti-Pit) Carrière, personal interview, May 12, 2010.

p. 91—**occasionally escaped**: Roger (Ti-Pit) Carrière, personal interview, May 12, 2010; Laurent Charbonneau, interview by Gerry Talbot, February 15, November 2, 2011; Edelta Turgeon, personal interview, November 12, 2008.

p. 91—**Pete**: *Toronto Daily Star*, "Can't Wipe Out Wolves by Rifle, Says Trapper," *Toronto Daily Star*, January 19, 1925, p. 23. The descriptions and explanations about wolves, including Pete, come from this article.

p. 93—**Strong Man of the North**: *Toronto Daily Star*, "You Can Never

Tell What Wives or Wolves Will Do, Says Joe," October 26, 1938, p. 24; Gisèle Laflamme Lanthier, personal interview, May 21, 2010; *Sudbury Star*, "'Wolfman of Gogama' Will Always Be Remembered Now," January 2, 1968, p. 7.

p. 93—**wrestling match**: *Sudbury Star*, "Moose, Badger, Wolves, Elk and Bears 'Friends' of the Mooseman of Gogama," February 8, 1965, p. 3. Gerald Payette, interview by Gerry Talbot, June 23, 2011. *Standard-Freeholder*, "Bushman Who Wrestles Wolves to Whet Appetite in Toils At Gogama," October 5, 1938; Maurice Desjardins, "Tous les sports: Avec Fernand dans la cage aux loups," *Photo-Journal*, August 17, 1950, p. 46.

p. 93—**feeding**: Leslie Avery, "Joe and Wolves Reach New York for Sport Show," *Oshkosh Northwestern*, February 17, 1939, p. 7; *Transport in the North*, Trenton (Ontario), ISN # 185638, Ontario Motion Picture Bureau, 1925; Rhéal Véronneau, personal interview, June 27, 2008; E.S. Telfer, "Moose," 1997, *Hinterland Who's Who* [website], http://www.hww.ca/en/species/mammals/moose.html; Roger (Ti-Pit) Carrière, personal interview, May 12, 2010.

p. 94—**back in the 1940s**: Personal interviews with Ernest (Dubby) Turcotte, May 2, 2009; Rhéo Beauchamp, June 27, 2008; Alfred (Médé) Secord, May 2, 2009.

p. 94—**Secord recalls**: Alfred (Médé) Secord, personal interview, November 10, 2008

p. 95—**"a fast sale of something"**: *Globe and Mail*, "Gogama's 'Paul Bunyan' Bringing Moose to City," January 24, 1947, p. 3; Rhéo Beauchamp, personal interview, June 27, 2008

p. 95—**play with the moose**: Roger (Ti-Pit) Carrière, personal interview, May 12, 2010; Ernest (Dubby) Turcotte, personal interview, May 2, 2009.

p. 95—**how to handle them**: Alfred (Médé) Secord, personal interviews, November 10, 2008, and May 2, 2009.

p. 95—**suddenly, the wolves stopped**: *Sudbury Star*, "Claims Wolf Pack Will Attack Man," January 27, 1939, p. 1; Maurice Desjardins, "Tous les sports: Avec Fernand dans la cage aux loups," *Photo-Journal*, August 17, 1950, p. 46.

p. 96—**Pete suddenly lunged**: *Sudbury Star*, "Joe Laflamme Out Again after Second Wolf Team," May 30, 1938, p. 6; *Sudbury Star*, "Claims Wolf Pack Will Attack Man," January 27, 1939, p. 2.

Notes to Chapter 17

p. 97—**gold ore**: The information on the 1932 gold rush came from the following articles: Bert Stoll, "Rushing on Wings to Seek Hidden Gold," *New York Times*, March 12, 1933, p. SM7; Bert Stoll, "Gold Fever Is High in North Ontario," *New York Times*, October 30, 1932, p. E6; *Winnipeg Free Press*, "Prospectors Head North to New Ontario Gold Rush," August 12, 1933, p. 1.

p. 99—**renewed his license**: Joe held prospecting licenses #C-12635 (1929) and #C-17655 (1938) according to Ontario Ministry of Northern Development, Mines, and Forestry records in the John B. Gammon Geoscience Library Archives, Sudbury, ON.

p. 99—**"Klondyke [sic] vein"**: Bert Stoll, "Gold Fever Is High in North Ontario," *New York Times*, October 30, 1932, p. E6;

p. 99—**gold claim**: Leslie Avery, "Joe and Wolves Reach New York for Sport Show," *Oshkosh Northwestern*, February 17, 1939, p. 7.

p. 99—**Marie Théoret died**: As per Marie Théoret's funeral card, and the article: "Feu Mme O. Laflamme," *La Presse*, February 4, 1933, p. 43.

p. 99—**1938 rush**: The information on the 1938 gold rush was taken from the following articles: *Sudbury Star*, "New Gold Rush Is under Way near Gogama," July 27, 1938, p. 1; *Sudbury Star*, "Gogama Woman First of Sex to New Field," August 8, 1938, p. 8; *Lethbridge Herald*, "'Beeg Joe' in News Again," September 20, 1938, back page; Percy T. Cole, "Latest Ontario Gold Find Better Than Yellowknife Old Prospector Contends," *Evening Telegram*, September 21, 1938.

p. 100—**"he dared me"**: *Sudbury Star*, "Gogama Woman First of Sex to New Field," August 8, 1938, p. 8; Lillie held prospecting license #C-17631 (1938) according to Ontario Ministry of Northern Development, Mines, and Forestry records in the John B. Gammon Geoscience Library Archives, Sudbury, ON.

p. 100—**"I beat Joe"**: Percy T. Cole, "Latest Ontario Gold Find Better Than Yellowknife Old Prospector Contends," *Evening Telegram*, September 21, 1938.

Notes to Chapter 18

p. 102—**his Waco VKS-7**: "Biplane," *Wikipedia*, http://en.wikipedia.org/wiki/Biplane. "Waco Standard Cabin Series," *Wikipedia*, http://en.wikipedia.org/wiki/Waco_Standard_Cabin_series. The events of the chapter have been reconstructed from the following sources: *Evening Telegram*, "Pilot's Skill Saves Self and Three," October 17, 1938, p. 1; *Dunkirk (NY) Evening Observer*, "Canadian Pilot with Propeller Off, Wing Shattered, Saved Plane," October 17, 1938, p. 1; *Albuquerque Journal*, "Planes Rescue Four Men Lost in Woods of Northern Ontario," October 17, 1938, p. 1; *Globe and Mail*, "Four Cheat Death by Pilot's Daring," October 17, 1938, p. 1; Gregory Clark, "Diving toward Death at 80 Miles an Hour Only Thought Repairs," *Toronto Daily Star*, October 17, 1938, p. 1; Larry Milberry, *Austin Airways: Canada's Oldest Airline*, Toronto: CANAV, 1985, pp. 27–29.

p. 104—**small, nameless lake**: Some articles mention that the men had landed on Fralek Lake, which is a fairly large one in the area.

Notes to Chapter 19

p. 107—**first wolf team**: *Montreal Gazette*, "Uses Wild Wolves For Hauling Sled," June 25, 1938, p. 13; Leslie Avery, "Joe and Wolves Reach New York for Sport Show," *Oshkosh Northwestern*, February 17, 1939, p. 7.

p. 107—**placed an order**: Leslie Avery, "Joe and Wolves Reach New York for Sport Show," *Oshkosh Northwestern*, February 17, 1939, p. 7.

p. 107—**New York–Boston Winter Show**: *La Presse*, "Le loup comme bête de trait," June 27, 1938, p. 15.

p. 108—**train her**: *Sudbury Star*, "Timber Wolves to Visit City," January 23, 1939, p. 1.

p. 108—**other wolves**: *Sudbury Star*, "Joe LaFlamme to Drive Wolves on Sudbury Streets Tomorrow," January 25, 1939, p. 1.

p. 108—**"this team"**: *Sudbury Star*, "Long Legs Aid in Capture of Dashing Wolf," January 27, 1939, p. 3. *Dunkirk (N.Y.) Evening Observer*, "Finds Trouble in Plane Load of Wild Wolves," January 26, 1939, p. 13.

p. 108—**Wolf**: Leslie Avery, "Joe and Wolves Reach New York for Sport Show," *Oshkosh Northwestern*, February 17, 1939, p. 7; *Sudbury Star*, "Thousands See Wolves Run on City Streets," January 27, 1939, p. 6; *Sudbury Star*, "Joe LaFlamme to Drive Wolves on Sudbury Streets Tomorrow," January 25, 1939, p. 1.

p. 108—**a lot of persuasion**: *Toronto Daily Star*, "Joe LaFlamme, the Wolfman of the North, May Pay Toronto a Flying Visit with His 11 Wolves," January 21, 1939, 2nd sec., p. 1; *Sudbury Star*, "Thousands See Wolves Run on City Streets," January 27, 1939, p. 6.

p. 108—**trial run**: *Sudbury Star*, "Joe LaFlamme to Drive Wolves on Sudbury Streets Tomorrow," January 25, 1939, p. 8. The sleigh, custom-made by ALP Paquin & Fils, is on exhibit at the Gogama Heritage Museum (although it is need of repair). Joe had abandoned his sleigh when leaving Gogama. A few years later, Fred (White Pine) Thomson bought it for $50 and had it shipped to Capreol in 1967. The sleigh found its way to Parry Sound, where the Gogama Heritage Museum retrieved it in 2002. See Louise McDonald, "Antlers with a Story," *Sudbury Star*, September 6, 1990, p. B5, for more details.

p. 109—**"Heigh, Calgary!"**: *Sudbury Star*, "Joe LaFlamme to Drive Wolves on Sudbury Streets Tomorrow," January 25, 1939, p. 8.

p. 110—**"with them myself"**: William Kinmond, "Joe Has Wife and Wolves and Says They Are Alike," *Toronto Daily Star*, October 26, 1938, sec. 2, p. 1.

p. 110—**paying passengers**: Details of this plane ride came from the following articles: William Kinmond, "Joe Fights Ten Wolves Trying to Escape Plane," *Toronto Daily Star*, January 26, 1939, p. 10; *Sudbury Star*, "Long Legs Aid in Capture of Dashing Wolf," January 27, 1939, p. 3; *Sudbury Star*, "Joe LaFlamme to Drive Wolves on Sudbury Streets Tomorrow," January 25, 1939, p. 8; Leslie Avery, "Joe and Wolves Reach New York for Sport Show," *Oshkosh Northwestern*, February 17, 1939, p. 7. All quotations come from Kinmond's article. Note that LaFlamme referred to Muckoos as male but the animal was actually a female.

Notes to Chapter 20

p. 114—**the Wolf Man's visit**: The visit to Sudbury was reconstructed from the following articles: *Sudbury Star*, "Joe LaFlamme to Drive Wolves on Sudbury Streets Tomorrow," January 25, 1939, p. 8; *Sudbury Star*, "Crowds

Throng Streets to Watch Laflamme's Wolves Run," January 27, 1939, p. 6; *Lethbridge Herald*, "Street Traffic Startles Trained Timber Wolves," January 27, 1939, p. 2; *Sudbury Star*, "Son Thrills at Father's Feat," January 27, 1939, p. 1; Sudbury Brewing and Malting Company, "All Famous in the North!" advertisement for Silver Foam beverages, *Sudbury Star*, January 30, 1939, p. 9; *Sudbury Star*, "Thousands See Wolves Run on City Streets," January 27, 1939, p. 6; William Kinmond, "Lashes Whip at Spectators as Crowd Stampede Wolves," *Toronto Daily Star*, January 26, 1939, 2nd sec., pp. 1, 25; *Sudbury Star*, "Claims Wolf Pack Will Attack Man," January 27, 1939, p. 1; Nettie Madger, "Wolf as Pet Seemed Fine Idea but 'What to Do' Is Worry Now," *Toronto Daily Star*, January 28, 1939, 2nd sec., p. 1; Nettie Madger, "Muckoos Is Nice Wolf but Law Is after Our Nettie," *Toronto Daily Star*, January 31, 1939, p. 17; Leslie Avery, "Joe and Wolves Reach New York for Sport Show," *Oshkosh Northwestern*, February 17, 1939, p. 7; *La Presse*, "Le loup déteste la muselière!" February 2, 1939, p. 11.

p. 115—**"through city streets"**: *Sudbury Star*, "Thousands See Wolves Run on City Streets," January 27, 1939, p. 6.

p. 115—**"hurry a wolf"**: *Sudbury Star*, "Thousands See Wolves Run on City Streets," January 27, 1939, p. 6.

p. 116—**"tickle a timber wolf"**: *Sudbury Star*, "Claims Wolf Pack Will Attack Man," January 27, 1939, p. 1.

p. 116—**"lot of kids"**: *Sudbury Star*, "Thousands See Wolves Run on City Streets," January 27, 1939, p. 6.

p. 116—**"feed the wolves"**: William Kinmond, "Lashes Whip at Spectators as Crowd Stampede Wolves," *Toronto Daily Star*, January 26, 1939, 2nd sec., p. 1.

p. 116—**"like my dad"**: *Sudbury Star*, "Son Thrills at Father's Feat," January 27, 1939, p. 1; Cécile Turcotte, personal interview, May 2, 2009; Roland (Bidou) Secord, personal interview, March 28, 2011.

p. 117—**"like a flash"**: *Sudbury Star*, "Thousands See Wolves Run on City Streets," January 27, 1939, p. 6.

p. 118—**"she's yours"**: Nettie Madger, "Wolf as Pet Seemed Fine Idea but 'What to Do' Is Worry Now," *Toronto Daily Star*, January 28, 1939, 2nd sec., p. 1.

p. 118—**"headaches enough"**: Nettie Madger, "Muckoos Is Nice Wolf but Law Is after Our Nettie," *Toronto Daily Star*, January 31, 1939, p. 17.

Notes to Chapter 21

p. 119—**taking wolf photos**: The event was reconstructed from the following articles: Nettie Madger, "Muckoos Is Nice Wolf but Law Is after Our Nettie," *Toronto Daily Star*, January 31, 1939, p. 17; *Sudbury Star*, "Laflamme Battles Wolf in Studio," January 30, 1939, pp. 1, 8. All quotations in this chapter come from the latter article.

p. 121—***Louise*, by Gustave Charpentier**: "[Met Performance] CID:124880: *Louise {24}* Matinee Broadcast ed. Metropolitan Opera House: 01/28/1939," *The Metropolitan Opera* [website], http://archives.metoperafamily.org

Notes to Chapter 22

p. 123—**transportation**: *North Bay Nugget*, "Laflamme and Wolves Bound for Boston in Small Truck," February 1, 1939, p. 14; Nettie Madger, "Muckoos Is Nice Wolf but Law Is after Our Nettie," *Toronto Daily Star*, January 31, 1939, p. 17.

p. 123—**the musher's clothes**: *Lethbridge Herald*, "Wolves Mushing New York Streets," February 2, 1939, p. 5.

p. 124—**Boston Sportsman's and Boat Show**: John F. Kenney, "The Lookout," *Lowell Sun*, February 7, 1939, p. 11.

p. 124—**National Sportsmen's Show**: Raymond R. Camp, "Wood, Field and Stream," *New York Times*, January 25, 1939, sports sec., p. 29; *New York Times*, "Angling Events on Show Card," February 12, 1939, sports sec., p. 92; Lincoln A. Werden, "Thousands at Opening Session of National Sportsmen's Show," *New York Times*, February 19, 1939, sports sec., p. 75; *Evening Independent*, "Canadian Trapper Prefers Wolves to Dogs," March 15, 1939, p. 10.

p. 124—**wolves "feel best"**: Leslie Avery, "Joe and Wolves Reach New York for Sport Show," *Oshkosh Northwestern*, February 17, 1939, p. 7.

p. 126—**Michigan Sportsmen's Show**: "2nd Annual Michigan Sportmen's Show" advertisement, *Detroit News*, April 3, 1939, p. 22.

p. 126—**"We know Joe"**: Fan-Fare, "Film Possibilities of Little Guilds

Lauded: Drama Festival Has Great Talent Array," *Windsor Daily Star*, April 13, 1939, p. 2.

p. 126—**in the footsteps**: According to *Wikipedia*, Grey Owl was a writer and conservationist; Jack Miner was a conservationist; and Ernest T. Seton, author and wildlife artist, was a founding pioneer of the Boy Scouts of America; the three men were Canadians, either of origin or naturalized.

p. 126—**Hamilton**: *Montreal Gazette*, "Joe Laflamme Going Home," April 14, 1939, p. 22.

p. 126—**Jim Curran**: *Globe and Mail*, "Do Wolves Attack Men? Editor, Tamer Disagree," January 28, 1939, 2nd sec., p. 15.

p. 126—**"thirteen years' experience"**: *Globe and Mail*, "Do Wolves Attack Men? Editor, Tamer Disagree," January 28, 1939, 2nd sec., p. 15; in fact, Joe's experience with wolves went back to 1923, some 16 years.

p. 126—**"will attack humans"**: *Toronto Daily Star*, "Wolves Will Attack Humans, Joe Insists," January 28, 1939, 2nd sec., p. 1.

p. 127—**mayoress for the day**: *Toronto Daily Star*, "Woman Mayor for a Day to Greet King at Gogama," June 1, 1939, p. 1; *South Side Story*, "Great Lives Lived in Greater Sudbury," January 2005, p. 27.

p. 127—**police forbade**: *Lethbridge Herald*, "Royal Brevities," June 6, 1939, back page.

p. 127—**wolf team was dispersed**: *Sudbury Star*, "'Wolfman of Gogama' Will Always Be Remembered Now," January 2, 1968, p. 7.

Notes to Chapter 23

p. 128—**two young moose**: Information about the moose comes from the following articles: *Toronto Daily Star*, "Wolf Man's Latest Pets Are Right At Home In Family Circle," October 11, 1939, 2nd sec., p. 1; Raymond R. Camp, "News of Wood, Field and Stream," *New York Times*, November 28, 1939, sports sec., p. 33; *Sudbury Star*, "'Wolfman of Gogama' Will Always Be Remembered Now," January 2, 1968, p. 7; *Montreal Gazette*, "Moose Train for Show: Joe Laflamme Taking Pets to Boston Sportsmen Display," January 27, 1940, p. 14; *La Presse*, "Personnage pittoresque attendu à Montréal," January 24, 1947, p. 3.

p. 128—**"that moose I have"**: Mike Bolton, "Moose Gets the Hot Seat," *Toronto Daily Star*, November 22, 1958, p. 54.

p. 129—**like pets**: *Emmetsburg (Iowa) Democrat*, "Outdoors with G.K. Jr.," April 3, 1947, p. 2.

p. 130—**"itchy fingers"**: *Montreal Gazette*, "Moose Train for Show: Joe Laflamme Taking Pets to Boston Sportsmen Display," January 27, 1940, p. 14; see also John Kieran, "Sports of the *Times*," *New York Times*, February 20, 1940, sports section, p. 25.

p. 130—**climb into a taxi**: *Sudbury Star*, "North Steals Spotlight at Gotham Show," February 20, 1940, p. 8.

p. 130—**moose mail**: *Toronto Daily Star*, "Will Bear Attack Moose? Maybe. Anyhow, Joe's Is Safe in Gotham," February 15, 1940, p. 5.

p. 130—**New York Sportsmen's Association**: *Toronto Daily Star*, "Will Bear Attack Moose? Maybe. Anyhow, Joe's Is Safe in Gotham," February 15, 1940, p. 5; Jim M. Taylor, letter to Division of Operation and Personnel of the Ontario Department of Lands and Forests, Toronto, December 31, 1946.

p. 131—**really good show**: *Sudbury Star*, "North Steals Spotlight at Gotham Show," February 20, 1940, p. 8; John Kieran, "Sports of the *Times*," *New York Times*, February 20, 1940, sports sec., p. 25.

p. 131—**warning anglers and hunters**: Raymond R. Camp, "Wood, Field and Stream," *New York Times*, February 16, 1940, sports sec., p. 28; *Sudbury Star*, "North Steals Spotlight at Gotham Show," February 20, 1940, p. 8.

p. 131—**Detroit's Sportsmen's Show**: *Windsor Daily Star*, "Joe LaFlamme and Tame Moose Draw Crowds in Detroit," March 4, 1940, p. 5; *Windsor Daily Star*, "Zoo Parade: Rare Tamed Moose," January 4, 1958, p. 36; *Sudbury Star*, "Moose, Badger, Wolves, Elk and Bears 'Friends' of the Mooseman of Gogama," February 8, 1965, p. 3; Jim M. Taylor, letter to Division of Operation and Personnel of the Ontario Department of Lands and Forests, Toronto, December 31, 1946.

p. 132—**feet of moose**: *Globe and Mail*, "Gogama's 'Paul Bunyan' Bringing Moose to City," January 24, 1947, p. 3.

p. 132—**"make tourists' eyes stick out"**: *Toronto Daily Star*, "Gogama Joe Gives Away Moose; Now He'll Train Some Wolves," April 12, 1940, p. 10.

p. 133—**"no match for wolves"**: *Toronto Daily Star*, "Finds Wolves are Like Women 'Can Never Really Tame Them,'" March 20, 1945, p. 2.

p. 133—**wartime travel restrictions**: Jim M. Tyalor, letter to Division of Operation and Personnel of the Ontario Department of Lands and Forests, Toronto, December 31, 1946.

p. 133—**trained to plow**: *Toronto Daily Star*, "There'll Be Indians If They Can Find Any," January 22, 1946, p. 3.

p. 133—**"local Joe Laflamme"**: T.A.K., "From Jingle Bells to Truck Rumble," *Montreal Gazette*, November 10, 1941, p. 8.

p. 133—*Joe and Bateese*: *Lost Battalion Survivors*, 1955, *Longwood's Journey*, http://www.longwood.k12.ny.us/history/upton/lbn1.htm.

p. 133—**frog-jumping contest**: *Lethbridge Herald*, "The Left Hand Corner," May 29, 1957, p. 1.

p. 133—**tall tales**: *Toronto Star Weekly*, "Tall Tales from the North," February 24, 1962, p. 18-20.

p. 134—**radio talk shows**: *Sudbury Star*, "Moose, Badger, Wolves, Elk and Bears 'Friends' of the Mooseman of Gogama," February 8, 1965, p. 3. This probably occurred at Toronto's CBC radio station as it was, at the time, the closest station to Gogama. Unfortunately, the program recordings no longer exist.

p. 134—*Canadian Cavalcade*: CBC, "Girls, He Tames Wolves" advertisement, *Winnipeg Free Press*, April 26, 1945, ent. sec., p. 17; Lorne Greene would later play Ben Cartwright in the television series *Bonanza*. For Lillie's love of the radio, see *Toronto Daily Star*, "Prefers Northern Life to Comforts of Paris," January 31, 1925, p. 18.

Notes to Chapter 24

p. 135—**put up an exhibit**: J.T. LaFlamme, letter to District Forester Jim M. Taylor, November 5, 1946; Jim M. Taylor, letter to Division of Fish and Wildlife, Department of Lands and Forests, Toronto, November 28, 1946. It is not known where LaFlamme got his deer as there were none in the Gogama area.

p. 135—**postcards and brochures**: *Sudbury Star*, "'Mooseman' Joe Laflamme Dies at 61," August 7, 1958, p. 3.

p. 136—**in Toronto**: *La Presse*, "'P'tit Mousse,' l'orignal bien-aimé,"

January 31, 1947, p. 29; *Globe and Mail*, "Gogama's 'Paul Bunyan' Bringing Moose to City," January 24, 1947, p. 3.

p. 136—**Santa Claus's double**: Maurice Desjardins, "Tous les sports : Avec Fernand dans la cage aux loups," *Photo-Journal*, August 17, 1950, p. 46; *Globe and Mail*, "Gogama's 'Paul Bunyan' Bringing Moose to City," January 24, 1947, p. 3; *Lethbridge Herald*, "Moose Are Like Women," January 25, 1947, p. 14.

p. 136—**in Toronto**: Moon, Robert. "Neglected Monarch. We Mourn the Moose." *Leader Post*, January 27, 1948, p. 5; "Royal York Hotel, Toronto—Building Info," *A View on Cities* [website], http://www.aviewoncities.com/buildings/toronto/royalyorkhotel.htm; *Globe and Mail*, "Gogama's 'Paul Bunyan' Bringing Moose to City," January 24, 1947, p. 3.

p. 138—**To Betty Davis with devotion**: A photo of cradle and note appear in *Boxoffice*, "'Moose Man' Sends a Papoose Board to Assist Bette Davis in Films," February 22, 1947, p. 99, www.boxoffice.com/the_vault/issue_page?issue_id=1947-2-22&page_no=107#page_start; in the magazine, the note in the photograph is illegible. The same photo is held in the City of Toronto Archives: see Alexandra Studio, "Joe La Flamme, 'The Moose Man,' with Glenn Ireton, Deer and Moose," [194-?], Commissioned photographs, Alexandra Studio fonds, f1257, s1057, it3326, City of Toronto Archives, Toronto, ON. The *Boxoffice* article states that Joe was the only honorary white chief ever elected by the Ontario Ojibway Indians; research has led to nothing that confirms this. However, Alan Corbiere, executive director of the Ojibwe Culture Centre on Manitoulin Island, explained, "the practice was fairly widespread but in most cases this was akin to somebody now getting the 'keys to the city' by the mayor." Corbiere added that the title was purely honorary and carried no authority (Alan Corbiere, e-mail to author, February 2, 2011).

p. 139—**moose were flown**: *New York Times*, "The 'King of the Northern Woods' Gets Balky" [photo], February 14, 1947, p. S26; see also *Sandusky Register-Star-News*, "Bull(headed) Moose Makes Air Debut," February 20, 1947, p. 1.

p. 140—**a moose can weigh**: E.S. Telfer, "Moose," 1997, *Hinterland Who's Who*, http://www.hww.ca/en/species/mammals/moose.html; *Sudbury Star*,

"Gotham Finds Joe LaFlamme Country Slicker in Hick City," February 20, 1947, p. 6.

p. 140—**1947 show**: Raymond R. Camp, "Wood, Field and Stream," *New York Times*, February 15, 1947, sports sec., p. 12; Oscar Farley, "Today's Sport Parade," *Olean Times Herald*, February 17, 1947, p. 8.

p. 141—**a sensational act**: *Sudbury Star*, "Gotham Finds Joe LaFlamme Country Slicker in Hick City," February 20, 1947, p. 6.

p. 141—**New York with Muskeg**: Izaak Hunter, "Rod and Gun," *Montreal Gazette*, February 9, 1965, p. 29.

p. 141—**"fund of stories"**: *Sudbury Star*, "Gotham Finds Joe LaFlamme Country Slicker in Hick City," February 20, 1947, p. 6.

p. 141—**self-appointed Gogama Mayor**: Joe and Morris LaFlamme, Letter to District Forester Jim M. Taylor, March 3, 1947; with this letter was a money order of $10 to cover the cost of the Tourist Outfitter's License for 1947.

p. 142—**National Sportsmen's Show of Canada**: V.A. Bower, "6,500 Attend Opening Performances of Sportsmen's Show," *Ottawa Citizen*, April 22, 1947, p. 12.

p. 142—**visit Sudbury**: *Sudbury Star*, "Moose, Badger, Wolves, Elk and Bears 'Friends' of the Mooseman of Gogama," February 8, 1965, p. 3.

Notes to Chapter 25

p. 143—**telegraph to Columbus**: *Windsor Daily Star*, "Moose Seek Real Thing: Old Joe Laflamme to Transport Animals," July 31, 1947, p. 8.

p. 143—**moose died**: James Stonerock, phone communication, July 19, 2010.

p. 143—**"bes' tam' woodsman"**: *Sandusky Register-Star-News*, "Joe LaFlamme Has Columbus-Bound Moose in Toronto," August 13, 1947, p. 1. Details of the trip to Toronto and fate of the moose came from this article; Terry Brady, "Letter from former Gogama resident," May 1986 [?]; and *Grape Belt*, "Joe LaFlamme at Moose Convention with a Real One," August 19, 1947, p. 9.

p. 144—**"dat moose money"**: *Sandusky Register-Star-News*, "Joe LaFlamme Has Columbus-Bound Moose in Toronto," August 13, 1947, p. 1.

p. 144—**in a refrigerator truck**: *Ruston Daily Leader*, "Heat Wave Hits

East after Leaving Trail across Midwest Belt," August 14, 1947, p. 1; Alexandra Studio, "Joe La Flamme, 'The Moose Man,' Loading Moose onto Dew the Mover Ltd. Truck, Bound for Columbus, Ohio," [194-?], Commissioned photographs, Alexandra Studio fonds, f1257, s1057, it3322, City of Toronto Archives, Toronto, ON.. Muskeg's antlers, as seen in the photo, seem to have been cut off, probably during his stay at the Toronto zoo.

p. 144—**stopover in Hamilton**: V.A. Bower. "6,500 Attend Opening Performances of Sportsmen's Show," *Ottawa Citizen*, April 22, 1947, p. 17.

p. 144—**the Moose convention**: Details of the convention were taken from the following: *Long Beach Press-Telegram*, "Joe LaFlamme Brings Big Pet to Convention," August 17, 1947, p. 1; *Grape Belt*, "Joe LaFlamme at Moose Convention with a Real One," August 19, 1947, p. 9. Quotations come from the former.

Notes to Chapter 26

p. 147—**"the Ex"**: *Time Magazine*, "Canada: Ontario: The Ex," September 1, 1947, http://www.time.com/time/magazine/article/0,9171,887606,00. html. For details about Moosie's experience, see also *Sudbury Star*, "Joe and His Moose at the Ex," September 2, 1947, p. 1.

p. 147—*Johnny at the Fair*: Rick Salutin, "Forward on Life's Tightrope," *Rabble.ca*, August 29, 2003, http://rabble.ca/print/columnists/forward-lifes-tightrope. For Pachter's description of his experience, see Charles Pachter, personal interview, May 6, 2010; and Charles Pachter, email to Gerry Talbot, March 21, 2010. See also *Johnny at the Fair*, dir. Jack Olsen, National Film Board, 1947.

p. 149—**Animal Man**: *Lethbridge Herald*, "Miss Byline, Black Bear Cub, to Fly to Sydney, Australia," September 5, 1947, p. 2. The same reporter called him "the Canadian naturalist," a label Joe also received in the *Winnipeg Free Press*, "Around the World: Animals," September 5, 1947, p. 2.

p. 149—**black bear cub**: *Lethbridge Herald*, "Miss Byline, Black Bear Cub, to Fly to Sydney, Australia," September 5, 1947, p. 2; *Toronto Daily Star*, "'That a Tree?' Louise Downs It, Urn Too, Then Dives under Bed," September 5, 1947, p. 20; *Montreal Gazette*, "'Animal Greeting' Brings Difficulty: Australia Protests Canadian Newsmen's Plan to Air-Ship Bear Cub," September 22, 1947, p. 9.

p. 150—**jail**: *Ottawa Citizen*, "Case Held Over till Show Ends," October 17, 1947, p. 10.

p. 150—**making Muskeg talk**: Roger Laflamme, personal interview, October 14, 2008; Suzanne Laflamme, personal interview, October 21, 2011.

p. 150—**hiding from the law**: Guy Laflamme, personal interview, October 14, 2008; Rhéal Véronneau, personal interview, June 27, 2008.

p. 150—**a check-up**: *Montreal Gazette*, "Joe LaFlamme Makes Brief Stop; Walks Moose to See Veterinary," January 30, 1948, p. 3.

p. 151—**"without indigestion"**: *North Bay Nugget*, "'Mooseman of Gogama' Joe LaFlamme Passes," February 8, 1965, p. 6.

p. 152—**guest appearances**: *Life*, "Mumbling Moose," March 15, 1948, p. 61; quotations from Craig and other details about the interview come from this article. See also D.A.L. MacDonald, "Sports on Parade," *Manitoba Ensign*, December 9, 1950, p. 10. "Muskeg" is the most common spelling of the moose's name; however, "Mushkeg," "Mushkig," "Muskeag," and "Mushki" also appear in various articles.

p. 152—**Glenn Ireton**: Gabriel Ireton, email to Gerry Talbot, December 13, 2007.

p. 153—**never liked the city**: Tom Dare, "'Stackie' Adds Thrills in Search for Santa," *Toledo News-Bee*, October 22, 1926, p. 1.

p. 153—**"enough of civilization"**: Raymond R. Camp, "Wood, Field and Stream," *New York Times*, February 22, 1948, sports sec., p. 3.

p. 153—**passed through customs**: *La Presse*, "À l'arrivée de Jos. LaFlamme à la gare centrale," March 29, 1948, p. 7.

p. 153—**Sportsman's Exhibition**: Izaak Hunter, "With Rod and Gun," *Montreal Gazette*, February 28, 1948, p. 15.

p. 153—**Joe's occupation**: *Detroit Border Crossings and Passenger and Crew Lists, 1905-1957, Ancestry.com*, http://search.ancestrylibrary.com.

p. 154—**"authority to capture"**: Jim M. Taylor, letter to J.T. LaFlamme, April 15, 1948.

Notes to Chapter 27

p. 155—**required medical attention**: *Sudbury Star*, "Been Reported Dead Twice before but Joe Laflamme in Best of Health," August 8, 1958, p. 1.

p. 155—**check his nine bears**: *Montreal Gazette*, "Bears Readied for Trip," August 4, 1948, p. 3. The photo accompanying the article shows LaFlamme wearing a white shirt and a tie. This is one of the first articles featuring Joe as a Montreal citizen, after his move from Gogama.

p. 155—**feed the animals**: *Northern Daily News*, "Gogama Mooseman Dies in Montreal at 75," February 8, 1965, p. 1.

p. 156—**Belmont Park**: "Belmont Park, Montreal," *Wikipedia*, http://en.wikipedia.org/wiki/Belmont_Park,_Montreal.

p. 156—**name was not listed**: *Montreal Directory* (*Annuaires Lovell*), Bibliothèque et archives nationales du Québec, http://bibnum2.banq.qc.ca/bna/lovell.

p. 156—**lots were sold**: Sudbury (No. 53) Land Registry Office, Roll # 53ER12, parcel 7492, p. 458; roll # 53ER16, parcel 10024, p. 773; roll # 53ER18, parcel 11823, p. B1.

p. 156—**tour of Quebec**: Information about this tour was taken from the following articles: *St. Maurice Valley Chronicle*, "Three Rivers Exhibition Gets under Way Saturday," August 19, 1948, p. 1; *St. Maurice Valley Chronicle*, "Game Association Backs Sportsman's Show; Public Invited to Visit Wild Game Exhibits at Exhibition," August 19, 1948, p. 3; C. Leney, "Heigh Ho, Come to the Fair," *Sherbrooke Telegram*, September 2, 1948, p. 5; *Sherbrooke Telegram*, "Joe Laflamme Explains the Aims of Convention," October 28, 1948, p. 4.

p. 156—**regularly practised**: Maurice Desjardins, "Tous les sports: Avec Fernand dans la cage aux loups," *Photo-Journal*, August 17, 1950, p. 46.

p. 157—**"poachers at heart"**: *Sherbrooke Telegram*, "Joe Laflamme Explains the Aims of Convention," October 28, 1948, p. 4; Leo Cassidy's praise appears in the same article.

p. 157—**wolf population**: Luigi Boitani, "Wolf Conservation and Recovery," in *Wolves: Behavior, Ecology, and Conservation*, ed. L. David Mech and Luigi Boitani, 321. Chicago: University of Chicago Press, 2006.

p. 158—**"biased or inaccurate"**: Steven H. Fritts et al., "Wolves and

Humans," in *Wolves: Behavior, Ecology, and Conservation*, ed. L. David Mech and Luigi Boitani, 298. Chicago: University of Chicago Press, 2006. See Fritts et al. (297) for educational approaches to wolf conservation recommended well after LaFlamme's day.

p. 158—**"human attitudes"**: L. David Mech and Luigi Boitani, Concl. to *Wolves: Behavior, Ecology, and Conservation*, ed. L. David Mech and Luigi Boitani, 341, Chicago: University of Chicago Press, 2006.

p. 158—**Aldo Leopold**: Steven H. Fritts et al., "Wolves and Humans," in *Wolves: Behavior, Ecology, and Conservation*, ed. L. David Mech and Luigi Boitani, 294, Chicago: University of Chicago Press, 2006.

p. 158—**"attest to his success"**: Jim M. Taylor, letter to Division of Operation and Personnel, Department of Lands and Forests, Toronto, ON, December 31, 1946.

p. 159—**Montreal sports show**: Gilles Vernier, personal interview, October 20, 2010.

p. 159—**unsuspecting reporter-in-training**: Jerry Williams, "A Man and His Moose; I Met Joe LaFlamme in 1949 and Was Asked to Keep Watch over His Menagerie," *Montreal Gazette*, June 6, 1993, p. C2. The account of LaFlamme's visit to the *Gazette* office, including all quotations, and Jerry Williams's encounter with the wolves, comes from this article.

Notes to Chapter 28

p. 160—**operated a zoo**: Mechel Hershcovich, email to Sarah Hartt-Snowbell, forwarded to Gerry Talbot, June 12, 2011.

p. 160—**"Impossible to reason"**: Maurice Desjardins, "Tous les sports: Avec Fernand dans la cage aux loups," *Photo-Journal*, August 17, 1950, p. 46; translation by the author.

p. 160—**lectures**: *Montreal Gazette*, "To Give Wildlife Lectures," October 4, 1950, p. 3.

p. 160—**"'talk' with the wolf"**: Sarah Hartt-Snowbell, email to Gerry Talbot, June 11, 2011.

p. 160—**LaFlamme worked**: Details of LaFlamme's employment come from the following articles: *Today Magazine* [*Toronto Star* insert], Q & A,

February 7, 1981; *Timmins Daily Press*, "North's Mooseman Legend in Canada," February 8, 1965, p. 5; Judy Hudson, "A Brief History of Trails," *Randolph Mountain Club Newsletter*, Summer 2003, http://www.randolphmountainclub. org/newsletters/summer2003.html#historyoftrails; Maurice Desjardins, "Tous les sports: Avec Fernand dans la cage aux loups," *Photo-Journal*, August 17, 1950, p. 46.

p. 162—**Maheegan ... escaped**: *Calgary Herald*, "Five Bullets from a City Policeman's Revolver," August 9, 1950, p. 3.

p. 162—**Muskeg caught a cold**: Gilles Vernier, personal interview, October 20, 2010.

p. 162—**Joe and his pet**: Marek Krasuski, "Moose Man: Hero or Heretic," *Challenge: A Journal of Male Perspectives* 1 (2004): 37-38; Edelta Turgeon, personal interview, November 22, 2008.

p. 162—**listed as a tenant**: *Montreal Directory* (*Annuaires Lovell*), Bibliothèque et archives nationales du Québec, http://bibnum2.banq.qc.ca/bna/lovell; all references to the *Montreal Directory* in this chapter come from this source.

pp. 162-163—**"he can hold his own"**: *Post-Register*, "New York Gets Coyote Problem," August 19, 1953, p. 16.

p. 163—**former policeman and friend**: *Sudbury Star*, "Been Reported Dead Twice before but Joe Laflamme in Best of Health," August 8, 1958, p. 1.

p. 164—**"more ferocious"**: Jean Côté, "L'homme aux loups a perdu son seul ami," *Le Nouveau Samedi*, April 11, 1964, p. 5; translation by the author.

p. 164—**"Go make war"**: Gisèle Laflamme Lanthier, personal interview, October 14, 2008.

p. 166—**not totally naked**: Diane Laflamme, personal interview, October 14, 2008; Simone Talbot, personal interview, November 15, 2008. Translation by the author.

p. 166—**diabetes**: Details of the last days of Joe LaFlamme are taken from Izaak Hunter, "Rod and Gun," *Montreal Gazette*, January 23, 1965, p. 44; January 30, 1965, p. 40; February 9, 1965, p. 29.

p. 167—**Ermitage Saint-Antoine**: *Ermitage Sainte Antoine*, http://www.st-antoine.org/. The name of the site was obtained from Father Maurice Labbé in a telephone communication with the author on June 17, 2011.

Notes to Chapter 29

p. 168—**operation**: *La Presse*, "Joe Laflamme, un sportif original, meurt à 75 ans," February 8, 1965, p. 37.

p. 168—**Wolf Man's passing**: Izaak Hunter, "Rod and Gun," *Montreal Gazette*, February 9, 1965, p. 29; *La Presse*, "Avis de décès," February 8, 1965, p. 37.

p. 168—**"thrill of his life"**: *Montreal Gazette*, "Uses Wild Wolves for Hauling Sled," June 25, 1938, p. 13.

p. 169—**dog-and-wolf pack arrived**: *New York Times*, "Temperature Drops to 17 Here, Cold to Stay; Up-State Suffers; Earthquake at Cambridge," January 23, 1926, p. 1; James P. Dawson, "Mushes 700 Miles with Dogs to See Hockey Here Tonight," *New York Times*, January 23, 1926, p. S11. The description of mushing in New York that follows is based on how Joe ran his other tours, and on the author's limited experience driving a dog-train.

p. 170—**call on Mayor**: No record has been found of a visit with the mayor.

p. 170—**Thousands of people**: *Montreal Gazette*, "Uses Wild Wolves for Hauling Sled," June 25, 1938, p. 13.

p. 170—**Times Square**: *Evening Independent*, "Canadian Trapper Prefers Wolves to Dogs," March 15, 1939, p. 10.

p. 170—**wolves on Broadway**: *Montreal Gazette*, "Wolf Tamer Stars as Court Witness," June 9, 1938, p. 31.

Chronology 1889-1965

1889	March 9: Télesphore Laflamme (Joe LaFlamme) is born in St. Télesphore, Quebec.
1893	August 18: Émilie Haigneré (Lillie LaFlamme) is born in Étaples-sur-Mer, northern France.
1910-1914	Télesphore works as a Montreal Street Railway conductor while training to become police officer for the City of Montreal. He continues to conduct trains until 1914, even though he is officially enrolled in the police force on July 29, 1910.
1914	April 28: Télesphore marries Florence May West at St. Aloysius, in Montreal.
1916	November 13: Télesphore resigns from the police force.
c1917	To avoid being recruited by the army, Télesphore changes his name to "Joe" Laflamme, which is the name of his brother who is a farmer.

1919	Émilie immigrates to Montreal and meets Joe. The couple starts a common-law relationship.
1920	Summer: Joe and Émilie (Lillie) Laflamme move to Gogama, in Northern Ontario.
	Joe works on the construction of a lumber mill and later starts raising huskies and bootlegging.
1923	Joe starts trapping wolves and training them to the harness.
1924	February 9: Joe raced his first team of nine wolves in a dog derby in Montreal.
	He starts writing his family name with a capital "F": LaFlamme.
1925	January 26 to February 2: Invited by the *Toronto Daily Star* on a week-long exhibition engagement in the city, Joe features his team of eleven dogs and four wolves.
	Winter: Joe is cast in a provincial government film titled *Transport in the North*.
1926	January 23: Joe mushes on Broadway Street, in New York, with a team of five wolves and eight dogs. He then starts a two-week exhibition engagement at Madison Square Garden.
	February 20-26: Joe races his wolf team at Alasa Farms in Alton, then in Rochester, New York State.
1926-1930	Joe raises mink in Gogama. In winter 1926, Pete, who is leading a team of undisciplined wolves, turns against Joe, deep in the forest.
1929	April 26: Morris LaFlamme is born in Gogama.
1931	March: Joe goes to court for the first time and is fined $100 for possession of liquor without a permit. He is accused of the same offence in September.
1932	September: Prospector Joe strikes gold during the first gold rush south of Gogama.

1936   October: Joe is sentenced to three months in jail for stealing a boat and gasoline. His brother Elzéar possibly serves his term.

1937   Joe is again accused of possession of liquor without a permit, but the case is dismissed for lack of evidence. He sells his lucrative gold claim to order a dozen wolves from the Hudson's Bay Company.

1938   Summer: Joe starts training wolves for his first all-wolf team for the upcoming American sportsmen's shows.

August 6: Lillie records three mine claims staked during the second gold rush in the Gogama area.

October: Joe is accused of supplying beer illegally to a Native.

October 14: Joe survives an airplane accident on a lake and is rescued two days later.

1939   January 25: Joe travels to Sudbury by plane with his ten wolves as paying passengers.

January 26-30: He exhibits his wolves to the Sudbury public.

February to April: Joe participates in sportsmen's shows in Boston, New York, Indianapolis, Detroit, Windsor, and Hamilton.

Summer: He obtains two moose, which he starts training.

1940   Winter: With his moose and a deer, Joe goes on a three-month US tour of Boston, New York, Detroit, and Buffalo.

1941   Early winter: Joe exhibits his wolves in New York. He starts suffering from low blood pressure.

May: He fights the monster fire that devastates the Gogama area.

1944   Joe wins the wrestling match against D. MacLaren, from Timmins.

Summer: He is featured in the Warner Brothers' documentary *The Forest Commandos*.

1945

Winter: Joe attends the "rushes" of the film in Toronto.

June: He runs unsuccessfully for Conservative MPP for the riding of Sudbury.

Summer: Twin Secord brothers steal liquor from Joe's hiding place in a shed.

1947

January 23-29: Joe visits Toronto with three moose and a deer. He offers a papoose carrier to actress Bette Davis. He starts a three-month tour of the US.

February 13: From Boston, Joe flies with his four animals as paying passengers to New York. After this sportsmen's show, he exhibits in Philadelphia, Buffalo, St. Louis, Chicago, Minneapolis, San Francisco, and Portland, ending the tour in Ottawa.

August 10-14: Joe is hospitalized in Toronto due to injuries from a battle with his bull moose while attempting to put the animal on the train in Gogama.

August 17: He collects a reward for bringing a live moose at the Royal Order of Moose convention in Columbus, Ohio.

August 22-September 8: With his moose, he attends the Ex in Toronto, where he meets young Charles Pachter.

October 17: Joe is accused of illegal possession of alcohol and is sentenced to three months in the Sudbury jail. To avoid this penalty, he moves in the Montreal area.

1948

February and March: Joe does another US tour starting with New York, where he exhibits a moose, a wolf, a badger, and a bear cub. His moose and wolf make a guest appearance on ABC radio.

April: He exhibits his menagerie in Montreal, then in Detroit, Buffalo, and Boston.

August: Joe ships to South Wales nine bear cubs he has trained in his wildlife zoo in Belmont Park, in Montreal.

Late summer: Joe exhibits his animals in Trois-Rivières, Sherbrooke, Quebec, and Shawinigan Falls.

1949   Winter: Joe exhibits his animals (a moose, a bear, a badger, a raccoon, two otters and three wolves) in Montreal.

1950   Joe retires as a school-crossing guard and a night watchman on the Montreal docks. He operates a wild animal zoo on Décarie Boulevard.

Summer: He works in a resort in Jefferson, New Hampshire, and then blazes trails for the Randolph Mountain Club.

1951   Summer: Joe blazes trails in New Hampshire for a second summer.

1952   Winter: Joe exhibits his moose and other animals in South Carolina. Muskeg dies on his return to Montreal, prompting Joe to retire from the animal business.

1958   Joe is working as a special guard for Barnes Investigation Bureau in Montreal; it is not known when he began this work, nor when he retired.

August: He visits Gogama after Elzéar's death in Sudbury.

1965   January: Joe is admitted to Montreal General Hospital to have his right leg amputated.

February 5: Joe LaFlamme dies shortly after surgery, at age 75.

1982   November 18: Lillie LaFlamme dies at Queen Elizabeth Hospital, in Montreal.

1996   July 22: Morris LaFlamme dies at Montreal General Hospital.

Joe LaFlamme's Territory

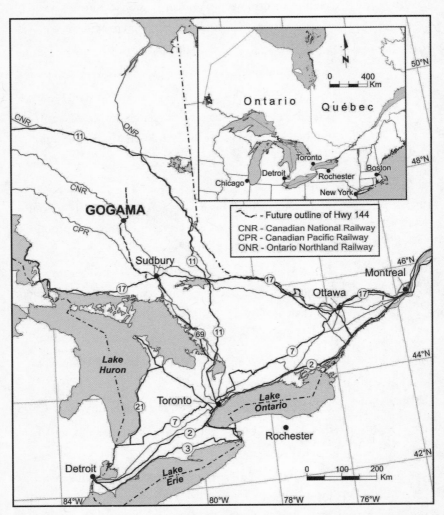

The map shows northeastern and southern Ontario, and southwestern Quebec, circa 1920-1950, when Joe LaFlamme was at the height of his fame as the Wolf Man and Moose Man of Gogama. Highway 144, running from Sudbury north to Gogama, is indicated by a broken line because it was not built until the late 1960s. The inset map shows the greater extent of Joe's travels, from Boston on the eastern seabord, west to Chicago. Credit: L.L. Lariviere—Laurentian University

Bibliography

Archival Institutions and Museums

Archives départementales du Pas-de-Calais, France. "Étaples—État civil: tables décennales." 1893-1902, 3 E 6141.

Association des familles Laflamme inc.

City of Toronto Archives, Alexandra Studio fonds.

Gogama Heritage Museum [Joe LaFlamme photos and dog sled].

Hudson's Bay Company Archives, Archives of Manitoba.

John B. Gammon Geoscience Library Archives, Ontario Ministry of Northern Development, Mines and Forestry. Joseph Laflamme: prospector's license #C-12635 (1929), #C-17655 (1938). Lillie Laflamme: prospector's license #C-17631 (1938).

P.S.S. #1 Noble/Gogama Public School. "Events and Changes to the School." 1939. Private collection.

Sudbury (No. 53) Land Registry Office. Roll #53ER12, parcel 7492, p. 458; roll #53ER16, parcel 10024, p. 773; and roll #53ER18, parcel 11823, p. B1.

Interviews, emails, personal communications

Beauchamp, Rhéo, Gogama resident. Interview by the author. Gogama, June 27, 2008.

Belisle, Eunice, daughter of Dave and Simone Ranger, former Gogama residents. Telephone interview by the author. September 3, 2010.

Bouchard, Clermont, great-nephew of Joe LaFlamme. Interview by the author. St. Polycarpe, October 21, 2011.

Bruneau, Wivine, Gogama resident. Interview by the author. Gogama, November 15, 2008.

Carrière, Annette. Gogama resident. Interview by the author. Gogama, May 12, 2010.

Carrière, Roger (Ti-Pit), Gogama resident. Interview by the author. Gogama, May 12, 2010.

Charbonneau, Laurent, Gogama resident. Interview by Gerry Talbot. Gogama, February 15, 2011.

———. Interview by Gerry Talbot. Gogama, November 2, 2011.

Charbonneau, Violette, former Gogama resident. Telephone interview by the author. January 31, 2010.

Corbiere, Alan. Email to the author. February 2, 2011.

de Nobile, Jean-Marc. Email to the author. March 1, 2011.

———. Telephone communication with the author. July 8, 2010.

Hartt-Snowbell, Sarah. Email to Gerry Talbot. June 11, 2011

Hershcovich, Mechel. Email to Sarah Hartt-Snowbell [forwarded to Gerry Talbot]. June 12, 2011.

Ireton, Gabriel. Email to Gerry Talbot. December 13, 2007.

———. Email to Gerry Talbot. December 20, 2007.

Kivi, Nicole. Email to the author. June 7, 2013.

Labbé, Father Maurice. Telephone communication with the author. June 17, 2011.

Laflamme, Diane, great-niece of Joe LaFlamme. Interview by the author. St. Polycarpe, October 14, 2008.

Laflamme, Guy, great-nephew of Joe LaFlamme. Interview by the author. St. Polycarpe, October 14, 2008.

LaFlamme, Joe. Letter to Jim M. Taylor. November 5, 1946.

LaFlamme, Joe, and Morris LaFlamme. Letter to Jim M. Taylor. March 3, 1947.

Laflamme, Margaret, great-niece of Joe LaFlamme. Interviews by the author. St. Polycarpe, October 14, 2008 and October 21, 2011.

Laflamme, Robert, great-nephew of Joe LaFlamme. Interviews by the author. St. Polycarpe, October 19, 2010 and October 21, 2011.

Laflamme, Roger, great-nephew of Joe LaFlamme. Interviews by the author in St. Polycarpe, October 14, 2008 and October 21, 2011.

Laflamme, Suzanne, great-niece of Joe LaFlamme. Interviews by the author. St. Polycarpe, October 20, 2010 and October 21, 2011.

Laflamme Lanthier, Gisèle, great-niece of Joe LaFlamme. Interviews by the author. St. Polycarpe, October 14, 2008, October 19, 2010 and October 21, 2011.

——. Telephone interview by the author. November 12, 2008.

——. Telephone interview by the author. May 1, 2009.

——. Telephone interview by the author. May 21, 2010.

——. Telephone interview by the author. August 22, 2010.

Lanthier, Gilbert. Interview by the author. St. Polycarpe, October 14, 2008.

Levac, Huguette (Laflamme), great-niece of Joe LaFlamme. Interviews by the author. St. Polycarpe, October 14, 2008 and October 21, 2011.

Mangan, Griff, grandson of Alvah Griffin Strong. Telephone interview by the author. June 19, 2008.

Michaud, Paul. Letter to Gerry Talbot. June 26, 2004.

Miller, Gordon, former Gogama resident. Telephone interview by the author. August 5, 2011.

Pachter, Charles. Email to Gerry Talbot. March 21, 2010.

——. Interview by the author. Toronto, May 6, 2012.

Payette, Gérald, Gogama resident. Interview by Gerry Talbot. Gogama, June 23, 2011.

Secord, Alfred (Médé), Gogama resident. Interview by the author. Gogama, May 2, 2009.

——. Telephone interview by the author. November 10, 2009.

——. Telephone interview by the author. March 28, 2011.

Secord, Roland (Bidou), Gogama resident. Telephone interview by the author. March 28, 2011.

Stonerock, James. Telephone communication by the author. July 19, 2010.

Talbot, Gerry, Gogama resident. Interview by the author. Gogama, April 29, 2011.

———. Telephone interview by the author. June 7, 2010.

Talbot, Simone, Gogama resident. Interview by the author. Gogama, November 15, 2008.

Taylor, Jim M. Letter to Division of Fish and Wildlife, Ontario Department of Lands and Forests, Toronto. November 28, 1946.

———. Letter to Division of Operation and Personnel, Ontario Department of Lands and Forests, Toronto. December 31, 1946.

———. Letter to Joe LaFlamme. April 15, 1948.

Turcotte, Cécile, Gogama resident. Interview by the author. Gogama, May 2, 2009.

Turcotte, Ernest (Dubby), Gogama resident. Interview by the author. Gogama, May 2, 2009.

Turgeon, Edelta, former Gogama resident. Interview by the author. Sudbury, November 12, 2008.

Vernier, Gilles, great-nephew of Joe LaFlamme. Telephone interview by the author. October 20, 2010.

Véronneau, Marguerite, Gogama resident. Interview by the author. Gogama, June 27, 2008.

Véronneau, Raoul, Gogama resident. Interview by the author. Gogama, November 15, 2008.

Véronneau, Reina, Gogama resident. Interviews by the author. Gogama, July 18, 2002, June 27, 2008 and November 15, 2008.

Véronneau, Rhéal, Gogama resident. Interviews by the author. Gogama, June 27, 2002, and July 18, 2002."

Films

Transport in the North. Ontario Motion Picture Bureau, 2010. DVD. Orig. prod. 1925.

Johnny at the Fair. Dir. Jack Olsen. National Film Board, 1947.

The Forest Commandos. By Glenn Ireton. Dir. Van Campen Heilner. Warner Brothers, in collaboration with the Province of Ontario, c1995. VHS. Orig. prod. 1946.

Published Sources

Albuquerque Journal. "Planes Rescue Four Men Lost in Woods of Northern Ontario." October 17, 1938, p. 1.

Allingham, Peter V. "Dickens in Montreal." November 2, 2007. *Victorian Web*, http://www.victorianweb.org./authors/dickens/montreal/montreal.html.

"Acquisition of Canadian Citizenship at Birth or by Derivation through a Parent or Spouse," *The Ships List*, http://www.theshipslist.com/Forms/CanCitAq_Natz.shtml.

Avery, Leslie. "Joe and Wolves Reach New York for Sport Show." *Oshkosh Northwestern*, February 17, 1939, p. 7.

Bee [Danville, VA]. "Takes Wolf He Caught to Zoo under His Arm." June 7, 1923, p. 3.

Boitani, Luigi. "Wolf Conservation and Recovery." In *Wolves: Behavior, Ecology, and Conservation*, ed. L. David Mech and Luigi Boitani, 317-40. Chicago: University of Chicago Press, 2006.

Bolton, Mike. "Moose Gets the Hot Seat." *Toronto Daily Star*, November 22, 1958, p. 54.

Border Cities Star [Windsor, ON]. "Toronto Gets Real 'Mush' Thrill." January 26, 1925, p. 2.

Bower, V.A. "6,500 Attend Opening Performances of Sportsmen's Show." *Ottawa Citizen*, April 22, 1947, p. 12.

——. "Rod and Gun." *Ottawa Citizen*, August 27, 1947, p. 17.

Bowness, E. Rendle. "Ontario." In *History of the Early Mink People in Canada*, n.p.: Canada Mink Breeders Association, 1980, pp. 54-70. http://www.jkcc.com/minkpeople/ontario.html.

Boxoffice. "Joe Laflamme Featured." 26 April 1947, p. 114, http://www.boxoffice.com/the_vault/issue_page?issue_id=1947-4-26&page_no=128#page_start.

——. "'Moose Man' Sends a Papoose Board to Assist Bette Davis in Films." February 22, 1947, p. 99, www.boxoffice.com/the_vault/issue_page?issue_id=1947-2-22&page_no=107#page_start.

Brady, Terry. "Letter from former Gogama resident." May 1986 [?]. (Appeared in a local Ontario newspaper following the Gogama Public School reunion May 19, 1986.)

Burton, D.H. *The Gogama Fire of 1941.* Toronto: Ontario Department of Lands and Forests, Division of Research, 1949.

Buse, Dieter K., and Graeme S. Mount. *Come On Over! Northeastern Ontario A to Z.* Sudbury: Scrivener Press, 2011.

Calgary Herald. "Five Bullets from a City Policeman's Revolver." August 9, 1950, p. 3.

Camp, Raymond R. "News of Wood, Field and Stream." *New York Times*, November 28, 1939, sports sec., p. 33.

———. "Wood, Field and Stream" *New York Times*, January 25, 1939, sports sec., p. 29.

———. "Wood, Field and Stream" *New York Times*, February 16, 1940, sports sec., p. 28.

———. "Wood, Field and Stream." *New York Times*, February 15, 1947, sports sec., p. 12.

———. "Wood, Field and Stream." *New York Times*, February 22, 1948, sports sec., p. 3.

Canadian Passenger Lists, 1865-1935. Ancestry.com, http://search.ancestrylibrary.com.

Carbone, Geneviève. *Destination loups.* Paris: Éditions Solar, 2007.

CBC. "Girls, He Tames Wolves" [advertisement]. *Winnipeg Free Press*, April 26, 1945, ent. sec., p. 17.

Chiasson, Herménégilde. *Climates.* Transl. Jo-Anne Elder and Fred Cogswell. Frederiction: Goose Lane, 1999.

Chopra, Deepak, Debbie Ford, and Marianne Williamson. *The Shadow Effect. Illuminating the Hidden Power of Your True Self.* New York: Harper Collins, 2010.

Clark, Gregory. "Diving Toward Death at 80 Miles an Hour Only Thought Repairs." *Toronto Daily Star*, October 17, 1938, p. 1.

Cole, Percy T. "Latest Ontario Gold Find Better Than Yellowknife Old Prospector Contends." *Evening Telegram* [Saint-John, NF], September 21, 1938.

———. "Pilot's Skill Saves Self and Three." *Evening Telegram*, October 17, 1938, p. 1.

———. "'Wild Wolf Man of Gogama' Plans to Drive 10 Wolves into New York and Boston." *Evening Telegram*, September 22, 1938.

Côté, Jean. "L'homme aux loups a perdu son seul ami." *Nouveau Samedi* [Montreal, QC], April 11, 1964, p. 5.

Cross, Harry. "New York Six Ties With Boston Again." *New York Times*, January 24, 1926, p. 1.

Dare, Tom. ""Stackie" Adds Thrills in Search for Santa." *Toledo News-Bee*, October 22, 1926, p. 1.

Dawson, James P. "Mushes 700 Miles with Dogs to See Hockey Here Tonight." *New York Times*, January 23, 1926, p. S11.

Democrat and Chronicle [Rochester, NY]. "Seen and Heard." February 24, 1926, p. 27.

——. "Team of Timber Wolves to Be Shown at Strong Country Home." February 19, 1926, p. 19.

——. "Thousands See Wolf Team Dash through Streets." February 25, 1926, pp. 17, 24.

——. "Timber Wolves and Huskies Give Exhibition." February 21, 1926, p. 25.

——. "Timber Wolves to 'Mush' To-Day." February 26, 1926, p. 17.

——. "Wolf and Dog Teams to Race Here Tomorrow and Thursday." February 23, 1926, p. 17.

——. "Wolf Team to Be Shown on Golf Course." February 21, 1926, p. 25.

Desjardins, Maurice. "Tous les sports: Avec Fernand dans la cage aux loups." *Photo-Journal* [Montreal, QC], August 17, 1950, p. 46.

Detroit Border Crossings and Passenger and Crew Lists, 1905-1957. Ancestry. com, http://search.ancestrylibrary.com.

Detroit News. "2nd Annual Michigan Sportmen's Show" [advertisement]. April 3, 1939, p. 22.

Le Droit [Ottawa, ON]. "Gogama, Ont." February 20, 1924, p. 6.

Dunkirk (N.Y.) Evening Observer. "Canadian Pilot with Propeller Off, Wing Shattered, Saved Plane." October 17, 1938, p. 1.

——. "Finds Trouble in Plane Load of Wild Wolves." January 26, 1939, p. 13.

Emmetsburg (Iowa) Democrat. "Outdoors with G.K. Jr." April 3, 1947, p. 2.

Ermitage Sainte Antoine, http://www.st-antoine.org/.

Erskine, Laurie York. "The Great Gray Wolf: Mighty Hunter of the Wilds." *Frontiers: A Magazine of Natural History*, December 1950. Condensed version at *Stillwater Woods* [blog], http://stillwoods.blogspot. ca/2008/06/gray-wolf_18.html.

Evening Independent [Massillon, OH]. "Canadian Trapper Prefers Wolves to Dogs." March 15, 1939, p. 10.

Evening Telegram [Saint-John, NF]. "Liquor Term is Cancelled: Gogama Man Turns in Appeal against Second Conviction." December 19, 1931, p. 2.

Fan-Fare. "Film Possibilities of Little Guilds Lauded: Drama Festival Has Great Talent Array." *Windsor Daily Star*, April 13, 1939, p. 2.

Farley, Oscar. "Today's Sport Parade." *Olean Times Herald*, February 17, 1947, p. 8.

Florida Passenger Lists, 1898-1951. Ancestry.com, http://search. ancestrylibrary.com.

Fressineau, Marcelle. *Le traîneau de la liberté: L'aventure extraordinaire d'une femme dans le Grand Nord*. Lausanne: Éditions Favre SA, 2004.

Fritts, Steven H., Robert O. Stephenson, Robert D. Hayes, and Luigi Boitani. "Wolves and Humans." In *Wolves: Behavior, Ecology, and Conservation*, ed. L. David Mech and Luigi Boitani, 289-316. Chicago: University of Chicago Press, 2006.

Funeral Card of Marie Théoret. Montreal: L. Roy Photo, December 1932.

Gaudreau, Serge. "Jack Renault." *Greb*, www.harrygreb.com/jackrenault.html.

Globe and Mail [Toronto, ON]. "Do Wolves Attack Men? Editor, Tamer Disagree." January 28, 1939, 2nd sec., p. 15.

——. "Four Cheat Death by Pilot's Daring." October 17, 1938, p. 1.

——. "Gogama's 'Paul Bunyan' Bringing Moose to City." January 24, 1947, p. 3.

——. "They Prefer Arrows to Bullets." November 2, 1938, p. 3.

Gogama Board of Trade. Minutes. 1929 to 1946. Gogama, ON.

Gogama Chamber of Commerce. *Crossing the High Portage: A Guide to the Gogama Area*. Sudbury: Journal Printing, c2000.

Gogama Community News. "The End of an Era." November 1996, p. 1.

Goodwin, Rutherfoord. "Wolves Race Dogs at A.G. Strong Farm; First Time Timber Beasts Ever Harnessed." *Rochester Times-Union*, February 20, 1926, Sat. night ed., p. 8.

Grape Belt [Dunkirk, NY]. "Joe LaFlamme at Moose Convention with a Real One." August 19, 1947, p. 9.

Historical Records: Birth, Marriage & Death. Ancestry.com, http://search. ancestrylibrary.com

Historical Records: Census & Voter Lists—1901 Census of Canada. Ancestry. com, http://search.ancestrylibrary.com.

"History of Kodak Milestones—Chronology 1878-1929." *Kodak* website, http://www.kodak.com/global/en/corp/historyOfKodak/1878.jhtml.

Hodgson, Robert G. *Let's Go Fur Farming*. Toronto: Fur Trade Journal of

Canada, 1953.

Hudson, Judy. "A Brief History of Trails." *Randolph Mountain Club Newsletter*, Summer 2003, http://www.randolphmountainclub.org/newsletters/summer2003.html#historyoftrails.

Hunter, Izaak. "Rod and Gun." *Montreal Gazette*, January 23, 1965, p. 44.

——. "Rod and Gun." *Montreal Gazette*, January 30, 1965, p. 40.

——. "Rod and Gun." *Montreal Gazette*, February 9, 1965, p. 29.

——. "Rod and Gun." *Montreal Gazette*, April 26, 1967, p. 24.

——. "With Rod and Gun." *Montreal Gazette*, January 29, 1947, p. 17.

——. "With Rod and Gun." *Montreal Gazette*, February 28, 1948, p. 15.

IMDb [*Internet Movie Database*]. IMDb.com, Inc., 2013, http://www.imdb.com/.

Institut Généalogique Drouin. *Répertoire alphabétique des mariages des Canadiens Français, 1760-1935: Ordre masculin*. Vol. 49. Ottawa: Institut Généalogique Drouin, 1990.

K., T.A. "From Jingle Bells to Truck Rumble." *Montreal Gazette*, November 10, 1941, p. 8.

Karr, Jack. "Movie-Go-Round." *Toronto Daily Star*, March 21, 1945, p. 11.

Kenney, John F. "The Lookout." *Lowell Sun*, February 7, 1939, p. 11.

Kieran, John. "Sports of the *Times*." *New York Times*, February 20, 1940, sports sec., p. 25.

Kinmond, William. "Joe Fights Ten Wolves Trying to Escape Plane." *Toronto Daily Star*, January 26, 1939, p. 10.

——."Joe Has Wife and Wolves and Says They Are Alike." *Toronto Daily Star*, October 26, 1938, p. 1, 2nd sec.

——. "Lashes Whip at Spectators as Crowd Stampede Wolves." *Toronto Daily Star*, January 26, 1939, 2nd sec., pp. 1, 25.

Krasuski, Marek. "Moose Man: Hero or Heretic." *Challenge: A Journal of Male Perspectives* 1 (2004): 37-38.

"Legend of Joe Laflamme—Mooseman/Wolfman of Gogama, Ontario, The." *Gogama* website, http://www.gogama.ca/joelaflamme_2.html.

Leney, C. "Heigh Ho, Come to the Fair." *Sherbrooke Telegram*, September 2, 1948, p. 5.

Lethbridge Herald [Lethbridge, AB]. "'Beeg Joe' in News Again." September 20, 1938, last page.

——. "The Left Hand Corner." May 29, 1957, p. 1.

——. "Miss Byline, Black Bear Cub, to Fly to Sydney, Australia." September 5, 1947, p. 2.

——. "Moose Are Like Women." January 25, 1947, p. 14.

——. "Royal Brevities." June 6, 1939, last page.

——. "Street Traffic Startles Trained Timber Wolves." January 27, 1939, p. 2.

——. "Wolves Mushing New York Streets." February 2, 1939, p. 5.

Life. "Mumbling Moose." March 15, 1948, pp. 61-62.

Long Beach Press-Telegram. "Joe LaFlamme Brings Big Pet to Convention." August 17, 1947, p. 1.

"Lost Battalion Survivors," 1955, *Longwood's Journey*, http://www.longwood.k12.ny.us/history/upton/lbn1.htm.

MacDonald, D.A.L. "Sports on Parade." *Manitoba Ensign*, December 9, 1950, p. 10.

MacDonald, Peter V. "Old Joseph Laflamme a Sudbury Lawyer's Dream." *Sudbury Star*, May 19, 1990, p. 16.

Madger, Nettie. "Muckoos Is Nice Wolf but Law Is after Our Nettie." *Toronto Daily Star*, January 31, 1939, p. 17.

——. "Wolf as Pet Seemed Fine Idea but 'What to Do' Is Worry Now." *Toronto Daily Star*, January 28, 1939, 2nd sec., p. 1.

McDonald, Louise. "Antlers with a Story." *Sudbury Star*, September 6, 1990, p. B5.

McNaughton, Janet. "Toronto in the 1920s." Homepage, www.janetmcnaughton.ca/Toronto,%201920s.html.

Mech, L. David, and Luigi Boitani. Concl. to *Wolves: Behavior, Ecology, and Conservation*, ed. L. David Mech and Luigi Boitani, 341-44. Chicago: University of Chicago Press, 2006.

Metropolitan Opera Company. "[Met Performance] CID:124880: *Louise* {24} Matinee Broadcast ed. Metropolitan Opera House: 01/28/1939." *The Metropolitan Opera* [website], http://archives.metoperafamily.org

Milberry, Larry. *Austin Airways: Canada's Oldest Airline*. Toronto: CANAV, 1985.

"Model T Facts." *Ford* website, http://media.ford.com.

Montreal Directory (*Annuaires Lovell*). Bibliothèque et archives nationales du Québec, http://bibnum2.banq.qc.ca/bna/lovell.

Montreal Gazette. "'Animal Greeting' Brings Difficulty: Australia Protests Canadian Newsmen's Plan to Air-Ship Bear Cub." September 22, 1947, p. 9.

——. "Bears Readied for Trip." August 4, 1948, p. 3.

——. "Joe Laflamme Going Home." April 14, 1939, p. 22.

——. "Joe LaFlamme Makes Brief Stop; Walks Moose to See Veterinary." January 30, 1948, p. 3.

——. "Moose Train for Show: Joe Laflamme Taking Pets to Boston Sportsmen Display." January 27, 1940, p. 14.

——. "To Give Wildlife Lectures." October 4, 1950, p. 3.

——. "Uses Wild Wolves for Hauling Sled." June 25, 1938, p. 13.

——. "Wolf Tamer Stars as Court Witness." June 9, 1938, p. 31.

Moon, Robert. "Neglected Monarch: We Mourn the Moose." *Leader Post*, January 27, 1948, p. 5.

Morning Leader [Regina, SK]. "Toronto Agitated as Wolf in Musher Team Makes Getaway." January 30, 1925, p. 1.

New York Evening Graphic. "Dangerous Dogs." February 2, 1926.

New York Times. "2,000 at Winter Fete." February 8, 1926, p. 16.

——. "Angling Events on Show Card." February 12, 1939, sports sec., p. 92.

——. "The 'King of the Northern Woods' Gets Balky." February 14, 1947, sports sec., p. S26.

——. "Temperature Drops to 17 Here, Cold to Stay; Up-State Suffers; Earthquake at Cambridge." January 23, 1926, p. 1.

North Bay Nugget. "Laflamme and Wolves Bound For Boston in Small Truck." February 1, 1939, p. 14.

——. "'Mooseman of Gogama' Joe LaFlamme Passes." February 8, 1965, p. 6.

Northern Daily News [Kirkland Lake, ON]. "Gogama Mooseman Dies in Montreal at 75." February 8, 1965, p. 1.

Ontario Department of Lands and Forests. *A History of Gogama Forest District*. District History Series no. 11. Toronto: Queen's Printer, 1964.

Ontario Treasury Department. *Public Accounts 1931; Estimates, Supplementary Estimates 1932*. Toronto: Baptist Johnston, 1932.

——. *Public Accounts 1947; Estimates 1948*, Toronto: Baptist Johnston, 1947.

Ottawa Citizen. "Case Held Over Till Show Ends." October 17, 1947, p. 10.
Paroisse de St. Télesphore, Quebec. Registre des baptêmes.

Popular Science Monthly, "Ontario Trapper Drives Team of Wolves," December 1924, p. 58.

La Presse [Montreal, QC]. "À l'arrivée de Jos. LaFlamme à la gare centrale." March 29, 1948, p. 7.

———. "Avis de décès." February 8, 1965, p. 37.

———. "Les chiens de Holt-Renfrew se classent bons premiers." February 11, 1924, p. 17.

———. "Feu Mme O. Laflamme." February 4, 1933, p. 43.

———. "Joe Laflamme, un sportif original, meurt à 75 ans." February 8, 1965, p. 37.

———. "Le loup comme bête de trait." June 27, 1938, p. 15.

———. "Le loup déteste la muselière!" February 2, 1939, p. 11.

———. "Personnage pittoresque attendu à Montréal." January 24, 1947, p. 3.

———. " P'tit Mousse,' l'orignal bien-aimé." January 31, 1947, p. 29.

Post-Register [Idaho Falls, ID]. "New York Gets Coyote Problem." August 19, 1953, p. 16.

Quebec Vital and Church Records (Drouin Collection), 1621-1967. Ancestry.com, http://search.ancestrylibrary.com.

Rochester Herald. "Thousands See Wolf Team in Races at Oak Hill and on Trip through Streets." February 25, 1926, p. 7.

"Rural and Urban Conflict: Congressional Reapportionment." In *American Decades: 1920-1929*, ed. Vincent Tompkins, vol. 3, Gale Cengage, 1995. *eNotes.com*, http://www.enotes.com/1920-government-politics-american-decades/rural-urban-conflict-congressional-reapportionment.

Ruston Daily Leader. "Heat Wave Hits East after Leaving Trail across Midwest Belt." August 14, 1947, p. 1.

Salutin, Rick. "Forward on Life's Tightrope." *Rabble.ca*, August 29, 2003, http://rabble.ca/print/columnists/forward-lifes-tightrope.

Sandusky Register-Star-News. "Bull(headed) Moose Makes Air Debut." February 20, 1947, p. 1.

———. "Joe LaFlamme Has Columbus-Bound Moose in Toronto." August 13, 1947, p. 1.

Sault Daily Star. "100 Take Part in Bar River Wolf Hunt Today." December 9, 1924, p. 1.

Schrag, Lex. "Progress Rocks Northern Ontario Village." *Globe and Mail*, December 3, 1959, p. 25.

Sherbrooke Telegram. "Joe Laflamme Explains the Aims of Convention." October 28, 1948, p. 4.

Sodus Record. "Sodus Residents Get Thrill from Timber Wolves." February 26, 1926, p. 1.

South Side Story [Sudbury, ON]. "Great Lives Lived in Greater Sudbury." January 2005, p. 27.

St. Maurice Valley Chronicle [Trois-Rivières, QC]. "Game Association Backs Sportsman's Show. Public Invited to Visit Wild Game Exhibits at Exhibition." August 19, 1948, p. 3.

——. "Three Rivers Exhibition Gets under Way Saturday." August 19, 1948, p. 1.

Standard-Freeholder [Cornwall, ON]. "Bushman Who Wrestles Wolves to Whet Appetite in Toils at Gogama." October 5, 1938, n.p.

Stoll, Bert. "Gold Fever Is High in North Ontario." *New York Times*, October 30, 1932, p. E6.

——. "Rushing on Wings to Seek Hidden Gold." *New York Times*, March 12, 1933, p. SM7.

Sudbury Star. "All Famous in the North!" [Advertisement for Silver Foam beverages by the Sudbury Brewing and Malting Co.] January 30, 1939, p. 9.

——. "And They Pulled Many a Stout Bow." November 2, 1938, p. 6.

——. "Been Reported Dead Twice before but Joe Laflamme in Best of Health." August 8, 1958, p. 1.

——. "Claims Wolf Pack Will Attack Man." January 27, 1939, p. 1.

——. "Crowds Throng Streets to Watch Laflamme's Wolves Run." January 27, 1939, p. 6.

——. "Gogama Anglicans Elect 1935 Officers." February 17, 1935, 2nd sec., p. 8.

——. "Gogama Tragedy." April 2, 1932, p.11.

——. "Gogama Woman First of Sex to New Field." August 8, 1938, p. 8.

——. "Gotham Finds Joe LaFlamme Country Slicker in Hick City." February 20, 1947, p. 6.

——. "Joe and His Moose at the Ex." September 2, 1947, p. 1.

——. "Joe Laflamme Dies in Sudbury." August 7, 1958, p. 1.

——. "Joe Laflamme out Again after Second Wolf Team." May 30, 1938, p. 6.

——. "Joe Laflamme Sent to Jail for 15 Days." October 16, 1936, p. 1.

——. "Joe LaFlamme to Drive Wolves on Sudbury Streets Tomorrow." January 25, 1939, pp. 1, 8.

——. "Joe Laflamme's Sentence Boosted to Three Months." October 23, 1936, p. 1.

——. "Judge Quashes L.C.A. Conviction on Wolf Tamer: Joe Laflamme Free; Evidence Conflicting." December 19, 1931, p. 1.

——. "Jury Declares Mrs. Fortin Did Not Set Fire: Cross-Questioning of Joe Laflamme Is Feature." June 10, 1938, p. 5.

——. "Laflamme Battles Wolf in Studio." January 30, 1939, pp. 1, 8.

——. "Laflamme's Reply Was a Boomerang." June 10, 1938, p. 5.

——. "Long Legs Aid in Capture of Dashing Wolf." January 27, 1939, p. 3.

——. "Moose, Badger, Wolves, Elk and Bears 'Friends' of the Mooseman of Gogama." February 8, 1965, p. 3.

——. "'Mooseman' Joe Laflamme Dies at 61." August 7, 1958, p. 3.

——. "New Gold Rush Is under Way Near Gogama." July 27, 1938, p. 1.

——. "North Steals Spotlight at Gotham Show." February 20, 1940, p. 8.

——. "Obituaries: Mooseman." August 7, 1958, p. 3.

——. "Resort Keeper Sent to Jail: Three Months Term for Joe Laflamme, of Gogama." September 19, 1931, p. 1.

——. "Son Thrills at Father's Feat." January 27, 1939, p. 1.

——. "Thousands See Wolves Run On City Streets." January 27, 1939, p. 6.

——. "Timber Wolves to Visit City." January 23, 1939, p. 1.

——. "'Wolfman of Gogama' Will Always Be Remembered Now." January 2, 1968, p. 7.

Swiernega, Robert P. "Going to America: Travel Routes of Zeeland Emigrants." Paper presented at the "Zeeland to America" conference, Roosevelt Studies Center, Middelburg, Netherlands, September 5, 1997, www.swierenga.com/RSC_pap.html.

Telfer, E.S. "Moose." 1997. *Hinterland Who's Who*, http://www.hww.ca/en/species/mammals/moose.html *Time*.

"Canada: Ontario: The Ex." September 1, 1947, http://www.time.com/time/magazine/article/0,9171,887606,00.html.

Timmins Daily Press. "North's Mooseman Legend in Canada." February 8, 1965, p. 5.

Today Magazine [*Toronto Star* insert]. "Q & A." February 7, 1981.

Toronto Daily Star. "12 Below To-night, Predicts Weatherman." January 27, 1925, p. 1.

——. "50,000 People Crowd Grenadier Pond and Hillsides at The Star's Winter Carnival." February 2, 1925, 2nd sec., p. 1.

——. "And Now Mrs. Joe LaFlamme and 'Sparky.'" January 31, 1925, p. 1.

——. "Can't Wipe Out Wolves by Rifle, Says Trapper." January 19, 1925, p. 23.

——. "Crowds Saw Wolves Perform at High Park." February 2, 1925, p. 24.

——. "Dog Team Is Greeted by a Capacity Curb." January 31, 1925, p. 4.

——. "Eerily, High Park Hills Re-echo Wolf Pack's Howls." January 31, 1925, p. 4.

——. "Finds Wolves Are Like Women 'Can Never Really Tame Them.'" March 20, 1945, p. 2.

——. "Fun and Exercise in The Star's "Wolf Hunt" at High Park." February 2, 1925, p. 24.

——. "Gogama Joe Gives Away Moose; Now He'll Train Some Wolves." April 12, 1940, p. 10.

——. "Howling Lupi Disturb Gogama People's Sleep, but There's Little Danger; They Are Tied Up." October 26, 1938, p. 24.

——. "Joe Backs Wolves With $100 Offer." January 31, 1925, 2nd sec., p. 17.

——. "Joe LaFlamme, Isaac Lewis, the Indian, and 'Tommy,' a Wolf." January 28, 1925, p. 17.

——. "Joe LaFlamme, the Wolfman of the North, May Pay Toronto a Flying Visit with His 11 Wolves." January 21, 1939, 2nd sec., p. 1.

——. "Lord and Lady Byng See Joe LaFlamme and Wolves." June 18, 1925, p. 7.

——. "Lumberman Honored." February 8, 1930, p. 34.

——. "Northern Racer Fined." March 26, 1931.

——. "Old and Young City Migrates High Parkwards." January 31, 1925, p. 17.

——. "Prefers Northern Life to Comforts of Paris." January 31, 1925, p. 18.

——. "Pretty Girls, Bear Cubs—Joe Laflamme." April 27, 1945, p. 2.

——. "Spend Night at Grenadier's with Wolves near Bedside." January 30, 1925, p. 2.

——. "The Star's Gogama Wolves and Dogs on City Streets and Grenadier Pond." January 30, 1925, 2nd sec., p. 1.

——. "Star's Wolves Captured in Long Trail over Hills." February 2, 1925, p. 6.

——. "There'll Be Indians If They Can Find Any." January 22, 1946, p. 3.

——. "'That a Tree?' Louise Downs It, Urn Too, Then Dives under Bed." September 5, 1947, p. 20.

——. "Will Bear Attack Moose? Maybe. Anyhow, Joe's Is Safe in Gotham." February 15, 1940, p. 5.

——. "Winter Sports Pow-wow near Grenadier Pond on Saturday Afternoon." January 29, 1925, p. 19.

——. "Wolf Captured after Half Day of Roaming." January 30, 1925, p. 9.

——. "Wolf Man's Latest Pets Are Right at Home in Family Circle." October 11, 1939, 2nd sec., p. 1.

——. "Wolf Team Driver Joe LaFlamme, Here." December 5, 1930, p. 10.

——. "Wolf-husky Cavalcade in Town as Star's Guest." January 26, 1925, p. 1.

——. "Wolves Will Attack Humans, Joe Insists." January 28, 1939, 2nd sec., p. 1.

——. "Wolves Will Run on Danforth and Other Streets To-morrow." January 27, 1925, p. 1.

——. "Woman Mayor for a Day to Greet King at Gogama." June 1, 1939, p. 1.

——. "You Can Never Tell What Wives or Wolves Will Do, Says Joe." October 26, 1938, p. 24.

Toronto Daily Telegraph. "The Wolf That Doesn't Whistle." January 18, 1951, p. 4.

Toronto Star Weekly. "Tall Tales from the North." February 24, 1962, pp. 18-20.

"Vermont Prohibition on the Sale of Intoxicating Liquor Act (1916)." *Ballotpedia*, June 14, 2012, http://ballotpedia.org/wiki/index.php/Vermont_Prohibition_on_the_Sale_of_Intoxicating_Liquor_Act_(1916).

A View on Cities. Van Ermengem bvba, 2013, http://www.aviewoncities.com.

Werden, Lincoln A. "Thousands at Opening Session of National Sportsmen's Show." *New York Times*, February 19, 1939, sports sec., p. 75.

Wikipedia. Wikimedia Foundation, Inc., 2013, http://en.wikipedia.org/wiki/Main_Page.

Williams, Jerry. "A Man and His Moose; I Met Joe LaFlamme in 1949 and Was Asked to Keep Watch over His Menagerie." *Montreal Gazette*, June 6, 1993, p. C2.

Windsor Daily Star. "Joe LaFlamme and Tame Moose Draw Crowds in Detroit." March 4, 1940, p. 5.

——. "Moose Seek Real Thing: Old Joe Laflamme to Transport Animals." July 31, 1947, p. 8.

——. "Zoo Parade: Rare Tamed Moose." January 4, 1958, p. 36.

Winnipeg Free Press. "Around the World: Animals." September 5, 1947, p. 2.

——. "Prospectors Head North to New Ontario Gold Rush." August 12, 1933, p. 1.

Yahoo Answers. Yahoo!, 2013, http://answers.yahoo.com/question/index?qid=20070128021723AAUwPqX.

Photographs *(see images in the text for full credits)*

Index of Proper Names

Note: The numbers in square brackets refer to chapter notes at the end of the book. The number preceding the colon is the chapter number; following the colon are the page/note numbers.

About the Author

Suzanne F. Charron has worked over 15 years in communications as well as teaching, administration and journalism. Born and raised in Sturgeon Falls, in Northern Ontario, she lives in Greater Sudbury where she works as a freelance writer. *Wolfman Joe LaFlamme: Tamer Untamed* is her first book.